ASP.NET Web API 2: Building a REST Service from Start to Finish

Jamie Kurtz
Brian Wortman

Apress·

ASP.NET Web API 2: Building a REST Service from Start to Finish

ISBN-13 (pbk): 978-1-4842-0110-7

ISBN-13 (electronic): 978-1-4842-0109-1

Publisher: Heinz Weinheimer
Lead Editor: James DeWolf
Development Editor: Douglas Pundick
Technical Reviewer: Fabio Ferracchiati
Editorial Board: Steve Anglin, Mark Beckner, Ewan Buckingham, Gary Cornell, Louise Corrigan, Jim DeWolf, Jonathan Gennick, Jonathan Hassell, Robert Hutchinson, Michelle Lowman, James Markham, Matthew Moodie, Jeff Olson, Jeffrey Pepper, Douglas Pundick, Ben Renow-Clarke, Dominic Shakeshaft, Gwenan Spearing, Matt Wade, Steve Weiss
Coordinating Editor: Kevin Walter
Copy Editor: Roger LeBlanc
Compositor: SPi Global
Indexer: SPi Global
Artist: SPi Global
Cover Designer: Anna Ishchenko

Distributed to the book trade worldwide by Springer Science+Business Media New York, 233 Spring Street, 6th Floor, New York, NY 10013. Phone 1-800-SPRINGER, fax (201) 348-4505, e-mail orders-ny@springer-sbm.com, or visit www.springeronline.com. Apress Media, LLC is a California LLC and the sole member (owner) is Springer Science + Business Media Finance Inc (SSBM Finance Inc). SSBM Finance Inc is a Delaware corporation.

For information on translations, please e-mail rights@apress.com, or visit www.apress.com.

Apress and friends of ED books may be purchased in bulk for academic, corporate, or promotional use. eBook versions and licenses are also available for most titles. For more information, reference our Special Bulk Sales–eBook Licensing web page at www.apress.com/bulk-sales.

Any source code or other supplementary material referenced by the author in this text is available to readers at www.apress.com. For detailed information about how to locate your book's source code, go to www.apress.com/source-code/.

I would like to dedicate this book to my loving wife and beautiful daughters, whose patience and grace for time spent on yet another book made all the difference in the world.

—Jamie

To Him who was, and is, and is to come.

—Brian

Contents at a Glance

Contents

About the Authors

Jamie Kurtz has over 17 years of experience working in a variety of roles as engineer and solution provider. While working as a developer and tester for an education software company, and working as a developer in a high-temperature super conductivity lab, he received his Bachelor of Science from Western Michigan University—double majoring in Physics and Mathematics and minoring in Computer Science.

From there, Jamie worked in DBA, project lead, team lead, manager, architect, advisor, tester, and developer roles in various industries, including: telecommunications, fulfillment, manufacturing, banking, and video intelligence/security. He is currently working as consultant and group manager at Fusion Alliance, Inc. in Indianapolis, Indiana.

In addition to love and enjoyment of his beautiful wife and two daughters (and dog and cat), and great times playing drums at an awesome local church, Jamie continually seeks opportunities to share his passion for helping software teams build and deliver real value to their customers.

Brian Wortman has been developing software for more than 20 years across a wide range of industries, including pharmaceutical, healthcare, telecommunications, surveillance, military, and financial. He received an M.S. in Computer Science from Johns Hopkins University in 1998. He is currently working as a senior consultant at Fusion Alliance, Inc. in Indianapolis, Indiana.

In addition to technology, Brian's interests include religion, politics, music, cars, and real estate. He has too many hobbies to mention (and to excel at any particular one), but most of them involve The Great Outdoors in one way or another. Yes, he even enjoys yard work!

Last but not least, Brian is a member of Christ Covenant Orthodox Presbyterian Church in Sheridan, Indiana, where he worships the Lord with his wife of 22 years (and counting) and his wonderful daughters, Jan and Danielle.

About the Technical Reviewer

Fabio Claudio Ferracchiati is a senior consultant and a senior analyst/developer using Microsoft technologies. He works at BluArancio SpA (`www.bluarancio.com`) as Senior Analyst/Developer and Microsoft Dynamics CRM Specialist. He is a Microsoft Certified Solution Developer for .NET, a Microsoft Certified Application Developer for .NET, a Microsoft Certified Professional, and a prolific author and technical reviewer. Over the past ten years, he's written articles for Italian and international magazines and coauthored more than ten books on a variety of computer topics.

Acknowledgments

We'd like to thank you, our reader. Without you, there wouldn't have been much point in writing this book! We look forward to learning from your comments and constructive criticisms. We are firm believers in the Agile way, which at its heart is all about feedback. Please feel free to share yours.

We'd like to thank Kevin Walter, Douglas Pundick, Roger LeBlanc, Jim DeWolf, and Fabio Claudio Ferracchiati of the Apress team. It was a pleasure to work with such a talented and encouraging group of individuals. Their input and efforts toward getting this book to market were invaluable.

For a similar reason, we'd like to thank our friends and colleagues Glenn Orr, Ray Clanan, and Jim Kelly. Though not part of the official editing team, these guys contributed their keen technical skills to help make sure the material contained herein is accessible and accurate.

I (Jamie) would also like to thank Brian Wortman for continuing to push me into excellence. Most people don't realize that Brian and I approach software very differently. I like to go fast and furious, seeking adventure and excitement along the way, growing bored quickly, usually skirting the details and finishing touches. Brian tackles every project with the application of tried-and-true patterns and practices, never stopping short of pure excellence, and never growing tired of the daily rigors that make up most of software development. He is truly the image of discipline. Without his (sometimes forceful) influence, I wouldn't have ever taken the time to learn so much of what makes me the developer I am today. Brian pushed me, kicking and screaming, into unit tests, design patterns, clean code, refactoring, and taking the time to complete with excellence that last 10% of a project that we all hate. So thanks a ton, Brian.

I (Brian) would like to thank my longtime friend (and boss) Jamie Kurtz for giving me the opportunity to coauthor this book. Yes, it was a lot of work . . . and yes, we're still friends (and I think I still have a job)! I'd also like to thank my pastor (Mark Melton), my friends, and my family for their prayers and encouragement. I'd especially like to thank my loving wife, Yvonne, and my precious daughters, Jan and Danielle. They are a constant reminder of how richly blessed I am.

Foreword

It's the end of the project. Project managers are happy, you've released the code on time, and it even works! Everyone is congratulating you for a job well done, but every pat on the back is like a lash from the whip of guilt. You harbor a dark secret that will soon be found out—your code. At first everything was great. You got to start from scratch, and hey, you even got to use a new framework! Then you built the code base, fixed bugs, and added features that were missed in the requirements document. But so many unexpected changes turned the code base into a tangled mess. It started new and shiny, but it ended as a crufty disaster. It works, but man, if you only had it to do all over again.

We all know that special sort of coding pain where you have this sense of accomplishment laced with frustration and guilt. Even worse, it's New Code 2.0! People are happy with it, and it may even end up as the core of many more projects to come. Too many projects and code bases start off with the guilt-laced code described. Every developer wants to rewrite it in a vain effort to erase their embarrassment from history and in the end make it right.

This book isn't about making it right. This book is about starting it right, written by brilliant and talented developers with many years of experience. The authors guide you through creating a REST API from start to finish. They cover SOLID principles, security, patterns, unit tests, integration tests, and backward compatibility for those clients that just can't understand that sometimes it is OK to drop the SOAP.

The authors, Jamie and Brian, will guide you through the entire process of designing and implementing a RESTful service—explaining what ASP.NET Web API 2 is, and what REST is and is not. They take you through the process of designing a task-management API and setting up the Visual Studio project. From there they show you how to implement the API, security, SOAP support, unit and integration tests, and then finally, a quick SPA web page to consume the service.

I hope you enjoy this book as much as I have. Usually technology books are very light on concept and more about demonstrating the technology at hand. To get information on clean code, you have to read a more abstract book and then spend a while experimenting to figure out how to correctly implement the idea with the technology. This process is usually shortened by having a developer experienced in the process on hand to help guide the project. This book is very similar to having that developer on hand, which I found very useful. Some concepts I formerly struggled to understand clicked, and overall I came out understanding not only ASP.NET Web API, or what a REST web service is, but also how to make a clean design overall and how to apply various SOLID concepts. I hope it does the same for you.

—Jim Kelly
Fusion Alliance, Inc.
Indianapolis, Indiana

Introduction

With the introduction of services technology over a decade ago, Microsoft made it relatively easy to build and support web services with the .NET Framework. Starting with XML Web Services, and then adding the broadly capable Windows Communication Foundation (WCF) several years later, Microsoft gave .NET developers many options for building SOAP-based services. With some basic configuration changes, you could support a wide array of communication protocols, authentication schemes, message formats, and WS-* standards with WCF. But as the world of connected devices evolved, the need arose within the community for a simple HTTP-only services framework—without all of the capabilities (and complexity) of WCF. Developers realized that most of their newer services did not require federated authentication or message encryption, nor did they require transactions or Web Services Description Language (WSDL)–based discovery. And the services really only needed to communicate over HTTP, not named pipes or MSMQ.

In short, the demand for mobile-to-service communication and browser-based, single-page applications started increasing exponentially. It was no longer just large enterprise services talking SOAP/RPC to each other. Now a developer needed to be able to whip up a JavaScript application, or 99-cent mobile app, in a matter of days—and those applications needed a simple HTTP-only, JSON-compatible back end. The Internet needs of these applications looked more and more like Roy Fielding's vision of connected systems (i.e., REST).

And so Microsoft responded by creating the ASP.NET Web API, a super-simple yet very powerful framework for building HTTP-only, JSON-by-default web services without all the fuss of WCF. Model binding works out of the box, and returning Plain Old CLR Objects is drop-dead easy. Configuration is available (though almost completely unnecessary), and you can spin up a RESTful service in a matter of minutes.

The previous edition of this book, *ASP.NET MVC 4 and the Web API: Building a REST Service from Start to Finish*, spent a couple chapters describing REST and then dove into building a sample service with the first version of ASP.NET Web API. In a little over a hundred pages, you were guided through the process of implementing a working service. But based on reader feedback, I discovered that a better job needed to be done in two major areas: fewer opinions about patterns and best practices and various open source libraries, and more details on the ASP.NET Web API itself. So when the second version of the ASP.NET Web API was released, Brian Wortman and I decided it was time to release a version 2 of the book. Brian wanted to help me correct some glaring "bugs," and also incorporate some great new features found in ASP.NET Web API 2. And so this book was born.

In this second edition, we will cover all major features and capabilities of the ASP.NET Web API (version 2). We also show you how to support API versioning, input validation, non-resource APIs, legacy/SOAP clients (this is super cool!), partial updates with PATCH, adding hypermedia links to responses, and securing your service with OAuth-compatible JSON Web Tokens. Improving upon the book's first edition, we continue to evolve the message and techniques around REST principles, controller activation, dependency injection, database connection and transaction management, and error handling. While we continue to leverage certain open source NuGet packages, we have eliminated the chatter and opinions around those choices. We also spend more time on the code—lots of code. Unit tests and all. And in the end, we build a simple KnockoutJS-based Single Page Application (SPA) that demonstrates both JSON Web Token authentication and use of our new service.

We have also made improvements in response to your feedback regarding the source code that accompanied the first book. Therefore, on GitHub you will find a git repository containing all of the code for the task-management service we will build together (`https://github.com/jamiekurtz/WebAPI2Book`). The repository contains one branch per chapter, with multiple check-ins (or "commits") per branch to help guide you step-by-step through the implementation. The repository also includes a branch containing the completed task-management service, with additional code to help reinforce the concepts that we cover in the book. Of course, feel free to use any of this code in your own projects.

I am very excited about this book. Both Brian and I are firm believers in the "Agile way," which at its heart is all about feedback. So we carefully triaged each and every comment I received from the first book and did our best to make associated improvements. And I'm really excited about all the new features in the second version of ASP.NET Web API. So many capabilities have been added, but Microsoft has managed to maintain the framework's simplicity and ease of use.

We hope you not only find this book useful in your daily developer lives, but also find it a pleasure to read. As always, please share any feedback you have. We not only love to hear it, but your feedback is key in making continuous improvements.

Cheers,
—Jamie Kurtz
(Brian Wortman)

CHAPTER 1

ASP.NET as a Service Framework

In the years since the first release of the .NET Framework, Microsoft has provided a variety of approaches for building service-oriented applications. Starting back in 2002 with the original release of .NET, a developer could fairly easily create an ASP.NET ASMX-based XML web service that allowed other .NET and non-.NET clients to call it. Those web services implemented various versions of SOAP, but they were available for use only over HTTP.

In addition to support for web services, the 1.0 release of .NET provided support for Remoting. This allowed developers to write services that weren't necessarily tied to the HTTP protocol. Similar to ASMX-based web services, .NET Remoting essentially provides object activation and session context for client-initiated method calls. The caller uses a proxy object to invoke methods, and the .NET runtime handles the serialization and marshaling of data between the client's proxy object and the server's activated service object.

Towards the end of 2006, Microsoft released .NET 3.0, which included the Windows Communication Foundation (WCF). WCF not only replaced ASMX web services and .NET Remoting, but also took a giant step forward in the way of flexibility, configurability, extensibility, and support for more recent security and other SOAP standards. For example, with WCF, a developer can write a non-HTTP service that supports authentication with SAML tokens and host it in a custom-built Windows service. These and other capabilities greatly broaden the scenarios under which .NET can be utilized to build a service-oriented application.

MORE ON WCF

If you're interested in learning more about WCF, I recommend reading either *Programming WCF Services* by Juval Lowy (O'Reilly Media, 2007) or *Essential Windows Communication Foundation (WCF): For .NET Framework 3.5* by Steve Resnick, Richard Crane, and Chris Bowen (Addison-Wesley Professional, 2008). Both of these books are appropriate for WCF novices and veterans alike, as they cover the spectrum from basic to advanced WCF topics. There is also an excellent introduction to WCF in *Pro C# 5.0 and the .NET 4.5 Framework, Sixth Edition* by Andrew Troelsen (Apress, 2012).

If you need to set up communication between two applications, whether they are co-located or separated by thousands of miles, rest assured WCF can do it. And if its out-of-the-box features don't suffice, WCF's tremendous extensibility model provides ample opportunity for plugging in just about anything you can think of.

And this is where we will take a bit of a left turn, off the evolutionary path of ever greater capability and flexibility and towards something simpler and more targeted at a small set of specific scenarios. As this books is about building RESTful services with the ASP.NET Web API, we want to start looking at the need for such services (in contrast to SOAP/RPC style services), and also what types of features and capabilities they provide.

In the Land of JavaScript and Mobile Devices

During much of the growth of the Internet over the past two-plus decades, web sites and pages have relied on server-side code for anything but basic HTML manipulation. But more recently, various AJAX-related tools and frameworks—including (but not limited to) JavaScript, jQuery, HTML5, and some tricks with CSS—have given rise to the need for services that are less about complex enterprise applications talking to each other and more about web pages needing to get and push small amounts of data. One significant example of these types of applications is the Single Page Application (SPA). You can think of these as browser-hosted "fat client" applications, where JavaScript code is connecting from your browser to a service back end. In cases such as these, communicating with a service over HTTP is pretty much a given, since the web sites themselves are HTTP applications. Further, security requirements of browser-based applications tend to be simpler than those of distributed out-of-browser applications, and thus support for all of the various security-related SOAP standards is not required of the service.

In addition to simpler protocol and security needs, web pages typically communicate with other applications and services using text-based messages rather than binary-formatted messages. As such, a service needs only to support XML or JSON serialization.

Beyond web applications, today's smartphones and tablets have created a huge demand for services in support of small, smart-client mobile applications. These services are very similar in nature to those that support AJAX-enabled web sites. For example, they typically communicate via HTTP; they send and receive small amounts of text-based data; and their security models tend to take a minimalist approach in order to provide a better user experience (i.e., they strive for less configuration and fewer headaches for users). Also, the implementation of these services encourages more reuse across the different mobile platforms.

In short, there is a recent and growing desire for a service framework that, out of the box, provides exactly what is needed for these simple, text-based HTTP services. While WCF can be used to create such services, it is definitely not configured that way by default. Unfortunately, the added flexibility and configurability of WCF make it all too easy to mess something up.

And this is where the ASP.NET Web API comes into the picture.

Advantages of Using the ASP.NET Web API

Once you know that you don't need the extended capabilities of WCF, you can start considering a smaller, more targeted framework like ASP.NET Web API. And now on its second version, the ASP.NET Web API provides even more capabilities out of the box, without sacrificing simplicity or its focus on the basics of HTTP service communication. In this section, you'll look at a few of these.

Configuration

As is the case when building a web site, there isn't much to configure to get an ASP.NET Web API-based service up and running. The concept of endpoints doesn't exist (as it does with WCF), and neither do contracts. As you'll see later, an ASP.NET Web API-based service is pretty loose in comparison to a WCF service. You pretty much just need a REST URL, a set of inbound arguments, and a response JSON or XML message.

REST by Default

Speaking of REST, building services with the ASP.NET Web API provides most of the nuts and bolts of what you need to adhere to the constraints of the REST architecture. This is largely due to the URL routing feature provided by the framework. Unlike WCF, where a service is an address to a physical file (i.e., an address that maps directly to a service class or .svc file), service addresses with the ASP.NET Web API are RESTful routes that map to controller methods. (We'll talk more about the basics of the REST architectural style in the next chapter.) As such, the paths lend themselves very nicely to REST-style API specifications.

This concept of routing is critical to understanding how the ASP.NET Web API can be used for building services, so let's look at an example. In this book, you will learn how to develop a simple task-management service. You can imagine having a SOAP-based service method to fetch a single task. This method would take a task's TaskId and return that task. Implemented in WCF, the method might look like this:

```
[ServiceContract]
public interface ITaskService
{
    [OperationContract]
    Task GetTask(long taskId);
}

public class TaskService : ITaskService
{
    private readonly IRepository _repository;

    public TaskService(IRepository repository)
    {
        _repository = repository;
    }

    public Task GetTask(long taskId)
    {
        return _repository.Get<Task>(taskId);
    }
}
```

With an appropriately configured .svc file and corresponding endpoint, you would have a URL that looks similar to this:

```
http://MyServer/TaskService.svc
```

The caller would then post a SOAP request with the SOAP action set to GetTask, passing in the TaskId argument. Of course, when building a .NET client, much of the underlying SOAP gunk is taken care of for you. But making SOAP calls from JavaScript or a mobile application can be a bit more challenging.

WHAT DO WE MEAN BY "TASK"?

We understand that "task" is an overloaded word, and the fact that the .NET Framework includes a Task class only complicates matters. Therefore, what we mean by the word "task" is based on the context in which it appears. The Task classes we will implement in the task-management service (there are three of them, at different layers in the application) map to the problem domain. Please take care to avoid confusing them with the .NET Framework's Task class.

This same example under the ASP.NET Web API would involve creating a controller instead of a WCF service class. The method for fetching a Task object exists on the controller, but it is no longer defined by a contract, as it is in WCF. The controller might look like this:

```
public class TasksController : ApiController
{
    private readonly IRepository _repository;
```

```
    public TasksController(IRepository repository)
    {
        _repository = repository;
    }

    public Task Get(long taskId)
    {
        return Json(_repository.Get<Task>(taskId));
    }
}
```

If you've built any RESTful services using the ASP.NET MVC Framework (as opposed to the ASP.NET Web API), one of the biggest differences you'll notice is the base class being used, ApiController. This base class was built specifically for enabling RESTful services, and you simply return the object (or objects in a collection) of the data being requested. Contrast this with the required use of ActionResult in an MVC-based REST controller method.

The URL for obtaining a specific Task from the preceding controller would be this:

```
http://MyServer/Tasks/123
```

Unlike with the MVC Framework, the URL doesn't need to include the controller's method name. This is because, with the ASP.NET Web API, HTTP verbs (e.g., GET, POST, PUT) are automatically mapped to corresponding controller methods. As you'll see in the next chapter, this helps you create an API that adheres more closely with the tenets of the REST architecture.

For now, the important thing to realize is that the entirety of this service call is contained in the URL itself; there is no SOAP message to go along with the address. And this is one of the key tenets of REST: resources are accessible via unique URIs.

A QUICK OVERVIEW OF REST

Created by Roy Fielding, one of the primary authors of the HTTP specification, REST is meant to take better advantage of standards and technologies within HTTP than SOAP does today. For example, rather than creating arbitrary SOAP methods, developers of REST APIs are encouraged to use only HTTP verbs:

- GET
- POST
- PUT
- DELETE

REST is also resource-centric; that is, RESTful APIs use HTTP verbs to act on or fetch information about resources. These would be the nouns in REST parlance (e.g., Tasks, Users, Customers, and Orders). Thus, you have verbs acting on nouns. Another way of saying this is that you perform actions against a resource.

Additionally, REST takes advantage of other aspects of HTTP systems, such as the following:

- Caching
- Security
- Statelessness
- Network layering (with various firewalls and gateways in between client and server)

This book will cover REST principles sufficiently for you to build services using the ASP.NET Web API. However, if you're interested, you can find several good books that cover the full breadth of the REST architecture. You might also find it interesting to read Chapter 5 of Fielding's doctoral dissertation, where the idea of REST was first conceived. You can find that chapter here:

```
http://www.ics.uci.edu/~fielding/pubs/dissertation/rest_arch_style.htm
```

Before moving on, let's quickly address a point that some may be thinking about: you can indeed create REST services with WCF. Looking around the Internet, you can certainly find arguments on both sides of the ASP.NET Web API versus WCF debate (for building RESTful services). Since this is a book on how to build services with the ASP.NET Web API, let's skip that debate altogether.

Abstraction with Routes

Somewhat similar to service interfaces and their implementations in WCF, routes give the ASP.NET Web API service developer a layer of abstraction between what the callers see and the underlying implementation. In other words, you can map any URL to any controller method. When the API signature (i.e., the REST URL) isn't hard-wired to a particular interface, class, or .svc file, you are free to update your implementation of that API method, as long as the URL specification for that method remains valid.

One classic example of using URLs to handle changing implementations is in the case of service versioning. By creating a new route with a "v2" (or similar) embedded in the URL, you can create an arbitrary mapping between an implementation and a versioning scheme or set of versions that doesn't exist until sometime later. Thus, you can take a set of controllers and decide a year from now that they will be part of the v2 API. Later on in this book, you learn about a few different options for versioning your ASP.NET Web API service.

Controller Activation Is, Well, Very Nice

Whether the subject is the older XML Web Services (a.k.a. ASMX services), WCF, services with ASP.NET MVC or with the ASP.NET Web API, the concept of *service activation* is present. Essentially, since by-and-large all calls to a service are new requests, the ASP.NET or WCF runtime activates a new instance of the service class for each request. This is similar to object instantiation in OO-speak. Note that service activation is a little more involved than simply having the application code create a new object; this book will touch on this topic in more depth in later chapters. Understanding activation and dependency resolution is very important if you want to have a solid grasp of any service application, including the ASP.NET Web API.

Simpler Extensible Processing Pipeline

ASP.NET Web API provides a highly-extensible, yet much simpler, processing pipeline. We will cover several examples of this in this book. For example, *delegating handlers* (a.k.a. "handlers") and *filters* are mechanisms providing pre- and post-processing capabilities.

Handlers allow you to execute custom code prior to any controller being activated within the application. In fact, handlers can be configured to handle routes that have no corresponding controller.

Filters are essentially classes that contain a few methods allowing you to run some code before and after specific controller methods are invoked. These come in a few different flavors: action filters, authorization filters, and exception filters. These filters take the form of attributes, and they are either decorated on specific controller methods, decorated on the controllers themselves, or configured globally for all methods.

It's a bit tough to describe, but once you write and debug a few controllers — along with a delegating handler and some action filters—you will start noticing how clean and easy Microsoft has made this arrangement. Nothing is hidden from you, making it simple to understand and step through an entire service call in the debugger.

Interoperability of JSON, XML, and REST

As mentioned previously, REST is based solely on existing HTTP standards, so it is extremely interoperable across all platforms capable of making HTTP requests. This not only includes computers, smartphones, and tablets, but it also gets into devices such as normal "old-fashioned" cell phones, DVRs, phone systems, ATM machines, refrigerators, alarm systems, browsers, smart watches, etc. As long as the device can make an HTTP request to a URL, it can "do" REST.

The same applies to JSON and straight XML data. Compared to the relative complexities of SOAP messaging, these technologies require very little in the way of proper formatting or an understanding of message specifications. Technically speaking, SOAP is an XML-based protocol. However, constructing a valid SOAP message (including envelope, header, and body) is quite a bit more complex than simply representing just your data with XML. The same can be said of parsing XML or JSON versus full-blown SOAP messages. And this complexity means that developers typically need SOAP libraries in order to construct and parse SOAP messages. The need for these libraries limits SOAP's usability on small or specialty devices.

One of the main advantages of JSON, other than its drop-dead simplistic formatting, is that, for a given data package, it is much smaller in size than the same data represented as XML/SOAP. Again, this makes JSON very appealing for occasionally-connected or low-power devices, as well as those that are most often used over cellular networks.

Of course, another key advantage of JSON is that it *is* JavaScript. So consuming, creating, and manipulating JSON-based objects within JavaScript code is very natural and very easy. JSON objects are themselves first-class citizens in JavaScript.

This is not to say SOAP isn't valuable or doesn't have its place; quite the contrary, actually. The capabilities of the SOAP protocol go far beyond those of REST and JSON (at this point in time, anyway). Most of these capabilities are defined by the WS-* specifications. ("WS" stands for "web services.") These specifications deal with more complex messaging needs, such as message security, transactions, service discovery, metadata publishing, routing, trust relationships, and identity federation. While some of these capabilities are available with a RESTful API, their implementations are not yet—as of this writing—fully worked out. For example, you can utilize something like OAuth to facilitate delegated authorization. But so far there is no specification for transactions or message security.

A Few Feature Highlights of the ASP.NET Web API

In this book's previous edition, we discussed how the MVC Framework provided a decent platform for building RESTful services. However, in response to feedback from our readers, in this edition we're focusing exclusively on the ASP.NET Web API, trusting you to explore MVC as a services platform on your own. This new edition will also cover many of the new capabilities and features found in the 2nd version of the ASP.NET Web API (released towards the end of 2013).

Let's briefly look at just a few of the features you'll be learning about later in this book:

- **Convention-based CRUD Actions:** HTTP actions (e.g., GET and POST) are automatically mapped to controller methods (also known as *controller actions*) by their names. For example, on a controller called Products, a GET request such as /api/products will automatically invoke a method named "Get" on the controller. Further, the ASP.NET Web API automatically matches the number of arguments given in the URL to an appropriate controller method. Therefore, the URL /api/products/32 would automatically invoke the Get(long id) method. The same magic also applies to POST, PUT, and DELETE calls.

- **Built-in Content Negotiation:** In MVC, controller methods that return JSON or XML have to be hard-coded to specifically return one of those content types. But with the ASP.NET Web API, the controller method need only return the raw data value, and this value will be automatically converted to JSON or XML, per the caller's request. The caller simply uses an Accept or Content-Type HTTP header to specify the desired content type of the returned data, and the ASP.NET Web API ensures your return value gets formatted appropriately. Rather than returning an object of type JsonResult, you simply return your data object (e.g., Product or IEnumerable<Product>).

- **Attribute Routing and Route Prefixes (new in ASP.NET Web API 2):** Sometimes you don't want to rely on convention-based routing. With v2, you can use the Route, RoutePrefix, and various Http* attributes (e.g., HttpGet, HttpPost) to explicitly define routes and associated HTTP actions for your controllers. As you'll see, this new feature makes supporting resource relationships much easier than was possible in v1.

- **Route Constraints (new in ASP.NET Web API 2):** This very cool feature provides a mechanism for constraining various controller methods and their routes to specific business rules. For example, rather than just {id} in your route, you can now include something like {id:int}, {id:min(10)}, {id:range(1,100)}, or even {phone:regex(^\d{3}-\d{3}-\d{4}$)}.

- **CORS Support (new in ASP.NET Web API 2):** The new EnableCors attribute allows you as the developer of an API to allow cross-origin requests from JavaScript applications not in your service's domain.

- **Global Error Handling (new in ASP.NET Web API 2):** This enormous improvement in error handling appeared in the ASP.NET Web API 2.1 release. All unhandled exceptions can now be caught and handled through one central mechanism. The framework now supports multiple exception loggers, which have access to the actual unhandled exception and the context in which it occurred.

- **IHttpActionResult (new in ASP.NET Web API 2):** Implementations of this HttpResponseMessage factory interface provide a reusable, unit-test-friendly way to encapsulate results of your Web API action methods. The created responses flow through the outbound processing pipeline, so content negotiation is honored. In the example task-management service, you will see this used to set the status code and location header in response to POST requests.

Summary

In this chapter, you learned how the ASP.NET Web API provides a great platform for building REST-style Web APIs. In scenarios where much of the power and flexibility of WCF and SOAP aren't needed, Web API can be a very simple and elegant alternative. These scenarios include applications that need to support only HTTP communication, as well as those that focus heavily on text-formatted messages.

■ ■ ■

CHAPTER 2

What Is RESTful?

This chapter explores what a service following the REST architectural style should look like to a caller. Considering that such an API is supposed to better leverage the HTTP protocol and its various aspects, focusing on HTTP verbs and resources, its interface will be markedly different from your typical RPC-style API. So, as we design the service, we will compare the REST approach with a more traditional RPC or SOAP approach.

Throughout this book, we will be working on a service for managing tasks. It's not terribly exciting; however, the lack of domain excitement will let you focus on the technical aspects of the service. Designing a RESTful interface is trickier than you might think, and you will need to reprogram your brain to some degree to go about modeling such an API.

The fact that this is more work up front certainly doesn't mean you shouldn't follow this path. As briefly covered in the previous chapter, there are many benefits to the REST architectural style. In fact, REST is effectively a restating or clarification of what an ideal web-based application should look like. But it will take some work to realize those benefits. Creating a REST API is not as simple as just converting your RPC methods into REST URLs, as many like to imagine. You must work within the constraints of the architecture, trusting that those constraints will result in a "better" API. And, in this case, you must also work within the constraints of the HTTP protocol because that will be your platform.

Here's what you'll learn about in this chapter:

- Leonard Richardson's maturity model for REST

- Working with URIs and resources

- Working with HTTP verbs

- Returning appropriate HTTP status codes

- What is the "Uniform Interface"?

Let's get started.

From RPC to REST

In November 2008, a fellow by the name of Leonard Richardson created a maturity model for REST. A maturity model, by definition, is a map that guides the user into ever-increasing levels of compliance with a given definition, architecture, or methodology. For example, the model called Capability Maturity Model Integration (CMMI) was created as a process-improvement approach to help organizations (typically, software organizations) improve performance and increase efficiencies. The model contains five *levels*, where each successive level is designed to provide the user or organization more process efficiency than the previous level.

Richardson's REST Maturity Model (RMM) provides service API developers the same type of improvement map for building RESTful web services. His model, in fact, starts at level 0 with an RPC-style interface, and then progresses up through three more levels—at which point you've achieved an API interface design that is, at least according to Roy Fielding,[1] a pre-condition for a RESTful service. That is, you cannot claim to have a RESTful service if you stop at levels 0, 1, or 2 of the RMM.

Figure 2-1 summarizes the levels in the RMM.

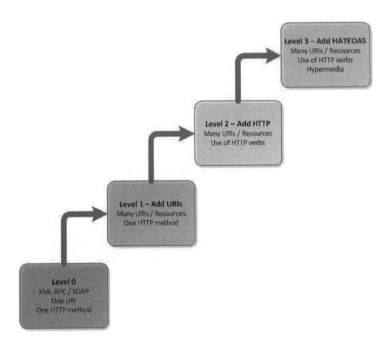

***Figure 2-1.** Diagram of Richardson's REST Maturity Model*

XML-RPC and SOAP

At Level 0, the API resembles most SOAP services. That is, the interface is characterized by having a single URI that supports only a single HTTP method or verb. You'll learn more about the available verbs in a bit; but for now, just know that HTTP provides a small set of known verbs that must be used if you intend to conform to and capitalize on the protocol.

Suppose, as mentioned in Chapter 1, that you want to build a task-management service, and you need to provide a way to create new tasks through a new API. If this were a Level 0 SOAP-based service, you might create a Windows Communication Foundation (WCF) service class called TaskService; and on it you might create a new method called CreateTask(). This method might take a request message that includes a task title, task category, perhaps a status, and so on. And the method's response message would likely include, among other things, a system-generated task number.

You also might create a method for fetching the details of a task. So, on your TaskService class, you might add a method called GetTask(). This new method would likely take as input a task ID of some kind, and then return a task object—serialized as XML.

---

[1]http://roy.gbiv.com/untangled/2008/rest-apis-must-be-hypertext-driven

To round out the `TaskService` class, you might also add the methods `UpdateTask()`, `SearchTasks()`, and `CompleteTask()`. Each of these would be designed to take in appropriate XML request messages and return some kind of response message.

The REST Maturity Model, and the work published by Roy Fielding, provides three distinct web-related attributes of an API that help you position yourself to be RESTful with HTTP:

- Unique URIs to resources

- Consistent use of HTTP verbs

- "Hypermedia as the engine of application state" (HATEOAS)

Let's examine the pretend `TaskService` service interface using these three attributes. (See Table 2-1.)

Table 2-1. *Task Service at Level 0 on the RMM*

Method	URI	HTTP verb	State changes/contract
CreateTask	/api/taskService.svc	POST	Caller required to know (e.g., WSDL)
GetTask	/api/taskService.svc	POST	Caller required to know (e.g., WSDL)
GetTaskAssignees	/api/taskService.svc	POST	Caller required to know (e.g., WSDL)
SearchTasks	/api/taskService.svc	POST	Caller required to know (e.g., WSDL)
UpdateTask	/api/taskService.svc	POST	Caller required to know (e.g., WSDL)
CompleteTask	/api/taskService.svc	POST	Caller required to know (e.g., WSDL)

As you can see, each operation or method on the service looks the same when looked at from the point of view of the Web. For example, whether fetching task 123 or task 456, the URI is the same. In fact, it is also the same URI used to create a task, update a task, complete a task, and so on. There's no sense of resource or resource addressability in our URI; that is, there's no URI that points directly to a specific task or list of tasks.

This example also does not utilize HTTP verbs as intended. This was discussed a bit in Chapter 1, and you'll learn about this in more detail later; however, every action available in the RPC-style API is essentially custom-made. To be RESTful on HTTP, you need to avoid creating custom actions and instead support actions that are consistent with HTTP. In other words, you need to use GET, PUT, POST, and DELETE (to name the primary actions).

And finally, clients of your RPC-style API are required to know all of the available actions ahead of time. This means there is an implicit binding between client and server, in that the caller is dependent on a contract and a given set of actions from the service. This does not feel very Web-like. When you browse to a public web site, all you are required to remember is the root address. From there, everything else is discoverable and linked to other elements via hypermedia (i.e., links and forms). Indeed, the Web dictates that hypermedia is the engine of application state. You can transition from one state to the next (where the state machine is a web site or the broader Internet) based solely on links and forms. You are not required to remember or know ahead of time the specific addresses for all of the pages you intend to traverse.

Similarly, you are not required to remember every field that must be filled out on a form when submitting a request (e.g., placing an order or signing up for a magazine subscription). Essentially, the server dictates all of the relationships, all of the URIs, and all of the forms, without you needing any prior knowledge; it provides all the information necessary to compose requests.

As you'll see shortly, this attribute of HATEOAS is key to a service's RESTfulness; however, it is often overlooked, as it requires a significant shift in thinking from the traditional RPC-style interface design.

URIs and Resources

As noted briefly in Chapter 1, building a RESTful interface means you end up with an API that is very resource-centric. As such, you need to intentionally design the interface with resources being at the center. Unlike RPC-style interfaces, where arbitrary service methods (i.e., the verbs) and their associated request and response messages rule the day, a REST interface will revolve around the resources (i.e., the nouns). The actions available to those resources are constrained by the use of HTTP. This is why you must map the available HTTP verbs into the API; you don't have the freedom to create other actions or verbs.

This concept is central to a REST design. So let's examine what the TaskService might look like if it were to move up to level 1 on the RMM. Table 2-2 shows how each individual resource is addressable by a unique URI.

Table 2-2. *Task Service at Level 1 on the RMM*

Method	URI	HTTP verb	State changes/contract
CreateTask	/api/tasks	POST	Caller required to know (e.g., WSDL)
GetTask	/api/tasks/1234	POST	Caller required to know (e.g., WSDL)
GetTaskAssignees	/api/tasks/1234	POST	Caller required to know (e.g., WSDL)
SearchTasks	/api/tasks	POST	Caller required to know (e.g., WSDL)
UpdateTask	/api/tasks/1234	POST	Caller required to know (e.g., WSDL)
CompleteTask	/api/tasks/1234	POST	Caller required to know (e.g., WSDL)

But you still must rely on specific messages for operations. In other words, the caller can't differentiate between the two different operations available with the /api/tasks URI unless the caller already has the contract. You're still using only the POST HTTP verb, so the request message itself dictates the desired action.

HTTP Verbs

You must look beyond URIs and their resources to the actions needed by the service. These actions will help you identify the HTTP verbs you need to use. Continuing to follow our example, there's no such thing as a CreateTask HTTP verb. In fact, there's not even a Create verb. If you're going to leverage the REST architectural style and the HTTP protocol, you must choose from the verbs available in that protocol, namely these:

- GET
- PUT
- POST
- DELETE

Intuitively, you can quickly eliminate GET and DELETE for the CreateTask action. But what is the difference in intent between PUT and POST? As shown in Table 2-3, PUT is designed to create or replace a resource with a known identifier, and hence a known unique URI. You use a POST when the system is generating the new resource's identifier.

Table 2-3. *Using HTTP Verbs with the Task Resource*

HTTP verb	(Collection URI) http://myserver.com/tasks	(Element URI) http://myserver.com/tasks/1234
GET	List of tasks, including URIs to individual tasks	Get a specific task, identified by the URI
PUT	Replace the entire collection of tasks	Replace or create the single task identified by the URI
POST	Create a new single task, where its identifier is generated by the system	Create a new subordinate under the task identified by the URI
DELETE	Delete the entire collection of tasks	Delete the tasks identified by the URI

Technically speaking, the REST architectural style is agnostic about any specific protocol. That includes the HTTP protocol. In other words, all you need is a protocol that provides a language and mechanism for describing both states (i.e., *representations*) and state changes. However, since this book is about building a REST service with the ASP.NET Web API, you'll focus on REST with HTTP. Fortunately, the HTTP protocol itself covers most of what you need.

Let's walk through some important concepts with this mapping. First, the exact meaning of each of the four verbs is dependent on the URI. So even though you have only four verbs, you actually have eight different actions available to you. The difference lies in whether the URI defines a collection or a unique element.

Second, when creating new instances of the resource (e.g., a new task), PUT is used with a unique URI in the scenario where the caller generates the new resource's identifier before submitting the request to the server. In Table 2-3, the PUT action is used with a unique element URI to create a new task with the specific identifier, 1234. If instead the system is to generate the identifier, the caller uses the POST action and a collection URI. This also ties into the concept of *idempotency*.

The GET, PUT, and DELETE methods are said to be idempotent; that is, calling them over and over will produce the same result without any additional side effects. For example, the caller should be able to call the DELETE action on a specific resource without receiving any errors and without harming the system. If the resource has already been deleted, the caller should not receive an error. The same applies to the PUT action. For a given unique resource (identified by an element URI), submitting a PUT request should update the resource if it already exists. Or, if it doesn't exist, the system should create the resource as submitted. In other words, calling PUT over and over produces the same result without any additional side effects (i.e., the new task will exist in the system per the representation provided by the caller, whether the system had to create a new one or update an existing one).

The GET action is also said to be *safe*. Safe means that nothing in the system is changed at all, which is appropriate for HTTP calls that are meant to query the system for either a collection of resources or for a specific resource.

It is important that the idempotency of the service's GET, PUT, and DELETE operations remain consistent with the HTTP protocol standards. Thus, every effort should be made to ensure those three actions can be called over and over without error.

Unlike the other three actions, POST is not considered to be idempotent. This is because POST is used to create a new instance of the identified resource type for every invocation of the method. Where calling PUT over and over will never result in more than one resource being created or updated, calling POST will result in new resource instances—one for each call. This is appropriate for cases where the system must generate the new resource's identifier and return it in the response.

As you model your task-management service, you will need to map each resource with a set of HTTP actions, defining which ones are allowed and which ones aren't supported.

Now let's take a new look at the task service. This time around, you'll use the available HTTP verbs, which will put you at level 2 on the RMM. (See Table 2-4.)

Table 2-4. *Task Service at Level 2 in the RMM*

Method	URI	HTTP verb	State changes/contract
CreateTask	/api/tasks	POST	Caller required to know (e.g., WSDL)
GetTask	/api/tasks/1234	GET	Caller required to know (e.g., WSDL)
GetTaskAssignees	/api/tasks/1234/users	GET	Caller required to know (e.g., WSDL)
SearchTasks	/api/tasks	GET	Caller required to know (e.g., WSDL)
UpdateTask	/api/tasks/1234	PUT	Caller required to know (e.g., WSDL)
CompleteTask	/api/tasks/1234	DELETE	Caller required to know (e.g., WSDL)

At this point, the service is utilizing unique URIs for individual resources, and you've switched to using HTTP verbs instead of custom request message types. That is, each of the PUT and POST actions mentioned previously will simply take a representation of a task resource (e.g., XML or JSON). However, the client must still have prior knowledge of the API in order to traverse the domain and to perform any operations more complex than creating, updating, or completing a task. In the true nature of the Web, you should instead fully guide the client, providing all available resources and actions via links and forms. This is what is meant by "hypermedia as the engine of application state."

HATEOAS

As you look at Tables 2-3 and 2-4, you can see that certain GET operations will return collections of resources. One of the guiding principles of REST with HTTP is that callers make transitions through application state only by navigating hypermedia provided by the server. In other words, given a root or starting URI, the caller should be able to navigate the collection of resources without prior knowledge of the possible navigation paths. Thus, whenever a resource is returned from the service, whether in a collection or by itself, the returned data should include the URI required to turn around and perform another GET to retrieve just that resource.

Here's an example of an XML response message that illustrates how each element in the collection should contain a URI to the resource:

```
<?xml version="1.0" encoding="utf-8"?>
<Tasks>
    <Task Id="1234" Status="Active" >
        <link rel="self" href="/api/tasks/1234" method="GET" />
    </Task>
    <Task Id="0987" Status="Completed" >
        <link rel="self" href="/api/tasks/0987" method="GET" />
    </Task>
</Tasks>
```

▓ **Note**   The actual href will include the URI's scheme, host, and where required, port (e.g., href="
http://www.foo.com/api/tasks/1234). We are omitting these details to focus on concepts and reduce clutter.

It is typically appropriate to return only a few attributes or pieces of data when responding with a collection, such as in the preceding example. Now the caller can use the URI to query a specific resource to retrieve all attributes of that resource. For example, the Tasks collection response (as just shown) might contain only the Task's Id and a URI to fetch the Task resource. But when calling GET to get a specific Task, the response might include TaskCategory, DateCreated, TaskStatus, TaskOwner, and so on.

Taking this approach can be a little trickier when using strongly typed model objects in .NET (or any other OO language). This is because you need to define at least two different variants of the Task type. The typical pattern is to have a TaskInfo class and a Task class, where the TaskInfo class exists only to provide basic information about a Task. The collection might look like this:

```
<?xml version="1.0" encoding="utf-8"?>
<Tasks>
    <TaskInfo Id="1234" Status="Active" >
        <link rel="self" href="/api/tasks/1234" method="GET" />
    </TaskInfo>
    <TaskInfo Id="0987" Status="Completed" >
        <link rel="self" href="/api/tasks/0987" method="GET" />
    </TaskInfo>
</Tasks>
```

And the single resource might look like this:

```
<?xml version="1.0" encoding="utf-8"?>
<Task Id="1234" Status="Active" DateCreated="2011-08-15" Owner="Sally" Category="Projects" >
    <link rel="self" href="/api/tasks/1234" method="GET" />
</Task>
```

Utilizing two different types like this is not a requirement for REST or any other service API-style. You may find that you don't need to separate collection type definitions from other definitions. Or you may find that you need many more than two. It all depends on the usage scenarios and how many different attributes exist on the resource. For example, if the Task resource included only five or six attributes, you probably wouldn't create a separate type for the collection objects. But if the Task object were to include 100 or more attributes (as is typical in something like a financial application), it might be a good idea to create more than one variation of the Task type.

Within the realm of HATEOAS, you also want to guide the user as to the actions available on a resource. You just saw how you can use a `<link>` element to provide a reference for fetching task details. You can expand this concept to include all available resources and actions. Remember, when browsing a web site, a user needs to have prior knowledge only of the root address to traverse the entire site. You want to provide a similar experience to callers of the API.

Here's what a full HATEOAS-compliant XML response might look like for the TaskInfo type:

```
<?xml version="1.0" encoding="utf-8"?>
<Tasks>
    <TaskInfo Id="1234" Status="Active" >
        <link rel="self" href="/api/tasks/1234" method="GET" />
        <link rel="users" href="/api/tasks/1234/users" method="GET" />
        <link rel="history" href="/api/tasks/1234/history" method="GET" />
        <link rel="complete" href="/api/tasks/1234" method="DELETE" />
        <link rel="update" href="/api/tasks/1234" method="PUT" />
    </TaskInfo>
    <TaskInfo Id="0987" Status="Completed" >
        <link rel="self" href="/api/tasks/0987" method="GET" />
        <link rel="users" href="/api/tasks/0987/users" method="GET" />
        <link rel="history" href="/api/tasks/0987/history" method="GET" />
        <link rel="reopen" href="/api/tasks/0987" method="PUT" />
    </TaskInfo>
</Tasks>
```

Note that the links available to each task are a little different. This is because you don't need to complete an already completed task. Instead, you need to offer a link to reopen it. Also, you don't want to allow updates on a completed task, so that link is not present in the completed task.

LINK PHILOSOPHY

We want to offer a disclaimer and a word of warning for the topic of links in REST messages. You find that, over the past several years, the debate over how the HTTP verbs are supposed to be used can be quite heated at times. This debate also extends into how to best design URIs to be most RESTful—without degenerating into a SOAP-style API.

For example, in the Task XML you just looked at, it specifies the "reopen" link as a PUT to the /api/tasks/0987 URI. It also specifies the "complete" link as a DELETE to the /api/tasks/1234 URI. These approaches are neither specified by the REST architectural style, nor are they even agreed upon by the folks who practice REST. And for whatever reason, people on various sides of the debate tend to get worked up about their way of doing things.

Instead of using a PUT against the resource URI for the "reopen" action, you could instead use a PUT against a URI like /api/tasks/0987/reopen. We tend to lean away from this approach, as it pushes you closer to specifying actions instead of resources (for the URI). However, we also think it's a bit unrealistic to assume you can accommodate all available actions on something like a Task object with only four HTTP verbs. Indeed, there are a few more verbs you can use, including PATCH, HEAD, and OPTIONS. But even so, the set of available verbs is limited, and the REST architectural style dictates that you don't add to those verbs. So at some point, you need to make a judgment call as to how to implement various actions on the Task object. The important thing is to conform as closely to HTTP standards as possible.

The use of the DELETE verb is also hotly debated. Most enterprise applications don't allow the caller to really delete a resource. More often, a resource is merely closed, inactivated, hidden, and so on. As such, it might seem reasonable to not waste one of your precious few verbs on an action that you never even allow, when instead you could use it for the "close" action.

As with most endeavors in the world of software, the devil's in the details. And you can usually find 101 ways to implement those details if you look hard enough. Our advice here is to simply do the best you can, don't be afraid to be wrong, and don't get stuck in an infinite loop of forever debating the very best approach to follow. Think, commit, and go.

You can now complete the table of task resources and operations using the three concepts you've learned from the RMM:

- URIs and resources
- HTTP verbs
- HATEOAS

Table 2-5 illustrates the task service under a more ideal RESTful design. That is, it shows the things you can do to make the service self-describing (i.e., related information and available operations are given to the caller via links contained in the service's responses). Again, following the RMM isn't sufficient in itself to being able to claim your service is a REST service. But you also can't claim compliance with REST without following it, either.

Table 2-5. *Task Service at Level 3 in the RMM*

Method	URI	HTTP verb	State changes/contract
CreateTask	/api/tasks	POST	HTTP POST used for creation
GetTask	/api/tasks/1234	GET	HTTP GET always fetches
GetTaskAssignees	/api/tasks/1234/users	GET	HTTP GET on users is self-describing
SearchTasks	/api/tasks	GET	HTTP GET on tasks is self-describing
UpdateTask	/api/tasks/1234	PUT	HTTP PUT on a task updates
CompleteTask	/api/tasks/1234	DELETE	HTTP DELETE on a task deletes or inactivates

Now that the API is in compliance with Level 3 in the RMM, you can see how self-describing it is. Those wanting to consume this API can glean a great deal of information simply from the URI and a basic understanding of the HTTP methods. For example, a POST to the tasks collection will create a new task, and a DELETE request on a uniquely identified task will delete it.

It is from this consistency (along with a few other infrastructural constraints) that building a RESTful API gains its many advantages over its SOAP version. The entire infrastructure of the Web, including a plethora of hardware and software, both relies on and leverages this consistent set of constraints that constitute what is known as the "Uniform Interface." Abiding by these constraints with your API means you automatically inherit this rich semantic and infrastructural value.

There is one last bit of guidance—one last aspect of the Uniform Interface—to discuss before wrapping up this exploration of REST...

HTTP Status Codes

So far in this chapter, you've learned about the constraints of the REST architectural style that led to creating an API where resources are the message of choice; where every resource and every action on a resource has a unique URI; where, instead of creating custom methods or actions, you're limiting yourself to the actions available with HTTP; and, finally, where you're giving the caller every action available on a given resource. All of these constraints deal with calls made by the caller. The last thing to discuss deals with the messages you send back from the server in response to those calls.

In the same way that you are constrained to using only the verbs available with HTTP, you are also constrained to using only the well-known set of HTTP status codes as return "codes" for your service calls. That is not to say you can't include additional information, of course. However, every web page you visit includes an HTTP status code, in addition to the HTML you see in the browser. The basic idea here is simply to properly utilize known status codes in the response headers.

Let's look first at a subset of the available HTTP status codes. You can find the complete official specification here: www.w3.org/Protocols/rfc2616/rfc2616-sec10.html. In this section, you will be examining only a small subset of these codes. Table 2-6 lists the most common status codes and their descriptions in the context of a RESTful API.

Table 2-6. *A List of Common HTTP Status Codes*

Status Code	API meaning
200	All is good; response will include applicable resource information, as well
201	Resource created; will include the Location header specifying a URI to the newly created resource
202	Same as 200, but used for async; in other words, all is good, but we need to poll the service to find out when completed
301	The resource was moved; should include URI to new location
400	Bad request; caller should reformat the request
401	Unauthorized; should respond with an authentication challenge, to let the caller resubmit with appropriate credentials
402	Reserved for future use, but many times used to indicate a failure in a business rule or validation check
403	Access denied; user successfully authenticated, but is not allowed to access the requested resource
404	Resource not found, or caller not allowed to access the resource, and we don't want to reveal the reason
409	Conflict; used as a response to a PUT request when another caller has dirtied the resource
500	Server error; something bad happened, and server might include some indication of the underlying problem

For example, assume a caller submitted the following HTTP request:

```
GET /api/tasks/1234 HTTP/1.1
```

The service should respond as follows (this is the raw HTTP response):

```
HTTP/1.1 200 OK
Content-Type: application/xml

<Task Id="1234" Status="Active" DateCreated="2011-08-15" Owner="Sally" Category="Projects" >
    <link rel="self" href="/api/tasks/1234" method="GET" />
    <link rel="users" href="/api/tasks/1234/users" method="GET" />
    <link rel="complete" href="/api/tasks/1234" method="DELETE" />
    <link rel="update" href="/api/tasks/1234" method="PUT" />
</Task>
```

Suppose now the caller is using a POST request to create a new task:

```
POST /api/tasks HTTP/1.1
Content-Type: application/xml

<Task Status="Active" DateCreated="2012-08-15" Owner="Jimmy" Category="Projects" >
```

The service should respond with a 201 code and the new task's URI (assuming the call succeeded):

```
HTTP/1.1 201 Created
Location: /api/tasks/6789
Content-Type: application/xml
```

```
<Task Id="6789" Status="Active" DateCreated="2012-08-15" Owner="Jimmy" Category="Projects" >
    <link rel="self" href="/api/tasks/6789" method="GET" />
    <link rel="owner" href="/api/tasks/6789/owner" method="GET" />
    <link rel="complete" href="/api/tasks/6789" method="DELETE" />
    <link rel="update" href="/api/tasks/6789" method="PUT" />
</Task>
```

The main point here, which is consistent with the topics discussed throughout this chapter, is to leverage the HTTP protocol as much as you can. That is really the crux of REST with HTTP: you both use HTTP and allow yourself to be constrained by it, rather than working around or against the protocol.

HAL, Collection+JSON, …

Now that we've reached the end of the chapter, you may be thinking that we've exaggerated the level of discoverability available in a REST-based API. After all, the server doesn't appear to be "providing **all** of the information necessary to compose requests," as we advertised back in the *"XML-RPC and SOAP"* section. For example, one can't create a Task without knowing what attributes are required, and nothing we've seen thus far in the server responses provides this information.

Well, this is one of those cases where a little bit of pragmatism comes into play. Consider the following:

- As discussed back in Chapter 1, REST-based APIs are often chosen because the messages tend to be relatively small and easy to process. Enriching messages with metadata may be unwanted, and even unnecessary, in certain situations (e.g., APIs for internal clients and/or for clients with good online usage documentation).

- As of this writing, there is no single, accepted standard for this metadata. The two most prominent ones are Mike Amundsen's *Collection+JSON* (`http://amundsen.com/media-types/collection/`) and Mike Kelly's *HAL* (`http://stateless.co/hal_specification.html`).

Where does this leave us? Well, there is really no good answer as of yet. So, for the sake of maintaining focus on the ASP.NET Web API, we aren't going to discuss message metadata options any further. For those interested in this topic, we encourage you to independently peruse the literature related to Collection+JSON and HAL.

Summary

In this chapter, you explored various characteristics of a service API that must exist before you can claim you are RESTful. Remember that adherence to these characteristics doesn't automatically mean your service qualifies as a REST service; however, you can at least claim its service interface qualifies as such.

You also walked through Leonard Richardson's maturity model for REST services and used the model as a platform for comparing a RESTful service to something more SOAP- or XML-RPC in nature. This allowed you to see that SOAP services do not capitalize on various aspects of HTTP, as your REST services should.

Next, in Chapter 3, you will put this new knowledge to good use by designing the task management service as a REST API.

■ ■ ■

Designing the Sample REST API

Thus far, you've learned some basic principles of the REST architecture using the HTTP protocol, and you're now ready to start developing your task-management service. First, you'll need to take some time to carefully build up tables of resource types, their available HTTP actions, and associated URIs. This design step is important, similar in kind to the importance of patiently and intentionally modeling a database. It pays to think it through and get it right. And, as you walk through the different resource types, you'll begin examining some code.

You may recall from the previous chapter that a programmer by the name of Leonard Richardson created what has become known as the REST Maturity Model (RMM). This model defines a pathway for turning a more traditional RPC-style API into a REST-style API. As you build your sample API, using this maturity model will help you map from something most developers know (i.e., non-REST) into something new and different (i.e., REST). You will need to be on the lookout for the natural tendency of the API to degenerate into an RPC-style API, thus falling back down the maturity model. We'll try to draw attention to those moments where a wrong choice could send you sliding back down.

Also in this chapter, you will model a small database for storing tasks and their supporting data. You won't spend much time doing so, as building a RESTful rather than a non-RESTful service doesn't change your approach to database modeling. Either way, you need to store instances of your resources and their relationships.

Finally, you will walk through what we believe to be good choices for components to use in your ASP.NET Web API service implementation. Since you're going to build a working service application, not just a trivial "Hello World" type of application, we'll show you components such as an Object Relational Mapper (ORM), a logger, an Inversion of Control (IoC) container, a type mapper, and so on.

Task Management Resource Types

Let's start by thinking about some things you want the callers of the API to be able to do. Since this service is focused on task management, most of the capabilities it offers will be centered on creating, viewing, and updating tasks. Again, a domain that is simple and well understood will allow you to focus on the nondomain concepts we're concerned about in this book—specifically, REST and the ASP.NET Web API.

First and foremost, the caller should be able to create a new task. And it should be able to do so without being required to provide anything more than a subject. Values such as start date, end date, and so on can be updated later if they're not known at the time the task is created. When creating a new task, we will have the system create its identifier, as opposed to the caller generating a custom identifier and passing it in.

The system will provide a listing of all tasks to the caller. This listing will support pagination, because the number of tasks in the system can be large. The caller should also be able to find, update, and delete a specific existing task.

The system will need to support zero or more users as assignees to a task. Most systems dealing with tasks allow only a single user assignment, which can be an inconvenient limitation. Our requirement to support multiple user assignments to a task will make the API a little more interesting.

Speaking of users, we need to provide a listing of all users to the caller. This listing will support pagination, because the number of users in the system can be large.

Finally, to support classification of the tasks, we will provide support for the task status. We can assume that the available values for status will be configured at the time of deployment.

The task-management example is about managing tasks and highlighting features of the ASP.NET Web API, so we won't discuss adding, updating, or deleting users or statuses.

Figure 3-1 illustrates what the resource types will look like as a class diagram in Visual Studio 2013.

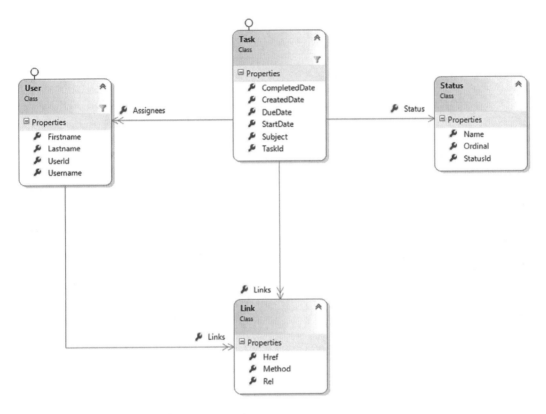

Figure 3-1. *A class diagram of resource types*

Recall, however, that one of the guiding rules of the REST architecture is to avoid coupling the client to the server by sharing type definitions. So, even though we will be using classes within server code to represent the resources received from and sent to the caller, these definitions are purely internal. This is markedly different from SOAP, where a Web Services Description Language (WSDL) document very explicitly defines all service interfaces, methods and their signatures, and all message types. Indeed this SOAP agreement is a contract, and it couples the client to the definitions on the server. But in REST, you want to avoid this coupling as much as possible and do your best to keep the "contractual" elements of your service limited to those required by the REST architectural style (i.e., HTTP verbs and URIs for accessing and updating resources, and utilizing hypermedia as the engine of application state).

Hypermedia Links

Speaking of hypermedia, you no doubt noticed the Link class in Figure 3-1, along with the associations with the other classes. Remember that we want to lead the API consumer through our application, similar to the way a user in a web browser is led through a web site with various hyperlinks and web forms. As such, each and every time you send a resource representation back to the caller, you need to give it a list of available actions (i.e., state changes).

Let's look at the Link class in more detail:

```
public class Link
{
    public string Rel { get; set; }
    public string Href { get; set; }
    public string Method { get; set; }
}
```

This should look familiar to you, as it is similar to the link HTML element. Indeed, you're trying to give the user very similar information to that provided by the link element:

- **Rel:** Specifies the relationship between the resource and the resource identified in the link

- **Href:** Specifies the linked resource's address

- **Method:** Specifies the HTTP method used to access the resource

As we discussed near the end of Chapter 2, one of the issues with using links like the one just specified is that the REST architecture doesn't define any specific standard for building hypermedia links in an API. If you search the Internet to find some semblance of a common approach, you will find many different opinions. And as we covered in Chapter 2, Collection+JSON and HAL appear to be the leading options right now.

RMM LOOKOUT

You might be tempted to use a set of more-specific links than just a collection of string-oriented link objects. For example, you could have Link properties for the following:

- Update

- Delete

- Assignees

- NewAssignment

But you need to remember that the RESTful service needs to look, act, and smell like a state machine. That means you must have resources moving through states via predefined state transitions. As defined by REST, your service must specify the allowed transitions for any given resource based on the current state of that resource. In other words, the available links (i.e., state transitions) will change from one call to the next, depending on what state you're in (e.g., the state of the Task and the permissions of the current user). Therefore, it is imperative that the list of links be dynamic.

There's another important reason for using a collection of links for the state transitions: the Single Responsibility Principle (SRP). Introduced by Robert C. Martin in 2002, the principle essentially states that a class should have only one reason to change; that is, it should only be responsible for one thing.

If you put those state transitions on your resource types, you violate SRP because now your resource definition will need to change every time you want to change any of the available state transitions. Your definition will also change if you add to or remove any transitions. Instead, the available transitions should be dictated by a separate class, not the resource type class. In other words, the rules that decide what actions the caller is allowed to take on a given resource should be external to that resource. If you keep the available transitions loose (your collection of Link objects), the service code doing the work of returning a resource can be the one to worry about creating appropriate links.

Before we get into modeling our resources against URIs and HTTP verbs, let's quickly look at the class code for our resource types:

```
public class Task
{
    public long? TaskId { get; set; }
    public string Subject { get; set; }
    public DateTime? StartDate { get; set; }
    public DateTime? DueDate { get; set; }
    public DateTime? CreatedDate { get; set;
    public DateTime? CompletedDate { get; set; }
    public Status Status { get; set; }
    public List<Link> Links { get; set; }
    public List<User> Assignees { get; set; }
}

public class Status
{
    public long StatusId { get; set; }
    public string Name { get; set; }
    public int Ordinal { get; set; }
}

public class User
{
    public long UserId { get; set; }
    public string Username { get; set; }
    public string Firstname { get; set; }
    public string Lastname { get; set; }
    public List<Link> Links { get; set; }
}
```

There's nothing particularly remarkable about these types, but note that their identifiers are integers, and those identifying values will be generated by the service, not provided by the caller. Also note that taskId is nullable. The reason for this will become clear when we deal with task updates.

Modeling the URIs and HTTP Verbs

We now want to model each resource type's allowed HTTP verbs and associated URIs. The operations (i.e., verbs) available will vary from type to type; there is no requirement for REST-based APIs to support all of the verbs on each resource type or URI.

Let's start with an easy one: Status. Table 3-1 illustrates that we want to support only one operation.

Table 3-1. *A List of Status Operations*

URI	Verb	Description
/api/statuses	GET	Gets the full list of all statuses

We don't need to allow the caller to modify statuses. The only requirement is to provide a method to get the list of statuses (e.g., to populate drop-down controls).

The URIs and verbs for the User resource type will be similar. The task-management service isn't going to allow the caller to modify the users in the system. Table 3-2 illustrates the two operations we will allow on User.

Table 3-2. *A List of User Operations*

URI	Verb	Description
/api/users	GET	Gets the full list of all users; optionally specifies a filter
/api/users/123	GET	Gets the details for a single user

The main difference between this resource type and the Status type is that we want to allow the caller to supply a filter for limiting the list of users returned. This will be in the form of URL query string arguments. We'll explore the details of user querying later, when we start building the service code.

ODATA

The /api/users URI in our task-management service will be providing limited filtering capability in the way of simple query strings. You might be tempted to allow more complex queries by supporting ANDs and ORs, parentheses, TOP, ORDERBY, and so on. However, it is for these capabilities that the Open Data Protocol (OData) exists. This protocol was created by Microsoft and a few other companies to standardize web-based data querying and updating.

Here's what the www.odata.org web site says:

> The Open Data Protocol (OData) enables the creation of REST-based data services, which allow resources, identified using Uniform Resource Identifiers (URIs) and defined in a data model, to be published and edited by Web clients using simple HTTP messages.

In fact, the ASP.NET Web API provides a simple mechanism for supporting OData with your REST service.

The downside to using OData with the Web API is that you must expose your domain model types over the wire. We'll be taking the approach of mapping domain model types over to resource types before returning the data to the caller. This approach reduces coupling between the client and server, which is one of the salient features of a REST-based API. But we can't do this if we want to implement an OData query interface using the built-in OData feature in ASP.NET Web API. It is for this reason, and the fact that OData is such a large topic in and of itself, that we trust our readers to explore OData on their own.

Finally, we need to define the URIs and HTTP verbs for the Task resource type. Table 3-3 shows the list of operations available for the Task.

Table 3-3. *A List of Task Operations*

URI	Verb	Description
/api/tasks	GET	Gets the full list of all tasks; optionally specify a filter
/api/tasks/123	GET	Gets the details for a single task
/api/tasks/123/users	GET	Gets the users assigned to the specified task
/api/tasks/123/users	PUT	Replaces all users on the specified task; returns the updated task in the response
/api/tasks/123/users	DELETE	Deletes all users from the specified task; returns the updated task in the response
/api/tasks/123/users/456	PUT	Adds the specified user (e.g., 456) as an assignee on the task; returns the updated task in the response
/api/tasks/123/users/456	DELETE	Deletes the specified user from the assignee list; returns the updated task in the response
/api/tasks	POST	Creates a new task; returns the new task in the response
/api/tasks/123	PUT	Updates the specified task; returns the updated task in the response

The relationships with users and statuses make task operations more interesting. For example, here you see something that wasn't present in the previous resource types: using PUT and DELETE on a collection of related resources. In order to add a new assignee to a task, the caller utilizes the users collection, adding or deleting specific users one at a time. Or, optionally, the caller can use PUT or DELETE against the entire collection. According to the HTTP protocol, this will replace or delete all users associated with the task.

Tasks are also related to statuses. In this example, let's imagine that there is a rules-based workflow that controls task status updates (i.e., updating a task's status isn't just a typical update operation in the "CRUD" sense of things). Instead, a series of processing steps must be executed within our service in order to change a task's status, possibly even sending an email—thereby making this update non-idempotent. How should we handle this from a REST-based API perspective?

We'll start by thinking about the required operations in the abstract, and then create conceptual resources to represent them. For example, we need to support the ability to begin, or "activate," a task. And, unless the system's prospective users are total slackers, we need to support the ability to eventually complete a task. Last, we probably should also support the ability to reopen, or "re-activate," a task that had been marked as completed.

Did you come up with a list of conceptual resources based on that last paragraph? We came up with Task Activations, Task Completions, and Task Re-activations. Table 3-4 summarizes this.

Table 3-4. *A List of Task Status Operations*

URI	Verb	Description
/api/tasks/123/activations	POST	Starts, or "activates," a task; returns the updated task in the response
/api/tasks/123/completions	POST	Completes a task; returns the updated task in the response
/api/tasks/123/reactivations	POST	Reopens, or "re-activates," a task; returns the updated task in the response

The situation of needing to support non–resource API operations using REST is fairly common. Having been through this little exercise with task status, you are now better prepared to deal with it on the job. It's okay if the list of "resources" you thought of didn't exactly match those in Table 3-4. The point is to keep thinking in terms of resources so that you don't degenerate into an RPC API.

And that wraps up this chapter's exploration of designing the resource types. Next, you will learn how to perform a quick modeling of the database.

The Task-Management Data Model

In this section, we're going to create the model for storing the task-management service data.

Logically, we have three categories of data to store:

- Reference data

- Tasks

- Users

Statuses are reference data. The Status table will include an identifier, a name, and an ordinal. The ordinal value can be used for sorting the data for display in drop-down or other list controls.

The task and user data is also straightforward. Note that we will use a many-to-many table to link tasks to users because a task can be associated with zero or more users, and a user can be associated with zero or more tasks.

Most of the model in Figure 3-2 looks similar to the resource types you designed earlier in this chapter. However, this model includes a column called ts for each table. As a matter of practice, it is a good idea to include a versioning column to be used for concurrency checking (i.e., checking for dirty data on update). We chose ts for the column name for a few reasons: it stands for *timestamp*, it's short, and it typically doesn't conflict with other column names. Later on, as we build the code, you'll see exactly how the ts column is used to ensure proper concurrency checking.

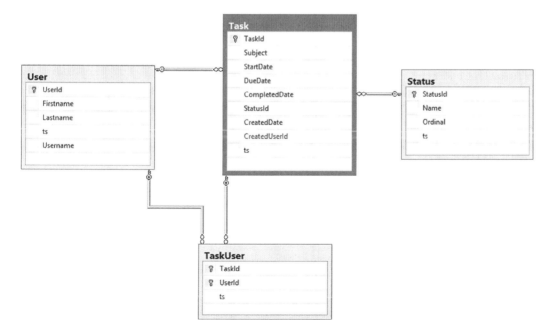

Figure 3-2. *Task and Reference Data Tables*

You also may have noticed the CreatedUserId column in the Task table, which we've included to help illustrate that the model objects exposed via the API can differ from the model objects, or "entities," used to persist the data.

At this point, we've designed all of the resource types, and we've laid out the URIs and HTTP verbs for those types. We've also just briefly modeled the underlying database to store our resources. Before closing out this chapter, let's spend a bit of time choosing the various architecture components we'll need to build our service application.

Choosing Architecture Components

The purpose of this book is to take you from a near-zero level of experience in writing .NET services, teach you about REST and the Web API, and have you end up with a reasonably robust, simple, yet fully functional, REST-style service. As such, we feel it prudent to introduce you to some components and tools that can greatly assist you in the implementation. So, now that we've done most of the high-level design of the system, let's explore some these.

Data Access

There are quite a few options available in .NET when it comes to data access and object persistence on SQL Server. Most of these options fall into one of two categories: using the various SqlClient objects (e.g., SqlConnection, SqlDataAdapter, and SqlCommand) with stored procedures or embedded SQL, or using an Object Relational Mapper (ORM). Sometimes the two approaches are used together, but more often developers choose one or the other.

We will be using the NHibernate ORM. The fact that you can do virtually all of your data access in C#, and the natural support for the Unit of Work pattern (via the ISession) are significant benefits. This is especially appropriate for web or service applications, where you want a given call to execute within the context of a single database session and transaction.

UNIT OF WORK AND REPOSITORY PATTERNS

Martin Fowler introduces some extremely valuable enterprise patterns in his book, *Patterns of Enterprise Application Architecture* (Addison-Wesley, 2002). If you aren't familiar with the definition and use-cases of Unit of Work as they apply to data access, we strongly encourage you to read up on them in Martin's book. For a free and quick summary of the patterns, you can also visit www.martinfowler.com, where he offers some brief descriptions and diagrams of some of the patterns found in the book. Possessing a solid understanding of such data access–related patterns is key to properly managing database connections and transactions, in-memory object state, and data cache. It is also critical to maintaining testability.

Type Mapper

A good type mapper liberates you from the tedium of manually mapping data between objects as processing flows up and down the stack. We will be using AutoMapper to map data between resources and their persistent representations, or entities. In other words, we can lean on AutoMapper to copy values from the domain or data model object to and from the corresponding—yet, slightly different—REST resource type. This allows us to easily account for differences in property names, data types, and even differences in the actual number of properties.

IoC Container

These days, whether you're working in .NET or in Java, not using an IoC container of some sort can almost be considered foolish. There are certainly special circumstances that might require you to manage dependencies yourself, but generally speaking, using one of the available frameworks is pretty much a no-brainer. The ASP.NET Web API provides the IDependencyResolver interface for the very purpose of resolving dependencies, and we will implement it with the Ninject container.

Logger

If you ask 10 people for their opinion on the best logger, you will likely get 11 different answers. We'll spare you the suspense and tell you now that we'll be using log4net. The log4net logging framework is simple to use, provides a logger interface that can be used with IoC containers, comes with numerous options for routing and filtering, and has been used all around the world in thousands of .NET applications for many years.

Testing Framework

The two most prominent testing frameworks for .NET are MSTest and NUnit. Both work very well, and both have their pros and cons. We tend to lean towards NUnit for its simplicity, full-featured Assert class, and available fluent interface, though MSTest also works just fine. We will be using NUnit.

Mocking Framework

We will use Moq for the test mocking framework. It is simple, powerful, and popular.

Summary

That wraps up the bulk of our exploration of the API design, including the SQL Server database and a selection of the most important components in your architecture.

At this point, using the modeling technique we introduced in this chapter, you should be able to properly design just about any RESTful service, complete with resource types, URIs, and HTTP verbs. You should also be aware of various tool and framework choices that can be leveraged in building a services application with ASP.NET Web API.

CHAPTER 4

■ ■ ■

Building the Environment and Creating the Source Tree

It's time to start working in Visual Studio! We've spent the first three chapters learning about REST and the ASP.NET Web API, as well as designing the task-management service and its underlying classes and database tables. More importantly, we've spent some time modeling the resource types and URLs we want to offer for the RESTful service.

In this chapter, we'll walk through the process of creating the task-management source tree. This will include a specific folder structure (in Windows Explorer) and a Visual Studio 2013 solution and its projects. We will also configure some external libraries using NuGet, as well as create a few project references. Last, we will lay down some initial code for the data model classes, service-resource types, logging, and the database.

It is important to set up the source tree properly or, rather, in a manner that allows for the benefits of separating architectural layers and components into discrete folders and projects. Think of it as the foundation on which we're going to build the "business" functionality. If this is done right, adding the task-management service operations and making sure they are fully testable will be simple. If this is done incorrectly, the service code will end up overly coupled and not conducive to clean and effective unit tests.

Speaking of the source code, feel free to download it from either www.apress.com or from the corresponding GitHub repository at https://github.com/jamiekurtz/WebApi2Book. Doing so will save you a ton of typing!

Let's start with a few basics that will help ensure your machine is ready for the code.

Configuring the Machine

In this section, you'll learn about the software prerequisites for building your task-management service. The list is actually quite short, so this won't take long. You may be able to get everything working by using a different bunch of software or versions. The specifications listed here simply note what has been tested (i.e., what is supported if you are going to utilize the example code that accompanies this book).

Windows 8 64-bit with .NET Framework 4.51

The code in this book was written on 64-bit Windows 8 with .NET Framework 4.51 installed. Our recommendation would be to follow suit, though Windows 7 64-bit (with .NET 4.51) would probably work as well in case you're one of the many who haven't "upgraded" to Windows 8.

For the web site you're going to build, you will use IIS Express during development, which is installed with Visual Studio 2013. Don't worry about needing to use the Professional Edition of Windows 8 (that supports running IIS) unless, of course, you'd rather use IIS over IIS Express.

SQL Server 2012

As discussed in Chapter 3, the task-management service will include a simple SQL Server database. Thus, you need to have some version of SQL Server installed on your local machine. We used SQL Server 2012 Developer Edition to write this book.

In general, we prefer to install SQL Server as the default instance (i.e., don't use a named instance). To run the code as-is, you will need to do the same. That said, if you use a named instance (e.g., SQLEXPRESS), you can simply update the connection string(s) before trying to run the example code.

Visual Studio 2013

Since you're working with the ASP.NET Web API 2, you will need to install the 2012 or 2013 version of Visual Studio. This code will not work with any of the previous versions. We used 2013 to write the code accompanying this book. And in terms of a specific edition, we used the Ultimate edition. The Professional and Premium editions will work fine, too.

One of the main reasons for using a non-Express edition of Visual Studio is that JetBrain's ReSharper is supported only on the "full" editions. And there's no way either of us would ever write code without ReSharper! For this book, we used ReSharper version 8.2; we highly recommend you do the same.

RESHARPER

ReSharper is one of those tools that, once you've used it for a bit, you can't go back to writing .NET code without it. Seriously, time and time again we hear developers refusing to code without ReSharper, even to the point where they will purchase their own personal copies if their employers won't pony up. It's that good!

So if you haven't used it, we strongly encourage you to visit `www.jetbrains.com` and take a look—and buy it. It will save you tons of time and effort, especially if you write code according to today's best practices with regard to dependency injection, unit tests, refactoring, variable naming, and so on.

NuGet Package Manager 2.6

We will use NuGet to set up the various libraries used in your task-management service. This Visual Studio add-in allows a developer to download and add project references for third-party libraries, each with a single command in the NuGet Package Manager console (window). For example, assume you run the following command with your test project selected:

```
install-package nunit
```

This code downloads the latest version of NUnit and adds it to your source tree, as well as a reference to all necessary DLLs from within your test project.

NuGet also takes care of library dependencies automatically. For example, if the latest NUnit package required another library, it would be downloaded and referenced, as well.

This book, and the example code, takes advantage of a new feature added back in NuGet version 2.1 that allows you to specify a custom folder location for the downloaded packages. As you'll see later, we prefer to put our libraries in a lib folder above the folder that holds the solution. By default, however, NuGet places the packages in the same folder as the solution file.

To ensure you have the 2.6 version (or greater) of the NuGet Package Manager, use the "Extensions and Updates" option under the Tools menu in Visual Studio. If you're starting from a clean install of Visual Studio 2013, your NuGet Package Manager version should already be at 2.6. The version number will appear on the right-hand side when you click the extension itself. If you already have a newer version, that will work fine, too (e.g., we're using 2.8).

Creating the Folder Structure

Part of the challenge of creating a source tree is making sure the top-level folder structure is created properly. That is, we want to create a set of folders and paths that allow for easy branching and merging; allow for the separation of libraries from source code, documents, and other types of artifacts; and are relatively easy and fast to type on the command line. We also want the folders to be intuitive to any developer who must look at the code.

While no real standard exists for a source-code folder structure, the folders we're going to create in this section are similar to what you can find in many of today's open source projects. The structure we'll use in this project is actually quite simple; we just want to have a root folder of some kind, with the following main folders under it: doc, lib, and src. Figure 4-1 shows what this would look like under a folder called WebApi2Book.

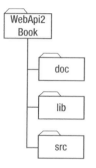

Figure 4-1. *The source tree folder structure*

What belongs in each of the folders just described should be fairly self-explanatory. But let's leave no doubt; the following list describes the intended content for each folder:

- **doc:** Contains documents related to the code base; this might include developer documents, installation guides, tips, requirements, images, and wireframes.

- **lib:** Contains all third-party libraries and packages used by the application(s) in this source tree; as stated previously, you will configure NuGet to place downloaded packages in this folder.

- **src:** Contains all of the source code, including the Visual Studio solution file(s) and all project folders.

Even though the task-management service is fairly simple and doesn't contain much in the way of application code, we think you'll find that this structure makes it much easier to navigate the tree than if we simply piled everything into a single folder (e.g., the root WebApi2Book folder).

If you're following along and have already completed the previous section for configuring your machine, go ahead and create the folder structure from Figure 4-1 in a root path similar to this:

```
C:\MyProjects\WebApi2Book\
```

At this point, you should now have a machine that contains all the software you need to build your task-management service. You should also have an empty source tree ready for creating an empty Visual Studio 2013 solution file.

Creating the Solution

You're now ready to create a blank Visual Studio solution file to which you can later add your projects. You create a blank solution first because you want the solution file to exist in the src folder. Unfortunately, Visual Studio doesn't let you create a new solution file without also creating a new folder with the same name; it's kind of a pain!

To put the solution file where you want it, follow these steps in Visual Studio:

1. Create a new solution file in the src folder by selecting Project from the File ➤ New menu.

2. Under the Installed ➤ Other Project Types ➤ Visual Studio Solutions section, select Blank Solution.

3. For this example, enter **WebApi2Book** for the solution Name.

4. For the Location, enter the full path to the src folder you created a bit ago.

5. Click OK.

This will create a new folder and solution in your src folder. Now either close Visual Studio or just close the solution. Then, using Windows Explorer, move the new solution file out of the folder that Visual Studio just created and into the src folder. Finally, delete the now-empty folder.

At this point, you should have something like Figure 4-2 in Windows Explorer.

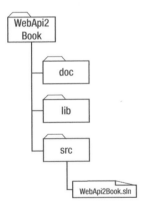

Figure 4-2. *Folders with a blank solution file*

Don't re-open the solution file quite yet; you still need to make a small tweak to the NuGet configuration for this solution.

NuGet Config File

The NuGet Package Manager was introduced in Visual Studio 2010 as a package-management system for .NET. It is similar to the Advanced Package Tool (APT) in many Linux distributions. The basic idea behind the tool is to provide a simple, reliable, and consistent mechanism for downloading libraries and their dependencies from a central repository, and then referencing them from Visual Studio projects. You will be using it to install most of the external libraries you need for your task-management service.

By default, NuGet downloads all packages to a folder called packages. This folder is created in the same folder where the solution file resides. But according to the folder structure shown in Figure 4-1, we want all of our external libraries to exist in the lib folder. As such, you need to provide NuGet with an override for the packages location.

To do this, create a new text file directly in the src folder (with Notepad or at the command line) and name this file **nuget.config**. Open the file and enter the following XML:

```
<settings>
    <repositoryPath>..\lib</repositoryPath>
</settings>
```

Save and close the file. Now when you open your new WebApi2Book solution file, NuGet will be configured to place all downloaded libraries into your lib folder.

Adding the Projects

In this section, we'll walk through adding all the projects to the new solution, and then configure some of their primary dependencies. When building an application, one wouldn't typically add all of the projects as a first step because it's usually easier to add them as you go. In this case, though, we want to provide an overview of the solution, so we will talk about all of them in one place.

Let's get started by double-clicking the new solution file (created in the previous section) to open it in Visual Studio 2013. Once it's open, add the projects listed in Table 4-1 with the configuration shown in Figure 4-3.

Table 4-1. *The Solution Projects*

Project Type	Project Name
Class library	WebApi2Book.Common
Class library	WebApi2Book.Data
Class library	WebApi2Book.Data.SqlServer
Class library	WebApi2Book.Web.Api.Models
Class library	WebApi2Book.Web.Common
ASP.NET Web Application. Use the Empty project template, and select only the Web API option (Figure 4-3).	WebApi2Book.Web.Api
SQL Server Database Project	WebApi2BookDb

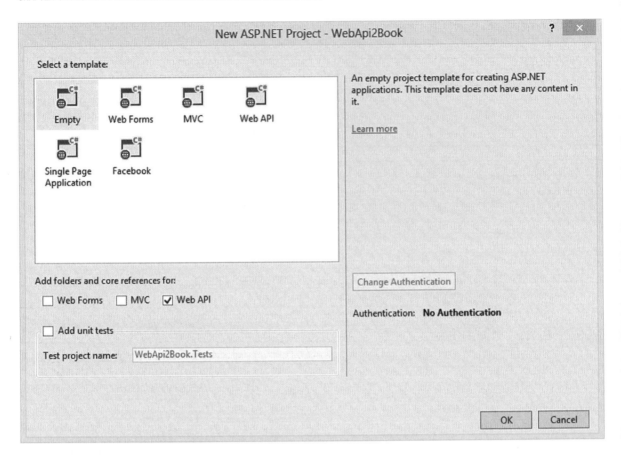

Figure 4-3. *Adding the ASP.NET Web application*

You also want to add a couple test projects to the solution. Begin by creating a new solution folder in Visual Studio called **Tests**, and then add the projects listed in Table 4-2 to that folder.

Table 4-2. *The Solution Test Projects*

Project Type	Project Name
Class library	WebApi2Book.Common.Tests
Class library	WebApi2Book.Data.SqlServer.IntegrationTests
Class library	WebApi2Book.Data.Tests
Class library	WebApi2Book.Web.Api.IntegrationTests
Class library	WebApi2Book.Web.Api.Tests
Class library	WebApi2Book.Web.Common.Tests

To help keep things clean, when you're finished adding these projects go ahead and delete the useless Class1.cs file that Visual Studio creates by default in each project.

Notice that we didn't add test projects for all projects. This is because not all projects have classes that need to be unit tested. For example, the WebApi2Book.Web.Api.Models project will contain only service-model classes, none of which lend themselves to any kind of unit tests.

As mentioned previously, we highly recommend using JetBrains' ReSharper when developing in .NET. Running unit tests is one of the benefits of this tool. It does a great job within the IDE of letting you run individual tests or all the tests in a class, category, project, or whatever. It also completely abstracts the underlying test framework, so the experience is the same whether you're using NUnit or MSTest.

At this point, you might be wondering why you have so many projects for such a simple application. There are a plethora of reasons why this separation works well, some of which are beyond the scope of this book. The main goal here is to separate your dependencies (e.g., not require the WebApi2Book.Common project to depend on NHibernate, and not require you to add SQL Server–specific code to anything but the WebApi2.Data.SqlServer project). This approach helps during development, but it also helps keep deployments and updates/patches much cleaner. Table 4-3 illustrates what each project is used for and what it will contain.

Table 4-3. *The Project Usage*

Project Name	Purpose and Contents
WebApi2Book.Common	Contains "framework-ish" functionality not specific to the API or the database.
WebApi2Book.Data	Contains the domain model Plain Old CLR Objects (POCOs); these are used by NHibernate to pull/push data from the database. Also contains the data-access interfaces and helper classes. However, nothing in this project is specific to SQL Server.
WebApi2Book.Data.SqlServer	Contains data-access implementations, as well as your NHibernate mappings. This project is what makes the Data project SQL Server–specific at runtime. As you build up your services application, you should note that no code references any types contained in this project; instead, the code references only the Data project.
WebApi2Book.Web.Api.Models	Contains the service's REST resource types (or models). We separate these into their own class library just to make unit testing a little easier. But remember that the client/caller never gets this DLL, because resource type definitions are not shared with REST service clients.
WebApi2Book.Web.Common	Contains functionality common to web and service applications.
WebApi2Book.Web.Api	This is the REST service application itself; it is hosted by IIS at runtime (though in development we use IISExpress). This project contains all of the Web API controllers and handlers, the REST routes, connection string(s), and so on.
WebApi2BookDb	Contains all the schema, code, and data for the SQL Server database. Once this project is compiled, use the output to publish the database to your preferred target. This works whether you want to create a new database or upgrade an existing one.
WebApi2Book.Common.Tests	Unit tests for the classes in the WebApi2Book.Web.Common project.
WebApi2Book.Data.SqlServer.IntegrationTests	Integration tests for the classes in the WebApi2Book.Data.SqlServer; these are used to test data access against the actual database.
WebApi2Book.Data.Tests	Unit tests for the classes in the WebApi2Book.Data project.

(*continued*)

Table 4-3. (*continued*)

Project Name	Purpose and Contents
WebApi2Book.Web.Api.IntegrationTests	Integration ("smoke") tests for the REST service.
WebApi2Book.Web.Api.Tests	Unit tests for the controllers and other classes in the WebApi2Book.Web.Api host project.
WebApi2Book.Web.Common.Tests	Unit tests for the classes in the WebApi2Book.Web.Common project.

Now that you have all of your Visual Studio projects in place, you need to add their respective external libraries and references using the NuGet Package Manager console. These commands will download the latest versions of the libraries (if needed), and then add appropriate references to the given projects. And because in a previous section you configured NuGet to download the packages to your lib folder, you can look there after running these commands to see what was downloaded.

From within the Visual Studio 2013 IDE, open the Package Manager console window and run the commands listed in Table 4-4. You can find the names of these packages and their corresponding install commands on the NuGet web site at www.nuget.org. Each command indicates which package to install and in which project to add the package reference.

Table 4-4. *A List of NuGet Commands*

NuGet Command
update-package Microsoft.AspNet.WebApi WebApi2Book.Web.Api
install-package automapper WebApi2Book.Common
install-package log4net WebApi2Book.Common
install-package nhibernate WebApi2Book.Data.SqlServer
install-package fluentnhibernate WebApi2Book.Data.SqlServer
install-package automapper WebApi2Book.Web.Api
install-package log4net WebApi2Book.Web.Api
install-package nhibernate WebApi2Book.Web.Api
install-package fluentnhibernate WebApi2Book.Web.Api
install-package Ninject.Web.Common.WebHost WebApi2Book.Web.Api
install-package log4net WebApi2Book.Web.Common
install-package nhibernate WebApi2Book.Web.Common
install-package ninject WebApi2Book.Web.Common
install-package ninject.web.common WebApi2Book.Web.Common

Note that the first statement in Table 4-4 is used to update the ASP.NET Web API libraries for the solution and WebApi2Book.Web.Api project. At the time of this writing, the Web API templates and references in Visual Studio 2013 included an older version of the libraries. So the update-package statement just ensures that we have the latest libraries configured.

If you get the feeling that you've seen these library names before, it's because they correspond to the components we mentioned in the "Choosing Architecture Components" section of the previous chapter. Though we may need to add more libraries later, this basic component mix provides a good start for pretty much any ASP.NET Web API application. As for the libraries used by the unit test projects, we'll address those as we build out the code later in the book.

Finally, let's add some project references that we already know about. More may be required later, but the ones listed in Table 4-5 are a good start. As for the project references used by the unit test projects, we'll also address those as we build out the code later in the book.

Table 4-5. *Project References*

Project	References
WebApi2Book.Data.SqlServer	WebApi2Book.Common WebApi2Book.Data
WebApi2Book.Web.Api	WebApi2Book.Common WebApi2Book.Data WebApi2Book.Data.SqlServer WebApi2Book.Web.Api.Models WebApi2Book.Web.Common
WebApi2Book.Web.Common	WebApi2Book.Common WebApi2Book.Data

If you've followed the steps outlined so far, you should see something similar to Figure 4-4 in the Solution Explorer for the WebApi2Book solution. Don't concern yourself with the WebApi2Book.Web.Legacy.Api or WebApi2Book.Windows.Legacy.Client projects at this point; we'll introduce them later as part of a special section on supporting legacy clients.

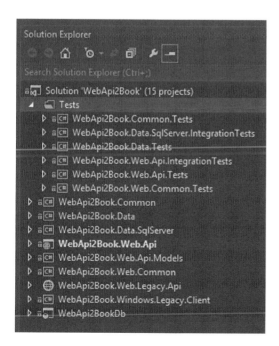

Figure 4-4. *The solution in Visual Studio 2013*

Basic Components

At this point, the solution should build successfully, even though we haven't added any real code yet. But with all the projects added and their libraries installed and referenced, we are ready to start building some of the easier components we'll need later on:

- Domain model (the persistent entities)
- Service resource types (the service model)
- Logging
- Database

Domain Model

In this section, we're going to add the POCO classes that make up your application's domain model. These will be used primarily to query and update the database.

Since these classes will be used by NHibernate and we want to support lazy loading, we need to make every property virtual.

■ **Note**   Lazy loading tells NHibernate to fetch related data only when it is needed—versus fetching all the data up front. For example, when a Task object is fetched from the database, lazy loading means that the Task object's status and assignments won't be fetched until code is executed that needs those values.

Other than that, they really are just POCOs. In other words, they don't derive from some special base class, nor do they return any special types for their properties. They aren't even tied to NHibernate at all, save for the virtual modifier to allow lazy loading.

So now let's look at all the class definitions, which are shown in the following code example. You will add these—one class per file, with each file name equal to the class name—to the WebApi2Book.Data project in a folder called Entities. We use the folder name of Entities to more easily distinguish in the code between the persistent model types and the service model types; don't let the name "Entities" fool you into thinking this has anything to do with Entity Framework. The namespace for all of the classes that follow is WebApi2Book.Data.Entities:

```
public class Status
{
    public virtual long StatusId { get; set; }
    public virtual string Name { get; set; }
    public virtual int Ordinal { get; set; }
    public virtual byte[] Version { get; set; }
}

public class Task
{
    private readonly IList<User> _users = new List<User>();

    public virtual long TaskId { get; set; }
    public virtual string Subject { get; set; }
    public virtual DateTime? StartDate { get; set; }
    public virtual DateTime? DueDate { get; set; }
```

```
    public virtual DateTime? CompletedDate { get; set; }
    public virtual Status Status { get; set; }
    public virtual DateTime CreatedDate { get; set; }
    public virtual User CreatedBy { get; set; }

    public virtual IList<User> Users
    {
        get { return _users; }
    }

    public virtual byte[] Version { get; set; }
}

public class User
{
    public virtual long UserId { get; set; }
    public virtual string Firstname { get; set; }
    public virtual string Lastname { get; set; }
    public virtual string Username { get; set; }
    public virtual byte[] Version { get; set; }
}
```

The Version byte array property on all of the domain model classes will be used by NHibernate to detect dirty data. As you'll see later, the column in SQL Server that the Version property maps to will be of type rowversion. This value is automatically incremented by SQL Server every time a new row is added or updated in the database. In this way, the system can detect when an update to a row will overwrite a previous update.

Service Model Types

Now let's add the classes that will make up the service model. These will be similar to the domain-model classes you just added and, like the domain model types, these classes are only used internally. Although the service-model types aren't sent to the client, they shape the data that will be going back and forth between the client and the service.

All of these class definitions go right in the root of the WebApi2Book.Web.Api.Models project; they use that name as their namespace, as well. Add these as one class per file, with each file name equal to the class name:

```
public class Link
{
    public string Rel { get; set; }
    public string Href { get; set; }
    public string Method { get; set; }
}

public class Status
{
    public long StatusId { get; set; }
    public string Name { get; set; }
    public int Ordinal { get; set; }
}
```

```csharp
public class Task
{
    private List<Link> _links;

    public long? TaskId { get; set; }
    public string Subject { get; set; }
    public DateTime? StartDate { get; set; }
    public DateTime? DueDate { get; set; }
    public DateTime? CreatedDate { get; set; }
    public DateTime? CompletedDate { get; set; }
    public Status Status { get; set; }
    public List<User> Assignees { get; set; }
    public List<Link> Links
    {
        get { return _links ?? (_links = new List<Link>()); }
        set { _links = value; }
    }

    public void AddLink(Link link)
    {
        Links.Add(link);
    }
}

public class User
{
    private List<Link> _links;

    public long UserId { get; set; }
    public string Username { get; set; }
    public string Firstname { get; set; }
    public string Lastname { get; set; }

    public List<Link> Links
    {
        get { return _links ?? (_links = new List<Link>()); }
        set { _links = value; }
    }

    public void AddLink(Link link)
    {
        Links.Add(link);
    }
}
```

Recall that one of the tenets of REST is to avoid coupling the client to the server. This means you shouldn't provide the DLL containing these resource types to callers of your API. These types are there simply to make it easier for the controller code to receive and respond to such data.

Logging

In this section, you will configure the web.config file. We'll deal with initializing log4net later, when tackling the Ninject container configuration. For now, begin by adding the following code to the WebApi2Book.Web.Api project's web.config file, near the top (and directly under the opening <configuration> tag). If the <configSections> section is already there, just add the log4net element:

```
<configSections>
  <section name="log4net" type="log4net.Config.Log4NetConfigurationSectionHandler, log4net" />
</configSections>
```

Next, directly under the closing </appSettings> tag, add the following log4net configuration section:

```
<log4net>
  <appender name="LogFileAppender" type="log4net.Appender.RollingFileAppender">
    <file type="log4net.Util.PatternString" value="..\\..\\logs\\WebApi2Book.Web.Api.log" />
    <appendToFile value="true" />
    <maxSizeRollBackups value="-1" />
    <countDirection value="1" />
    <maximumFileSize value="5MB" />
    <rollingStyle value="Composite" />
    <preserveLogFileNameExtension value="true" />
    <staticLogFileName value="false" />
    <lockingModel type="log4net.Appender.FileAppender+MinimalLock" />
    <layout type="log4net.Layout.PatternLayout">
      <conversionPattern value="%date %-5level [%thread] %logger - %message%newline%exception" />
    </layout>
  </appender>
  <logger name="NHibernate">
    <level value="ERROR" />
  </logger>
  <logger name="NHibernate.SQL">
    <level value="ERROR" />
  </logger>
  <root>
  <level value="ALL" />
    <appender-ref ref="LogFileAppender" />
  </root>
</log4net>
```

There are about 101 ways to configure logging with log4net. If you want to log a target other than a rolling log file, or if you are interested in modifying the behavior just covered, you should read the log4net configuration documentation to learn more. Here are a couple of useful links:

- http://logging.apache.org/log4net/release/manual/configuration.html

- http://logging.apache.org/log4net/release/sdk/log4net.Layout.PatternLayout.html

As-is, the preceding configuration logs to a file called WebApi2Book.Web.Api.YYYY-MM-DD.count.log (e.g., " WebApi2Book.Web.Api.2014-04-19.3.log") in a system-created logs folder in the WebApi2Book root directory. Each new day, the system will create a new log file, and it will roll over to a new file if the current file gets to be 5 MB in size. This configuration also logs only errors from NHibernate (to help guard against file bloat).

The Database

We explored the tables included in the database in Chapter 3 when we designed the service API. In this section, we will look at the SQL Server Database Project in Visual Studio 2013 and add the necessary files to it.

To start, add two folders to the project: Scripts and Tables. Figure 4-5 shows what the database project should look like when we are finished with this section.

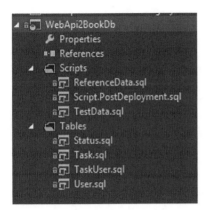

Figure 4-5. *The database project*

The Scripts folder will contain your deployment scripts for adding lookup data and test data. The Tables folder should be self-explanatory.

We should point out one thing regarding lookup data: the scripts in the project will run every time they are applied to a target database. In other words, you need to be very aware of existing data and avoid INSERT statements that will cause primary-key violations. For this reason, any time you add or update lookup data, the SQL statements need to first check that the data doesn't exist already. The ReferenceData.sql file demonstrates this:

```
if not exists(select * from dbo.Status where Name = 'Not Started')
    insert into dbo.Status(Name, Ordinal) values('Not Started', 0);
if not exists(select * from dbo.Status where Name = 'In Progress')
    insert into dbo.Status(Name, Ordinal) values('In Progress', 1);
if not exists(select * from dbo.Status where Name = 'Completed')
    insert into dbo.Status(Name, Ordinal) values('Completed', 2);
```

Go ahead and add the ReferenceData.sql file to the Scripts folder using the "Script (Not in build)" template option. Do the same for the TestData.sql script:

TestData.sql

```
declare @statusId int,
    @taskId int,
    @userId int

if not exists (select * from [User] where Username = 'bhogg')
    INSERT into [dbo].[User] ([Firstname], [Lastname], [Username])
        VALUES (N'Boss', N'Hogg', N'bhogg')

if not exists (select * from [User] where Username = 'jbob')
    INSERT into [dbo].[User] ([Firstname], [Lastname], [Username])
        VALUES (N'Jim', N'Bob', N'jbob')
```

```
if not exists (select * from [User] where Username = 'jdoe')
    INSERT into [dbo].[User] ([Firstname], [Lastname], [Username])
        VALUES (N'John', N'Doe', N'jdoe')

if not exists(select * from dbo.Task where Subject = 'Test Task')
begin
    select top 1 @statusId = StatusId from Status order by StatusId;
    select top 1 @userId = UserId from [User] order by UserId;

    insert into dbo.Task(Subject, StartDate, StatusId, CreatedDate, CreatedUserId)
        values('Test Task', getdate(), @statusId, getdate(), @userId);

    set @taskId = SCOPE_IDENTITY();

    INSERT [dbo].[TaskUser] ([TaskId], [UserId])
        VALUES (@taskId, @userId)
end
```

After that, add the following file to the Scripts folder using the "Post-Deployment Script" template option:

Script.PostDeployment.sql

```
:r .\ReferenceData.sql
:r .\TestData.sql
```

For ReferenceData.sql and TestData.sql, ensure the file properties are set as shown in Figure 4-6. For Script. PostDeployment.sql, ensure the file properties are set as shown in Figure 4-7.

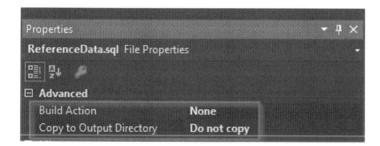

Figure 4-6. *File Properties for ReferenceData.sql and TestData.sql*

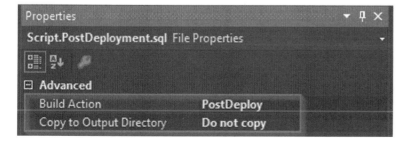

Figure 4-7. *File Properties for Script.PostDeployment.sql*

45

Now it's time to populate the Tables folder with the following:

Status.sql

```sql
CREATE TABLE [dbo].[Status] (
    [StatusId] BIGINT          IDENTITY (1, 1) NOT NULL,
    [Name]     NVARCHAR (100) NOT NULL,
    [Ordinal]  INT            NOT NULL,
    [ts]       rowversion     NOT NULL,
    PRIMARY KEY CLUSTERED ([StatusId] ASC)
);
```

Task.sql

```sql
CREATE TABLE [dbo].[Task] (
    [TaskId]         BIGINT         IDENTITY (1, 1) NOT NULL,
    [Subject]        NVARCHAR (100) NOT NULL,
    [StartDate]      DATETIME2 (7)  NULL,
    [DueDate]        DATETIME2 (7)  NULL,
    [CompletedDate]  DATETIME2 (7)  NULL,
    [StatusId]       BIGINT         NOT NULL,
    [CreatedDate]    DATETIME2 (7)  NOT NULL,
    [CreatedUserId]  bigint  NOT NULL,
    [ts]             rowversion     NOT NULL,
    PRIMARY KEY CLUSTERED ([TaskId] ASC),
    FOREIGN KEY ([StatusId]) REFERENCES [dbo].[Status] ([StatusId]),
    FOREIGN KEY ([CreatedUserId]) REFERENCES [dbo].[User] ([UserId])
);
```

TaskUser.sql

```sql
CREATE TABLE [dbo].[TaskUser]
(
    [TaskId] bigint NOT NULL,
    [UserId] bigint not null,
    [ts] rowversion not null,
    primary key (TaskId, UserId),
    foreign key (UserId) references dbo.[User] (UserId),
    foreign key (TaskId) references dbo.Task (TaskId)
)
go

create index ix_TaskUser_UserId on TaskUser(UserId)
go
```

User.sql

```sql
CREATE TABLE [dbo].[User](
    [UserId] BIGINT  IDENTITY (1, 1) NOT NULL,
    [Firstname] [nvarchar](50) NOT NULL,
    [Lastname] [nvarchar](50) NOT NULL,
    [Username] NVARCHAR(50) NOT NULL,
    [ts] [rowversion] NOT NULL,
    CONSTRAINT [PK_User] PRIMARY KEY ([UserId])
);
```

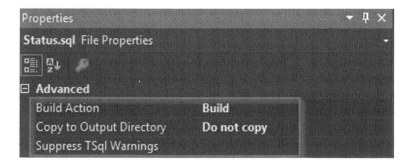

Figure 4-8. *File Properties for files in the Tables folder*

All of the files in the Tables folder should have the file properties shown in Figure 4-8.

With all that in place, you should be able to build and publish the WebApi2BookDb project! Please do so now to prepare for the next chapter, where we will implement posting a new task via our Web API.

Summary

In this chapter, you learned how to configure a clean Windows 8 machine with the software required to build the task-management service. You also created the folder structure you need to start adding code, libraries, and documents to the source tree. Next, you created an empty solution and added to it all of the projects we plan on using, including various library and project references. Finally, you created a bunch of basic classes and the various application configuration settings needed to support the service.

At this point, your solution should build successfully. You are now ready to start creating some of the framework-level components needed to manage controller and database session lifetimes, security, and the Ninject dependency injection container.

■ ■ ■

CHAPTER 5

Up and Down the Stack with a POST

In the previous chapter, we started with an empty folder, created a basic source-tree structure, added a new Visual Studio 2013 solution, and added the projects we know we'll need for this little REST service. We also added some of the more basic code components and set up the project and library references we anticipate needing. We wrapped things up by creating the database.

In this chapter, we will implement our first controller method (or "action method"). Along the way, we will need to deal with some of the more complex infrastructural concerns in the task-management service and highlight several great ASP.NET Web API features. We'll cover the following topics:

- Routing (convention and attribute-based)

- API versioning using attribute-based routing and a custom controller selector

- Management of dependencies

- NHibernate configuration and mappings

- Database unit-of-work management

- Database transaction control

- Diagnostic tracing

- Error handling

- IHttpActionResult

You may be wondering why security is missing from this infrastructure-heavy chapter. Well, security merits its own chapter; so don't worry, we will get to it soon. For now, we want to focus on getting the basic infrastructure in place so that we can begin implementing our task-management business logic.

Yes, this is a lot of material to cover in this rather long chapter. We'll take it step-by-step so that it will make sense in the end. Now let's get started.

CODING CONVENTION

Unless otherwise noted, we implement one public type per file. The file name should match the type name, and the file location should match the namespace name.

For example, the `WebApi2Book.Web.Common.Routing.ApiVersionConstraint` class is in a file named "ApiVersionConstraint.cs," which is located in a project folder named "Routing" in the `WebApi2Book.Web.Common` project.

We will initially provide detailed instructions to help you implement the solution according to this coding convention. However, to avoid becoming excessively repetitive and tedious, we will gradually provide less detail, under the assumption that you will have become familiar with the pattern.

Routing

Although a request to an ASP.NET Web API–based service can be processed by a message handler without any need for a controller (and you'll see an example of this in a later chapter when we discuss processing SOAP messages for legacy callers), ASP.NET Web API–based services are normally configured to route messages to controllers for processing. Such an arrangement allows services to benefit from model binding, controller-specific and action-specific filters, and result conversion (i.e., it fully utilizes the ASP.NET Web API's extensible processing pipeline). Leveraging routes and associated controllers is the kind of arrangement we will be discussing in this chapter.

HTTP MESSAGE LIFECYCLE IN ASP.NET WEB API

The official Microsoft ASP.NET Web API site has an excellent poster illustrating the complete ASP.NET Web API HTTP message lifecycle. The poster is available at `http://www.asp.net/posters/web-api/ASP.NET-Web-API-Poster.pdf`. A highly-simplified version illustrating some main elements of the processing pipeline is shown in Figure 5-1.

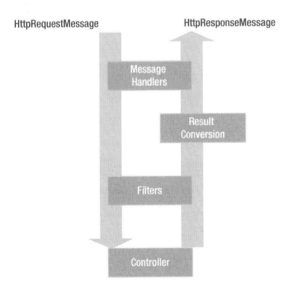

Figure 5-1. ASP.NET Web API message processing pipeline

Be sure to visit the official Microsoft site (`http://www.asp.net`) for this poster and many other useful resources.

When a service request comes over the network and into Internet Information Services (IIS), IIS routes it to a worker process that is hosting the ASP.NET runtime. Inside this process (or in an equivalent host process for self-hosted applications and applications running in IIS Express), the ASP.NET Web API framework uses the routes configured in the application to determine which controller should respond to the request. When the appropriate controller class is found, the ASP.NET Web API framework creates an instance of that controller class and forwards the web request to the appropriate controller action.

Let's look at some examples. Suppose you have the following route configured in the WebApiConfig.cs file (which is actually the default route set up by Visual Studio when you create a new Web API project):

```
config.Routes.MapHttpRoute(
    name: "DefaultApi",
    routeTemplate: "api/{controller}/{id}",
    defaults: new {id = RouteParameter.Optional});
```

Using the power of URL routing, the framework will try to match the URLs of requests against this and other routes. In this particular route, the framework will use the portion of the URL specified after api/ to determine the appropriate controller to activate. Assume you were to make either of the following calls against the service:

```
/api/tasks
/api/tasks/123
```

In both cases, the framework would activate the controller class called TasksController. Note that even though the URL specifies only tasks, the class name to be activated will be TasksController. By convention, the framework will automatically append the word Controller to the name taken from the URL.

At this point, you may be asking the question, "Which specific controller action method will get invoked?" Well, unlike with ASP.NET MVC, the URL route doesn't have to include an {action} segment. This is because the ASP.NET Web API framework automatically invokes controller methods based on the HTTP verb the caller is using. For example, if the caller performs a GET on the URL /api/tasks, the framework will invoke the Get method on the TasksController class. If the caller were performing a POST instead, the framework would invoke the Post method on the controller.

As you can see in the preceding route configuration, there is an optional {id} segment in the URL mapping. If the caller includes some sort of identifier at the end of the URL, the framework will select the corresponding controller method that matches a signature containing a single argument. Table 5-1 shows a few examples based on the task-management service's TasksController.

Table 5-1. *Examples of URLs, Verbs, and Matching Controller Methods*

URL	Verb	Controller Method
/api/tasks	GET	Get()
/api/tasks/123	GET	Get(long id)
/api/tasks/123	DELETE	Delete(long id)
/api/tasks	POST	Post()
/api/tasks/123	PUT	Put(long id)

The RESTful features and associated conventions of ASP.NET Web API help ensure that you are coding to the HTTP verbs discussed in Chapters 2 and 3. This is much cleaner and much truer to the REST style of services than trying to implement REST with ASP.NET MVC.

In addition to using arguments that come from the URL, you can add method arguments for data that arrives via the message body. Model binding, similar to that utilized with ASP.NET MVC, will be used to translate the incoming data into the appropriate model class. You can even add an argument of .NET type HttpRequestMessage, which the framework will provide automatically. As an example, here's the signature of the Post method that existed on the CategoriesController in the previous edition of this book:

```
Post(HttpRequestMessage request, Category category)
```

Let's examine each of these arguments.

Adding an HttpRequestMessage Argument

The HttpRequestMessage is an object that you can use to examine all kinds of properties of the incoming request. It provides access to the request headers, the body, the URL used to invoke the call, client certificates, and many other valuable properties. You can also use the HttpRequestMessage object to create a response that is pre-wired to the given request object.

Note that you could instead use the controller's Request property to access the request object, because all ASP.NET Web API controllers inherit the property from the framework's ApiController base class. However, as a matter of good design and clean code, you should be careful not to couple your controller to anything going on in a base class. Doing so generally makes it much more difficult to test, and it increases the fragility of your code. This is why we prefer to have the request object passed in as an argument when needed.

Adding a Model Object Argument

The second argument, the Category object, is also inserted auto-magically by the framework. When the caller puts a JSON or XML representation of a specific model object into the body of an HTTP request, the framework will do the work of parsing the textual data into an instance of that model type.

The same applies to a PUT request where the URL also contains an identifier. Suppose you have the following CategoriesController method:

```
Put(HttpRequestMessage request, long id, Category category)
```

Now suppose the caller submits a PUT request to the following URL:

```
/api/categories/123
```

The framework will invoke the controller's Put method with a framework-provided HttpRequestMessage as the request parameter, 123 as the id, and a category object parsed from the message body as the category. This is quite amazing because you don't need to do any special parsing of the JSON or XML content; the framework does it for you. Nor do you need to define any data contracts, as would normally be required in a WCF-based service. In line with the more recent trend toward "convention over configuration," it just works! And as we discussed in Chapter 2, this lack of strict client-server contract is also a foundational principle with the RESTful architecture.

Attribute-Based Routing

While certainly powerful, the convention-based routing in ASP.NET Web API version 1 had some limitations. For example, let's say we needed to support the operations shown in Table 5-2.

Table 5-2. URLs, Verbs, and Controller Methods for Attribute-Based Routing Example

URL	Verb	Controller Method
/api/tasks/123	GET	Get(long id)
/api/tasks/abc	GET	Get(string taskNum)

Here's the controller implementation:

```
public class TasksController : ApiController
{
    public string Get(int id)
    {
        return "In the Get(int id) overload, id = " + id;
    }

    public string Get(string taskNum)
    {
        return "In the Get(string taskNum) overload, taskNum = " + taskNum;
    }
}
```

If convention-based routing were the only option, we'd be out of luck. The framework picks the first action method based on the route and verb, and it ignores other method overloads that would be more appropriate based on the parameter's data type. To illustrate, here are some (excerpted) HTTP message requests and responses captured using Fiddler, a popular web debugging proxy (that you can download from http://www.telerik.com/fiddler):

Request #1

```
GET http://localhost:50101/api/tasks/123 HTTP/1.1
```

Response #1

```
HTTP/1.1 200 OK
"In the Get(int id) overload, id = 123"
```

Request #2

```
GET http://localhost:50101/api/tasks/abc HTTP/1.1
```

Response #2

```
HTTP/1.1 400 Bad Request
{"Message":"The request is invalid.","MessageDetail":"The parameters dictionary contains a null entry...
```

Things are even worse if we rename the taskNum parameter to id in order to match the configured route, so that the controller appears as follows:

```
public class TasksController : ApiController
{
    public string Get(int id)
    {
        return "In the Get(int id) method, id = " + id;
    }

    public string Get(string id)
    {
        return "In the Get(string id) method, id = " + id;
    }
}
```

53

So now we've not only compromised some of the semantic meaning in our business domain by renaming "taskNum" to "id" (in this example they are distinct concepts), but we've also put ourselves in a situation where we have multiple actions matching the configured route. By not taking the parameter types on the methods into account, the framework has no way to determine which route is correct; therefore, it just gives up and responds with an internal server error:

```
HTTP/1.1 500 Internal Server Error
{"Message":"An error has occurred.","ExceptionMessage":"Multiple actions were found that
match the request: ...
```

The good news is that attribute-based routing is now available, and it solves this and many other routing problems. It is enabled by default for ASP.NET Web API 2 applications. Let's take a look at the controller code and those same HTTP messages when attribute-based routing is used.

First, the controller code. Note the Route attributes over the methods. Not only do they specify the path to be matched against the URL, but they also contain constraints describing the action parameters. This enables the framework to make a more informed action method selection:

```
public class TasksController : ApiController
{
    [Route("api/tasks/{id:int}")]
    public string Get(int id)
    {
        return "In the Get(int id) overload, id = " + id;
    }

    [Route("api/tasks/{tasknum:alpha}")]
    public string Get(string taskNum)
    {
        return "In the Get(string taskNum) overload, taskNum = " + taskNum;
    }
}
```

Request #1

```
GET http://localhost:50101/api/tasks/123 HTTP/1.1
```

Response #1

```
HTTP/1.1 200 OK
"In the Get(int id) overload, id = 123"
```

Request #2

```
GET http://localhost:50101/api/tasks/abc HTTP/1.1
```

Response #2

```
HTTP/1.1 200 OK
"In the Get(string taskNum) overload, taskNum = abc"
```

That certainly looks better! With that victory behind us, we're now ready to dive into a much more complex example. Let's look at a controller that uses the ASP.NET Web API's RoutePrefixAttribute and a mix of attribute-based and convention-based routing. We'll also add a new convention-based route so that we can avoid conflating "taskNum" and "id".

First, the convention-based route configuration, this time showing the entire WebApiConfig class (note the new FindByTaskNumberRoute route):

```
public static class WebApiConfig
{
    public static void Register(HttpConfiguration config)
    {
        // Enables attribute-based routing
        config.MapHttpAttributeRoutes();

        // Matches route with the taskNum parameter
        config.Routes.MapHttpRoute(
            name: "FindByTaskNumberRoute",
            routeTemplate: "api/{controller}/{taskNum}",
            defaults: new { taskNum = RouteParameter.Optional }
        );

        // Default catch-all
        config.Routes.MapHttpRoute(
            name: "DefaultApi",
            routeTemplate: "api/{controller}/{id}",
            defaults: new { id = RouteParameter.Optional }
        );
    }
}
```

And next, the controller class:

```
[RoutePrefixAttribute("api/employeeTasks")]
public class TasksController : ApiController
{
    [Route("{id:int:max(100)}")]
    public string GetTaskWithAMaxIdOf100(int id)
    {
        return "In the GetTaskWithAMaxIdOf100(int id) method, id = " + id;
    }

    [Route("{id:int:min(101)}")]
    [HttpGet]
    public string FindTaskWithAMinIdOf101(int id)
    {
        return "In the FindTaskWithAMinIdOf101(int id) method, id = " + id;
    }

    public string Get(string taskNum)
    {
        return "In the Get(string taskNum) method, taskNum = " + taskNum;
    }
}
```

There are a lot of things happening here:

- First, the controller class' `RoutePrefixAttribute` is overriding the default behavior where the framework determines the controller class by the route name. The normal route to activate this controller is `api/tasks`, as you saw earlier, but this attribute has changed it to `api/employeeTasks` for all methods except the non-attributed, convention-based Get method.

- Now look at the `GetTaskWithAMaxIdOf100` method. The method name begins with *Get*, which is normal for controller action methods that implement GET requests. However, the `Route` attribute contains a constraint limiting id to an integer with a maximum value of 100.

- The `FindTaskWithAMinIdOf101` method is even more interesting. Note that the method name does not begin with *Get* (or any other HTTP method name for that matter), so we've added an `HttpGet` attribute to the method to inform the framework that this is an action method suitable for GET requests. Also note the `Route` attribute contains a constraint limiting id to an integer with a minimum value of 101.

- And last but not least, the `Get` method. This is plain-old vanilla, convention-based routing. But do note that we had to add the route named `FindByTaskNumberRoute` to the `WebApiConfig` class to enable the framework to match this action method with its nonstandard "taskNum" parameter name.

We'll wrap up this section on routing by looking at the (excerpted) HTTP message requests and responses, captured using Fiddler, with this highly-customized routing in place:

Request #1

```
GET http://localhost:50101/api/employeeTasks/100 HTTP/1.1
```

Response #1

```
HTTP/1.1 200 OK
"In the GetTaskWithAMaxIdOf100(int id) method, id = 100"
```

Request #2

```
GET http://localhost:50101/api/employeeTasks/101 HTTP/1.1
```

Response #2

```
HTTP/1.1 200 OK
"In the FindTaskWithAMinIdOf101(int id) method, id = 101"
```

Request #3

```
GET http://localhost:50101/api/tasks/abc HTTP/1.1
```

Response #3

```
HTTP/1.1 200 OK
"In the Get(string taskNum) method, taskNum = abc"
```

Excellent! Just what we expected. And though we've reconfigured paths, added constraints, and changed controller method names, we've been able to maintain the characteristics of a RESTful interface throughout the course of this little exercise.

At this point, we've touched on some of the main capabilities of attribute-based routing, and we know enough to move forward with our task service implementation. If you'd like to dive deeper, we recommend you visit the official Microsoft ASP.NET Web API site. There you'll find an excellent piece by Mike Wasson titled "Attribute Routing in Web API 2" (`www.asp.net/web-api/overview/web-api-routing-and-actions/attribute-routing-in-web-api-2`). Be sure to check it out!

Versioning

In this section, we are going to implement the first controller action method in our task-management service. Before we start slinging code, though, we need to consider the API design we documented in Chapter 3. It is lacking an important feature—one that should be addressed before we "break ground." Security? Well, yes, but we're going to cover that later. Localization? OK, yes, but let's assume that's not a requirement. How about versioning? Correct! And in case it's not totally obvious from the title of this section, we will create our first controller action method in a way that supports API versioning.

IMPLEMENTATION VERSUS API VERSIONING

Note that in this section we aren't talking about assembly or DLL versioning. The versioning of assemblies relates more to changes within the underlying implementation. Rather, we are interested here in the versioning of the public API (i.e., the interface). As such, changes to a DLL don't necessarily require a change to the API's version. But changes to URL, or breaking changes to a resource type, would require a new API version.

Currently within the software community, there are four basic approaches to versioning the RESTful way:

1. **URI Path** This approach takes the following form:

   `http://api/v2/Tasks/{TaskId}`

2. **URI Parameter** This approach takes the following form:

   `http://api/Tasks/{TaskId}?v=2`

3. **Content Negotiation** This is done in the HTTP header.

   `Content Type: application/vnd.taskManagerApp.v2.param.json`

4. **Request Header** This is also done in the HTTP header.

   `x-taskManagerApp-version: 2`

Out there on the Web, you can find passionate arguments for using each of these, and even combinations of these, different approaches. We encourage you to research this on your own and determine what best fits your current project. However, for the sake of maintaining focus on the ASP.NET Web API, we decided to use the first option in our task-management service. We are combining API and content versioning, so a change to the resource content (e.g., changing properties on a Web model class) constitutes a change to the API.

With that as an introduction, we will be implementing a controller action method to match the request shown in Table 5-3, so go ahead and open the solution in Visual Studio.

Table 5-3. *URL and HTTP Verb for Versioned POST*

URI	Verb	Description
/api/{apiVersion}/tasks	POST	Creates a new task; returns the new task in the response

Implementing POST

Add two folders to the `Controllers` folder: "V1" and "V2". The API project should then look like Figure 5-2.

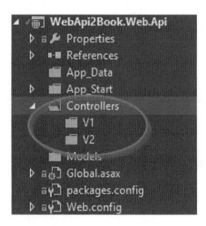

Figure 5-2. *API project with version-specific controller folders*

Add a new controller named `TasksController` to each folder using the empty Web API 2 controller template. (See Figures 5-3 and 5-4.)

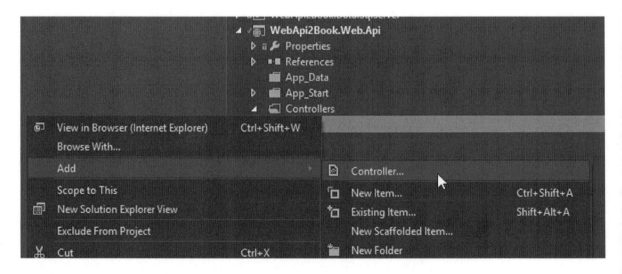

Figure 5-3. *Adding a controller*

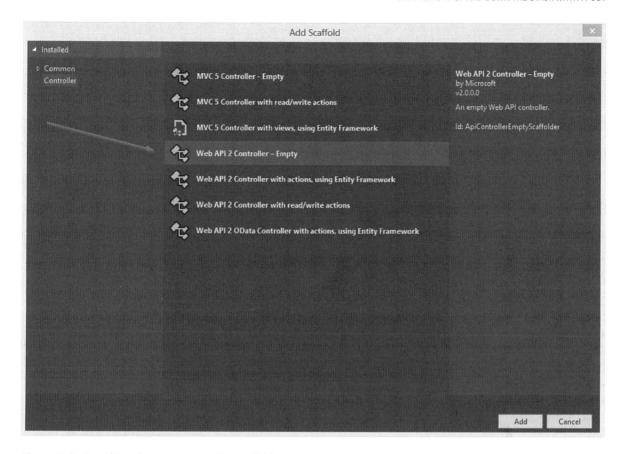

Figure 5-4. *Specifying the empty controller scaffold*

Now there will be two `TasksController` classes in the project, but the project will compile because they are in different namespaces. However, requests will always be routed to the controller in the `WebApi2Book.Web.Api.Controllers.V1` namespace because the framework only matches on the controller class name without regard to the controller class' namespace, and the V1 controller is the first match it finds. This is the case with both convention-based and attribute-based routing.

To work around this shortcoming (and, more importantly, to show off some ASP.NET Web API 2 goodness), we will use attribute-based routing with custom constraints, and we will also add a custom controller selector that takes the namespace into account when looking for the matching controller class. First, let's deal with the constraint.

A Custom IHttpRouteConstraint

The first thing we need to do is add some dependencies to the `WebApi2Book.Web.Common` project. With the solution open, run the following commands in the Package Manager console:

```
install-package Microsoft.AspNet.WebApi WebApi2Book.Web.Common
```

Next, add a folder named Routing to the WebApi2Book.Web.Common project, and then add a class named ApiVersionConstraint to the new folder. Implement the class as follows:

```
using System.Collections.Generic;
using System.Net.Http;
using System.Web.Http.Routing;

namespace WebApi2Book.Web.Common.Routing
{
    public class ApiVersionConstraint : IHttpRouteConstraint
    {
        public ApiVersionConstraint(string allowedVersion)
        {
            AllowedVersion = allowedVersion.ToLowerInvariant();
        }

        public string AllowedVersion { get; private set; }

        public bool Match(HttpRequestMessage request, IHttpRoute route, string parameterName,
            IDictionary<string, object> values, HttpRouteDirection routeDirection)
        {
            object value;
            if (values.TryGetValue(parameterName, out value) && value != null)
            {
                return AllowedVersion.Equals(value.ToString().ToLowerInvariant());
            }
            return false;
        }
    }
}
```

This class implements the IHttpRouteConstraint.Match method. Match will return true if the specified parameter name equals the AllowedVersion property, which is initialized in the constructor. But where does the constructor get this value? It gets it from a RoutePrefixAttribute, which we'll implement now.

A Custom RoutePrefixAttribute

Add a class named ApiVersion1RoutePrefixAttribute to the WebApi2Book.Web.Common.Routing folder. Implement it as follows:

```
using System.Web.Http;

namespace WebApi2Book.Web.Common.Routing
{
    public class ApiVersion1RoutePrefixAttribute : RoutePrefixAttribute
    {
        private const string RouteBase = "api/{apiVersion:apiVersionConstraint(v1)}";
        private const string PrefixRouteBase = RouteBase + "/";
```

```
    public ApiVersion1RoutePrefixAttribute(string routePrefix)
        : base(string.IsNullOrWhiteSpace(routePrefix) ? RouteBase : PrefixRouteBase + routePrefix)
    {
    }
    }
}
}
```

The main purpose of this attribute class is to encapsulate the api/v1 part of the route template so that we don't have to copy and paste it over all of the controllers (we will be using it a lot); it's just a bit of syntactic sugar to enhance the RoutePrefixAttribute base class. Oh, and it also allows us to demonstrate that cool new ASP.NET Web API 2 constraint we just added. (Note the constraint in the RouteBase string constant.)

Let's add an ApiVersion1RoutePrefixAttribute to the appropriate TasksController, and then we'll review what's going on with all this. Here's the controller with the attribute applied to it:

```
using System.Web.Http;
using WebApi2Book.Web.Common.Routing;

namespace WebApi2Book.Web.Api.Controllers.V1
{
    [ApiVersion1RoutePrefix("tasks")]
    public class TasksController : ApiController
    {
    }
}
```

Studying the ApiVersion1RoutePrefixAttribute class and the TasksController class, we can see that this TasksController implementation is equivalent to the following:

```
using System.Web.Http;
using WebApi2Book.Web.Common.Routing;

namespace WebApi2Book.Web.Api.Controllers.V1
{
    [RoutePrefix("api/{apiVersion:apiVersionConstraint(v1)}/tasks")]
    public class TasksController : ApiController
    {
    }
}
```

Recalling what you learned in the "Attribute-Based Routing" section earlier in the chapter, you can now recognize that this RoutePrefix attribute is configured to match a URL path of api/{apiVersion}/tasks. You also can see that the apiVersion parameter is constrained by our custom IHttpRouteConstraint to a value of "v1". Again, using the custom ApiVersion1RoutePrefix attribute helps you avoid silly errors in routing caused by copy/paste/syntax mistakes.

Now let's finish up stubbing out the controllers. We'll flesh out the real implementation later; for now, we're trying to demonstrate that we can properly support versioned routes. First, "implement" the V1 controller:

```
using System.Net.Http;
using System.Web.Http;
using WebApi2Book.Web.Api.Models;
using WebApi2Book.Web.Common.Routing;

namespace WebApi2Book.Web.Api.Controllers.V1
{
    [ApiVersion1RoutePrefix("tasks")]
    public class TasksController : ApiController
    {
        [Route("", Name = "AddTaskRoute")]
        [HttpPost]
        public Task AddTask(HttpRequestMessage requestMessage, Task newTask)
        {
            return new Task
            {
                Subject = "In v1, newTask.Subject = " + newTask.Subject
            };
        }
    }
}
```

And now implement the V2 controller:

```
using System.Net.Http;
using System.Web.Http;
using WebApi2Book.Web.Api.Models;

namespace WebApi2Book.Web.Api.Controllers.V2
{
    [RoutePrefix("api/{apiVersion:apiVersionConstraint(v2)}/tasks")]
    public class TasksController : ApiController
    {
        [Route("", Name = "AddTaskRouteV2")]
        [HttpPost]
        public Task AddTask(HttpRequestMessage requestMessage, Models.Task newTask)
        {
            return new Task
            {
                Subject = "In v2, newTask.Subject = " + newTask.Subject
            };
        }
    }
}
```

Note that for the V2 controller we're using the RoutePrefix attribute directly rather than subclassing it. The purpose is to emphasize that the custom ApiVersion1RoutePrefixAttribute is merely syntactic sugar; it doesn't affect the routing in any way. Also note that the two route names are unique between the two controllers. We need to ensure globally unique route names, as required by ASP.NET Web API.

OK, now we're almost ready to process a request. First, we'll implement the custom controller selector. (As we mentioned earlier, a custom controller selector is necessary because the framework only matches on the controller class name without regard to the controller class' namespace.) Then, after that, we will wire up the custom constraint and the custom controller selector with the ASP.NET Web API framework. So without further ado. . .

A Custom IHttpControllerSelector

Our controller selector implementation was inspired by Mike Wasson's MSDN blog post "ASP.NET Web API: Using Namespaces to Version Web APIs" (http://blogs.msdn.com/b/webdev/archive/2013/03/08/using-namespaces-to-version-web-apis.aspx). The implementation borrowed heavily from the official Microsoft CodePlex NamespaceControllerSelector sample referenced in that blog post. We made some simplifications (e.g., eliminated the code that checked for duplicate paths), and we made some enhancements required to address changes in the ASP.NET Web API framework (e.g., note the use of IHttpRouteData subroutes), but the basic design and implementation comes straight from CodePlex.

Anyway, go ahead and implement the custom controller selector as follows in the root of the WebApi2Book.Web.Common project:

```
using System;
using System.Collections.Generic;
using System.Globalization;
using System.Linq;
using System.Net;
using System.Net.Http;
using System.Web.Http;
using System.Web.Http.Controllers;
using System.Web.Http.Dispatcher;
using System.Web.Http.Routing;

namespace WebApi2Book.Web.Common
{
    public class NamespaceHttpControllerSelector : IHttpControllerSelector
    {
        private readonly HttpConfiguration _configuration;
        private readonly Lazy<Dictionary<string, HttpControllerDescriptor>> _controllers;

        public NamespaceHttpControllerSelector(HttpConfiguration config)
        {
            _configuration = config;
            _controllers = new Lazy<Dictionary<string,
                HttpControllerDescriptor>>(InitializeControllerDictionary);
        }

        public HttpControllerDescriptor SelectController(HttpRequestMessage request)
        {
            var routeData = request.GetRouteData();
            if (routeData == null)
            {
                throw new HttpResponseException(HttpStatusCode.NotFound);
            }
```

```
        var controllerName = GetControllerName(routeData);
        if (controllerName == null)
        {
            throw new HttpResponseException(HttpStatusCode.NotFound);
        }

        var namespaceName = GetVersion(routeData);
        if (namespaceName == null)
        {
            throw new HttpResponseException(HttpStatusCode.NotFound);
        }

        var controllerKey = String.Format(CultureInfo.InvariantCulture, "{0}.{1}",
            namespaceName, controllerName);

        HttpControllerDescriptor controllerDescriptor;
        if (_controllers.Value.TryGetValue(controllerKey, out controllerDescriptor))
        {
            return controllerDescriptor;
        }

        throw new HttpResponseException(HttpStatusCode.NotFound);
    }

    public IDictionary<string, HttpControllerDescriptor> GetControllerMapping()
    {
        return _controllers.Value;
    }

    private Dictionary<string, HttpControllerDescriptor> InitializeControllerDictionary()
    {
        var dictionary = new Dictionary<string,
            HttpControllerDescriptor>(StringComparer.OrdinalIgnoreCase);

        var assembliesResolver = _configuration.Services.GetAssembliesResolver();
        var controllersResolver = _configuration.Services.GetHttpControllerTypeResolver();

        var controllerTypes = controllersResolver.GetControllerTypes(assembliesResolver);

        foreach (var controllerType in controllerTypes)
        {
            var segments = controllerType.Namespace.Split(Type.Delimiter);

            var controllerName =
                controllerType.Name.Remove(controllerType.Name.Length -
                                    DefaultHttpControllerSelector.ControllerSuffix.Length);

            var controllerKey = String.Format(CultureInfo.InvariantCulture, "{0}.{1}",
                segments[segments.Length - 1], controllerName);
```

```
            if (!dictionary.Keys.Contains(controllerKey))
            {
                dictionary[controllerKey] = new HttpControllerDescriptor(_configuration,
                    controllerType.Name,
                    controllerType);
            }
        }

        return dictionary;
    }

    private T GetRouteVariable<T>(IHttpRouteData routeData, string name)
    {
        object result;
        if (routeData.Values.TryGetValue(name, out result))
        {
            return (T)result;
        }
        return default(T);
    }

    private string GetControllerName(IHttpRouteData routeData)
    {
        var subroute = routeData.GetSubRoutes().FirstOrDefault();
        if (subroute == null) return null;

        var dataTokenValue = subroute.Route.DataTokens.First().Value;
        if (dataTokenValue == null) return null;

        var controllerName =
            ((HttpActionDescriptor[])dataTokenValue).First()
                .ControllerDescriptor.ControllerName.Replace("Controller", string.Empty);
        return controllerName;
    }

    private string GetVersion(IHttpRouteData routeData)
    {
        var subRouteData = routeData.GetSubRoutes().FirstOrDefault();
        if (subRouteData == null) return null;
        return GetRouteVariable<string>(subRouteData, "apiVersion");
    }
  }
}
```

There's a lot going on in that controller selector, but it's explained well in Wasson's blog post, so we will refer you to it rather than continue to dwell on this topic:

```
http://blogs.msdn.com/b/webdev/archive/2013/03/08/using-namespaces-to-version-web-apis.aspx
```

We've still got a long way to go, so we're going to move on now to the configuration step, where all of this routing and versioning finally comes together.

Configuration

We need to register our constraint with ASP.NET Web API so that it gets applied to incoming requests. We also need to configure our custom controller selector. We accomplish this by implementing the WebApiConfig class as follows (go ahead and type/copy it in, replacing the default implementation provided by Visual Studio):

```
using System.Web.Http;
using System.Web.Http.Dispatcher;
using System.Web.Http.Routing;
using WebApi2Book.Web.Common;
using WebApi2Book.Web.Common.Routing;

namespace WebApi2Book.Web.Api
{
    public static class WebApiConfig
    {
        public static void Register(HttpConfiguration config)
        {
            var constraintsResolver = new DefaultInlineConstraintResolver();
            constraintsResolver.ConstraintMap.Add("apiVersionConstraint", typeof
                                    (ApiVersionConstraint));
            config.MapHttpAttributeRoutes(constraintsResolver);

            config.Services.Replace(typeof (IHttpControllerSelector),
                new NamespaceHttpControllerSelector(config));
        }
    }
}
```

The first part of the Register method configures the version constraint. Our ApiVersionConstraint is registered with a constraint resolver, which the framework uses to find and instantiate the appropriate constraint at runtime. The last part of the method wires-in our custom controller selector, replacing the default, namespace-unaware, controller selector.

With that in place, we are now finally ready to build and test the app.

The Demo

With the WebApi2Book.Web.Api project configured as the startup project in Visual Studio (please perform this configuration if you haven't done so already), we'll hit F5 to start the application. If you're following along, you'll see it load an error page in your browser (Figure 5-5).

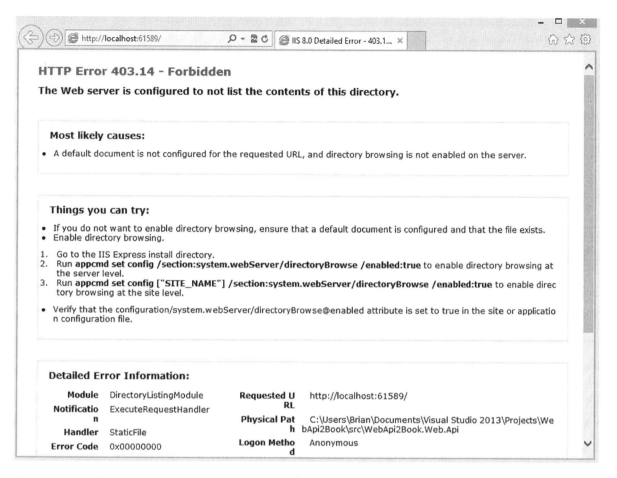

Figure 5-5. *Application error page*

Don't worry, this is expected. There are no routes configured in our application that match this base address.

Now we need to send an HTTP POST message via the V1 route, so go ahead and send the following request message using Fiddler (or your favorite web proxy debugging tool):

V1 Request

```
POST http://localhost:61589/api/v1/tasks HTTP/1.1
Content-Type: text/json

{"Subject":"Fix something important"}
```

You should see the following response:

V1 Response (abbreviated)

```
HTTP/1.1 200 OK
Content-Type: text/json; charset=utf-8
```

```
{"TaskId":null,"Subject":"In v1, newTask.Subject = Fix something important",
"StartDate":null,"DueDate":null,"CreatedDate":null,"CompletedDate":null,"Status":null,
"Assignees":null,"Links":[]}
```

Excellent! Note the Subject value in the response…just as we implemented it! You may also note that the TaskId is null, but that's because we're not actually persisting anything yet.

OK, now do the same for V2:

V2 Request

```
POST http://localhost:61589/api/v2/tasks HTTP/1.1
Content-Type: text/json

{"Subject":"Fix something important"}
```

V2 Response (abbreviated)

```
HTTP/1.1 200 OK
Content-Type: text/json; charset=utf-8

{"TaskId":null,"Subject":"In v2, newTask.Subject = Fix something important",
"StartDate":null,"DueDate":null,"CreatedDate":null,"CompletedDate":null,"Status":null,
"Assignees":null,"Links":[]}
```

Perfect! OK, this is great. You learned about routing, including many of the new capabilities made available by ASP.NET Web API 2. You learned about constraints and controller selectors. And you successfully processed an HTTP request. However, we must admit that this is rather "hello world-ish"; our controller actions aren't doing anything meaningful. This leads us to our next topic: dependencies. Inside of these dependencies is where the real work gets done, at least from a business perspective. Anything related to data access, calculations, file I/O, date/time, etc., will all be handled by such dependencies.

Dependencies

If the controllers are going to do anything useful, and if they are going to be implemented in a well-architected manner using SOLID design principles, they will depend heavily upon functionality provided by other classes. An example of this is a database accessor, which is an object that can be used to query and save changes back to the database. The database accessor is considered a dependency of the controller class that uses it—that is, the controller depends on it for functionality not implemented within the controller itself.

SOLID DESIGN PRINCIPLES

If you don't know with what we mean by the SOLID design principles, do yourself a huge favor and familiarize yourself with them. These principles were defined by Robert C. Martin in the early 2000s and have been reviewed and explained numerous times by quite a few people over the last decade.

The acronym SOLID stands for the following: Single responsibility principle, Open/closed principle, Liskov substitution principle, Interface segregation principle, and Dependency inversion principle. You can read up on these five principles in the following related articles written by Bob Martin:

- S - http://www.objectmentor.com/resources/articles/srp.pdf

- O - http://www.objectmentor.com/resources/articles/ocp.pdf

- L - http://www.objectmentor.com/resources/articles/lsp.pdf

- I - http://www.objectmentor.com/resources/articles/isp.pdf

- D - http://www.objectmentor.com/resources/articles/dip.pdf

The main idea is that the methods in the controllers should not be doing much more than simply using the functionality offered by various dependencies. And that brings us to the point of this section: **managing dependencies within the application**. Once you adopt the approach of using dependencies for most or all functionality, you need a pattern and appropriate tool(s) for configuring and obtaining those dependencies. The easiest way to approach this is summarized in these two points:

- Push dependencies up to the constructor.

- Configure the application to use dependency injection.

Constructor Injection of Dependencies

The concept of pushing dependencies up to the constructor is really quite simple, but it can be tough to grasp and put into practice for the Dependency Injection (DI) novice. Don't worry if you are new to DI, because you will become quite familiar with it as we continue to implement the task service.

To start, think of it this way: a class should not use any behavior that does not come through the constructor in the form of an abstraction (i.e., an interface). This includes even seemingly harmless classes such as System.DateTime, System.IO.File, System.Environment, and many other basic utility classes within the .NET Framework. If a class is using the services of another class, that other class needs to be injected in through the constructor. This also applies to static properties and methods. For example, if some piece of code needs to use the static DateTime.Now property, the DateTime.Now functionality should be wrapped in an injectable adapter class instead of used directly. There are exceptions to this "constructor injection mandate," such as when constructor injection isn't even possible (we'll see examples of this), but you get the point: use constructor injection wherever you can.

Again, you will see working examples of all of this later. But first, let's configure a DI tool to provide our code with the dependencies it needs at runtime. Of particular importance is the way in which controllers are activated by the runtime. All API requests will revolve around a controller method. As such, configuring our controllers to obtain their dependencies through their respective constructors provides the "root" we need to ensure all objects are managed properly.

Configuring Ninject Dependency Injection

As we mentioned in Chapter 3, we've chosen to use the open source Ninject DI tool. The same principles apply to all DI tools, though, so if you prefer a different one you probably just need to account for the differences in syntax.

There are three things we need to take care of regarding Ninject in the service. The first two need to be done in any kind of application, while the third is somewhat unique to an ASP.NET Web API service. Table 5-4 briefly describes each of these activities.

Table 5-4. *Ninject-Related Activities*

Activity	Implementation	Description
Container configuration	NinjectWebCommon	Make sure a DI container is created during application start-up and remains in memory until the application shuts down. (You can think of the container as the object that contains the dependencies.)
Container bindings	NinjectConfigurator	This is where we bind or relate interfaces to concrete implementations so that the dependencies can be resolved at run time. For example, if a class requires an IDateTime object, the bindings tell the container to provide a DateTimeAdapter object.
Dependency resolver for Ninject	NinjectDependencyResolver	This tells ASP.NET Web API to ask Ninject for all dependencies required at run time by the dependent objects. This is the key that allows you to push dependencies up to the constructor on the controllers. Without this resolver, ASP.NET won't use your configured Ninject container for dependencies.

Container Configuration

In order for the DI container to be useful for creating objects and injecting them into constructors, and to control the lifetime of those objects, the container must be available for the entire duration that the application is running. In other words, a single container instance must meet these criteria:

- Be created early in the application start-up process
- Be available at all times while the application is running
- Be destroyed as one of the last steps the application takes during shutdown

While it is certainly possible to wire up Ninject manually, the easiest and most reliable option for making sure the container is always available is to install the Ninject.Web.Common.WebHost NuGet package. If you were following the steps in Chapter 4, you already did this. The package generates code that handles creating and destroying a container instance within the Start and Stop methods of the NinjectWebCommon class it adds to the App_Start folder of the WebApi2Book.Web.Api project. The generated NinjectWebCommon class does require some tweaking to establish the container bindings and to register itself with the Web API framework's global configuration, but hey, it gets you 99 percent of the way there by hooking into the ASP.NET application's startup and shutdown events. We'll take a look at it soon.

Container Bindings

Now that the container itself is configured to be available while the application is running, we need to give it the type mappings so that it can instantiate and help inject dependencies into the objects that require them. This step is essentially just mapping interface types to implementation types, and in some cases, to implementation methods or variables. In a previous example, we mentioned wrapping `DateTime.Now` in an adapter class and injecting the interface into the dependent class(es). The particular mapping to accomplish this is as follows:

```
container.Bind<IDateTime>().To<DateTimeAdapter>().InSingletonScope();
```

Note that this isn't actually creating an instance of `DateTimeAdapter`; Ninject does that as such instances are required. Also note that by specifying `InSingletonScope` we are directing Ninject to provide a shared instance to all dependent objects for the entire lifetime of the application. This is an example of letting the container (and its associated configuration) manage the lifetime of an application's objects, thereby removing that burden from consumers of those objects.

Another lifetime scope we'll be using very frequently is `InRequestScope`, which provides a shared instance to all dependent objects processing the same HTTP request. We also sometimes use the `ToConstant` lifetime scope, which manages an application-level singleton instance that our code—not Ninject—has instantiated. And while we're on the subject of configuring dependencies with Ninject, we should mention that we occasionally use the `ToMethod` factory method to specify a method or delegate for Ninject to call whenever a new object of a given interface/abstract type is needed.

Armed with this vast knowledge about dependencies, DI, and Ninject, let's get back to writing some code! First off, let's go ahead and implement that `DateTimeAdapter` class and corresponding interface in the root of the `WebApi2Book.Common` project as follows:

IDateTime Interface

```
using System;

namespace WebApi2Book.Common
{
    public interface IDateTime
    {
        DateTime UtcNow { get; }
    }
}
```

DateTimeAdapter Class

```
using System;

namespace WebApi2Book.Common
{
    public class DateTimeAdapter : IDateTime
    {
        public DateTime UtcNow
        {
            get { return DateTime.UtcNow; }
        }
    }
}
```

Next, anticipating the need for logging (doesn't every significant application need some form of diagnostic logging?), add a project folder named Logging to the `WebApi2Book.Common` project. Then add the following interface and adapter class to that folder; this is to prevent tight coupling to the static log4net `LogManager.GetLogger` method. Remember, we want to push dependencies up to the controller, and not rely on specific static properties or methods.

ILogManager Interface

```
using System;
using log4net;

namespace WebApi2Book.Common.Logging
{
    public interface ILogManager
    {
        ILog GetLog(Type typeAssociatedWithRequestedLog);
    }
}
```

LogManagerAdapter Class

```
using System;
using log4net;

namespace WebApi2Book.Common.Logging
{
    public class LogManagerAdapter : ILogManager
    {
        public ILog GetLog(Type typeAssociatedWithRequestedLog)
        {
            var log = LogManager.GetLogger(typeAssociatedWithRequestedLog);
            return log;
        }
    }
}
```

And now we're ready to configure our first actual dependency bindings. So let's add a new class, named NinjectConfigurator, to the App_Start folder of the WebApi2Book.Web.Api project. Implement it as follows:

```
using log4net.Config;
using Ninject;
using WebApi2Book.Common;
using WebApi2Book.Common.Logging;

namespace WebApi2Book.Web.Api
{
    public class NinjectConfigurator
    {
        public void Configure(IKernel container)
        {
            AddBindings(container);
        }

        private void AddBindings(IKernel container)
        {
            ConfigureLog4net(container);

            container.Bind<IDateTime>().To<DateTimeAdapter>().InSingletonScope();
        }
```

```
        private void ConfigureLog4net(IKernel container)
        {
            XmlConfigurator.Configure();

            var logManager = new LogManagerAdapter();
            container.Bind<ILogManager>().ToConstant(logManager);
        }
    }
}
```

See the IDateTime and ILogManager bindings? Hopefully, they make sense now. However, how does this get invoked? We see that AddBindings calls ConfigureLog4net (by the way, that call to XmlConfigurator.Configure is required to configure log4net), and we see that Configure calls AddBindings, but what calls Configure? The answer to this question lies in the aforementioned NinjectWebCommon class, which we will explore at the end of this section on dependencies.

IDependencyResolver for Ninject

Here is the NinjectDependencyResolver we will use for our task-management service. Note that it takes an instance of a Ninject container in its constructor. Go ahead and implement it in the root of the WebApi2Book.Web.Common project:

```
using System;
using System.Collections.Generic;
using System.Web.Http.Dependencies;
using Ninject;

namespace WebApi2Book.Web.Common
{
    public sealed class NinjectDependencyResolver : IDependencyResolver
    {
        private readonly IKernel _container;

        public NinjectDependencyResolver(IKernel container)
        {
            _container = container;
        }

        public IKernel Container
        {
            get { return _container; }
        }

        public object GetService(Type serviceType)
        {
            return _container.TryGet(serviceType);
        }
```

CHAPTER 5 ■ UP AND DOWN THE STACK WITH A POST

```csharp
        public IEnumerable<object> GetServices(Type serviceType)
        {
            return _container.GetAll(serviceType);
        }

        public IDependencyScope BeginScope()
        {
            return this;
        }

        public void Dispose()
        {
            GC.SuppressFinalize(this);
        }
    }
}
```

The methods to note are GetService and GetServices. All they really do is delegate to the Ninject container to get object instances for the requested service types. Also note that in the GetService method we are using the TryGet method instead of the Get method. This is to prevent Ninject from blowing up if it is asked for a dependency that it can't provide because the dependency—or one of its dependencies—was never registered. We simply want to return null if we haven't explicitly registered a given type.

And now it's time to put it all together; it's time for us to complete the implementation of the NinjectWebCommon class.

Completing NinjectWebCommon

Take a look at the NinjectWebCommon class that the Ninject.Web.Common.WebHost NuGet package added, and then modify the implementation so that it appears as follows:

```csharp
using System;
using System.Web;
using System.Web.Http;
using Microsoft.Web.Infrastructure.DynamicModuleHelper;
using Ninject;
using Ninject.Web.Common;
using WebActivatorEx;
using WebApi2Book.Web.Api;
using WebApi2Book.Web.Common;

[assembly: WebActivatorEx.PreApplicationStartMethod(typeof (NinjectWebCommon), "Start")]
[assembly: ApplicationShutdownMethod(typeof (NinjectWebCommon), "Stop")]

namespace WebApi2Book.Web.Api
{
    public static class NinjectWebCommon
    {
        private static readonly Bootstrapper Bootstrapper = new Bootstrapper();

        public static void Start()
        {
            DynamicModuleUtility.RegisterModule(typeof (OnePerRequestHttpModule));
            DynamicModuleUtility.RegisterModule(typeof (NinjectHttpModule));
```

```
            IKernel container = null;
            Bootstrapper.Initialize(() =>
            {
                container = CreateKernel();
                return container;
            });

            var resolver = new NinjectDependencyResolver(container);
            GlobalConfiguration.Configuration.DependencyResolver = resolver;
        }

        public static void Stop()
        {
            Bootstrapper.ShutDown();
        }

        private static IKernel CreateKernel()
        {
            var kernel = new StandardKernel();
            try
            {
                kernel.Bind<Func<IKernel>>().ToMethod(ctx => () => new Bootstrapper().Kernel);
                kernel.Bind<IHttpModule>().To<HttpApplicationInitializationHttpModule>();

                RegisterServices(kernel);
                return kernel;
            }
            catch
            {
                kernel.Dispose();
                throw;
            }
        }

        private static void RegisterServices(IKernel kernel)
        {
            var containerConfigurator = new NinjectConfigurator();
            containerConfigurator.Configure(kernel);
        }
    }
}
```

Our modified version is different in some subtle ways. First, here are the significant changes that we made:

- We modified the Start method to register our dependency resolver with the Web API configuration. In doing so, we have directed the framework to hit our configured Ninject container instance to resolve any dependencies that are needed.

- We modified the RegisterServices method to configure the container bindings using the NinjectConfigurator class. So now we've finally answered the question about what calls the Configure method: NinjectWebCommon.RegisterServices does!

It's important to note that the registration of our dependency resolver with Web API and configuration of container bindings by the `NinjectConfigurator.Configure` method are both called (the former directly, the latter indirectly) from the `Start` method, which is called during application start-up. In this way, all of this setup is completed before the application accepts and processes any HTTP requests, and thus before any of the controllers—which rely on dependencies being injected into them—are ever created.

Now, for completeness, here are the insignificant changes that we made:

- We removed the comments. Nothing against comments, we're just pressed for space!

- We changed the namespace to `WebApi2Book.Web.Api`. It's common practice to use this namespace for files in the `App_Start` folder. Case in point: look at the namespace of the `WebApiConfig` class that Visual Studio automatically added to the `WebApi2Book.Web.Api` project.

- We moved the `using` directives outside of the namespace. There's no particular reason for this other than personal preference.

As we build the task-management service, we will find ourselves coming back to the `NinjectConfigurator` fairly often. This is because the classes used for various behaviors will continue to change as the application evolves. Simply put, these mappings are not etched in stone, and you should expect to modify this class as time goes on.

NHibernate Configuration and Mappings

We now turn our attention to configuring NHibernate to work with the database and with the domain model, or "entity," classes. We'll be using the Fluent NHibernate NuGet library that we installed in Chapter 4 for this.

To reiterate what we first mentioned in the previous chapter, we will continue to refer to the domain model classes as "entities" to more easily distinguish between the persistent domain model types (i.e., the entities) and the service model types.

Database Configuration: Overview

As with any approach to data access, at some point the underlying framework must be told how to connect to the database. And because NHibernate is database-provider agnostic, we must also tell it which provider we're using, and even which version of which provider. This allows NHibernate to load the appropriate driver for dynamically generating the DML (Data Manipulation Language) it needs to interact with the database—i.e., SELECT, INSERT, UPDATE, and DELETE statements. For example, creating a SELECT statement in SQL Server will be a little different in some cases than creating a SELECT statement in Oracle or MySQL. Indeed, one of the advantages of using an Object Relational Mapper (ORM) like NHibernate is that one can, in theory, change database providers without having to change anything about the domain model or any code that uses it. One would most likely need to update the NHibernate configuration and mapping definitions, however. It is for this reason that we have split the data layer into two separate projects:

- The `WebApi2Book.Data` project, which includes the entire domain model (i.e., all of the entity classes). None of this code is dependent on a specific database provider; that is, the entities will be the same whether you're working with SQL Server or Oracle.

- The `WebApi2Book.Data.SqlServer` project, which contains the NHibernate mapping definitions. These could possibly change when swapping out database providers.

Actually wiring-in the database configuration with the ASP.NET Web API framework requires a small bit of code located in the application's start-up logic, along with some supporting classes (that are easy to isolate) and some config file-based configuration. That means deciding to switch from SQL Server to Oracle, for example, can be accomplished relatively noninvasively.

So let's begin database configuration for the task-management service. You'll notice that although the wire-in itself doesn't require many lines of code, it does involve many related moving parts. So let's go through this carefully!

Adding Concurrency Support to Entities

The first thing we'll do is add concurrency support to the entities that we introduced back in Chapter 4. Start this off by adding a new interface to the WebApi2Book.Data.Entities namespace:

IVersionedEntity Interface

```
namespace WebApi2Book.Data.Entities
{
    public interface IVersionedEntity
    {
        byte[] Version { get; set; }
    }
}
```

Then have each of the entity classes implement that interface. This is trivial, because the Version property is already defined in each entity class (as created in the previous chapter). As an example, the Status class should now look like this:

```
namespace WebApi2Book.Data.Entities
{
    public class Status : IVersionedEntity
    {
        public virtual long StatusId { get; set; }
        public virtual string Name { get; set; }
        public virtual int Ordinal { get; set; }
        public virtual byte[] Version { get; set; }
    }
}
```

Entity Mapping

Next, we need to provide all of the code that will map between the entities and the database's tables and columns. Depending on the database model you're trying to map, and depending on how much you are trying to abstract away the domain model itself, building these mappings can be anywhere from very simple to very complex. We're focusing on the ASP.NET Web API, so we have designed the task-management service to be on the very simple end of the scale.

Since we've already gone through the entity classes and the data model in Chapter 4, these mapping definitions should be fairly self-explanatory. We'll point out a few key things after looking at the code; speaking of which, go ahead and add all the following classes to a new folder named Mapping in the WebApi2Book.Data.SqlServer project:

VersionedClassMap Class

```
using FluentNHibernate.Mapping;
using WebApi2Book.Data.Entities;

namespace WebApi2Book.Data.SqlServer.Mapping
{
    public abstract class VersionedClassMap<T> : ClassMap<T> where T : IVersionedEntity
```

```
    {
        protected VersionedClassMap()
        {
            Version(x => x.Version)
                .Column("ts")
                .CustomSqlType("Rowversion")
                .Generated.Always()
                .UnsavedValue("null");
        }
    }
}
```

StatusMap Class

```
using WebApi2Book.Data.Entities;

namespace WebApi2Book.Data.SqlServer.Mapping
{
    public class StatusMap : VersionedClassMap<Status>
    {
        public StatusMap()
        {
            Id(x => x.StatusId);
            Map(x => x.Name).Not.Nullable();
            Map(x => x.Ordinal).Not.Nullable();
        }
    }
}
```

TaskMap Class

```
using FluentNHibernate.Mapping;
using WebApi2Book.Data.Entities;

namespace WebApi2Book.Data.SqlServer.Mapping
{
    public class TaskMap : VersionedClassMap<Task>
    {
        public TaskMap()
        {
            Id(x => x.TaskId);
            Map(x => x.Subject).Not.Nullable();
            Map(x => x.StartDate).Nullable();
            Map(x => x.DueDate).Nullable();
            Map(x => x.CompletedDate).Nullable();
            Map(x => x.CreatedDate).Not.Nullable();

            References(x => x.Status, "StatusId");
            References(x => x.CreatedBy, "CreatedUserId");

            HasManyToMany(x => x.Users)
                .Access.ReadOnlyPropertyThroughCamelCaseField(Prefix.Underscore)
```

```
                .Table("TaskUser")
                .ParentKeyColumn("TaskId")
                .ChildKeyColumn("UserId");
        }
    }
}
```

UserMap Class

```
using WebApi2Book.Data.Entities;

namespace WebApi2Book.Data.SqlServer.Mapping
{
    public class UserMap : VersionedClassMap<User>
    {
        public UserMap()
        {
            Id(x => x.UserId);
            Map(x => x.Firstname).Not.Nullable();
            Map(x => x.Lastname).Not.Nullable();
            Map(x => x.Username).Not.Nullable();
        }
    }
}
```

The first thing you might notice is that all of the mapping code is contained within each class's constructor. Second, notice the use of the VersionedClassMap<T> base class for each of the map classes. This custom class leverages NHibernate's ability to check for dirty records in the database, based on a Rowversion column on each table. The crazy-long statement in the VersionedClassMap implementation can be broken down as follows:

- Use the Version property on each entity class as a concurrency (or, version) value.

- The database column supporting versioning is named ts.

- The SQL data type is a Rowversion.

- NHibernate should always let the database generate the value, as opposed to you or NHibernate supplying the value.

- Prior to a database save, the in-memory value of the Version property will be null.

Again, all of this is to let NHibernate protect against trying to update dirty records. Placing this statement in the constructor of the base class means it will automatically be executed by every ClassMap implementation in the Mapping folder. Implementing the IVersionedEntity interface just ensures that the class contains a Version property, and because of what we implemented in the previous section, we know that each of the entity classes implements this interface.

ClassMap<T>, the base class of VersionedClassMap<T>, is defined in the Fluent NHibernate library, and it simply provides a means of configuring entity-to-database mapping through code (as opposed to using XML files). This mapping code is placed in each mapping class's constructor. For example, the StatusMap mapping class constructor contains all of the mapping for the Status entity.

The two main ClassMap<T> methods used in the application's mapping classes are the Id and Map methods. The Id method can be called only once, and it's used to tell NHibernate which property on the entity class is used as the object identifier.

The Map is used to configure individual properties on the entities. By default, NHibernate will assume the mapped column name is the same as the given property name. If it's not, an overload can be used to specify the column name. Additionally, because this is a fluent-style interface, we can chain other property and column specifics together.

For example, the UserMap class's Firstname mapping also includes a specification telling NHibernate to treat the column as not nullable.

We have implemented one ClassMap<T> for each entity. The StatusMap and UserMap mapping classes are straightforward. They each have their properties mapped, the first of which is the class's identifier. We don't need to specify the column name, because the column name happens to match the property name.

The TaskMap class is slightly more complicated; it is used to map the Task's relationships to other entities. We'll explore it next.

Mapping Relationships

Mapping many-to-one references is actually relatively simple. For example, the Task class has a Status property that references an instance of a Status class. We then see in TaskMap that a Task has a reference to a Status. The corresponding column name in the Task table is StatusId. The reference to the user that created the task is similar.

Many-to-many relationships are more complicated because you must identify the linking table in the database, as well as the linking table's parent and child columns. For example, to link a set of users to a task, the TaskUser table will contain a record for each user linked to that task. The users will be loaded into the Users collection property on the Task object.

Regarding that collection, the Task class defines the Users property with only a getter, to prevent the developer from replacing the entire collection. Note that we also create an empty collection upon class instantiation, which allows us to immediately call Add on the property without having to create a new collection first. As such, the TaskMap class defines the Users property map with this bit of code:

```
.Access.ReadOnlyPropertyThroughCamelCaseField(Prefix.Underscore)
```

This tells NHibernate to "access the Users read-only property through a camel-cased field that is named with an underscore prefix." That's right, NHibernate will use reflection to access the collection of users via your private _users field—as opposed to the public getter.

Database Configuration: Bringing It All Together

OK, now that we've laid the groundwork for it, let's finish off this section by hooking NHibernate up to the ASP.NET Web API. First, add the following using directives and methods, respectively, to the NinjectConfigurator class we discussed previously.

Additional Using Directives

```
using FluentNHibernate.Cfg;
using FluentNHibernate.Cfg.Db;
using NHibernate;
using NHibernate.Context;
using Ninject.Activation;
using Ninject.Web.Common;
using WebApi2Book.Data.SqlServer.Mapping;
```

Additional Methods

```
private void ConfigureNHibernate(IKernel container)
{
    var sessionFactory = Fluently.Configure()
        .Database(
            MsSqlConfiguration.MsSql2008.ConnectionString(
```

```
                c => c.FromConnectionStringWithKey("WebApi2BookDb")))
        .CurrentSessionContext("web")
        .Mappings(m => m.FluentMappings.AddFromAssemblyOf<TaskMap>())
        .BuildSessionFactory();

    container.Bind<ISessionFactory>().ToConstant(sessionFactory);
    container.Bind<ISession>().ToMethod(CreateSession).InRequestScope();
}

private ISession CreateSession(IContext context)
{
    var sessionFactory = context.Kernel.Get<ISessionFactory>();
    if (!CurrentSessionContext.HasBind(sessionFactory))
    {
        var session = sessionFactory.OpenSession();
        CurrentSessionContext.Bind(session);
    }

    return sessionFactory.GetCurrentSession();
}
```

Then modify the AddBindings method so that it is implemented as shown (adding the call to ConfigureNHibernate):

```
private void AddBindings(IKernel container)
{
    ConfigureLog4net(container);
    ConfigureNHibernate(container);

    container.Bind<IDateTime>().To<DateTimeAdapter>().InSingletonScope();
}
```

Finally, add the following code to the Web.Api project's web.config file, right below the closing configSections tag that we added in Chapter 4:

```
<connectionStrings>
  <add name="WebApi2BookDb" providerName="System.Data.SqlClient" connectionString="Server=.;
        initial catalog=WebApi2BookDb;Integrated Security=True;
          Application Name=WebApi2Book API Website" />
</connectionStrings>
```

Let's review what we just did, starting with the ConfigureNHibernate method. This method sets four properties and then builds the ISessionFactory object:

- The first property indicates that we are using a version of SQL Server that is compatible with SQL Server 2012.

- The second property specifies the database connection string, and that it should be loaded from the web.config file's WebApi2BookDb connection string value.

- The third property tells NHibernate that we plan to use its web implementation to manage the current session object. We'll explore session management more in the next section, but this essentially scopes a single database session to a single web request (i.e., one database session per call).

- The fourth property tells NHibernate which assembly to use to load mappings. The WebApi2Book.Data.SqlServer project contains all of those mappings, so we just gave it a class name that exists in that assembly.

Then the method calls BuildSessionFactory, which returns a fully configured NHibernate ISessionFactory instance. The ISessionFactory instance is then placed into the Ninject container with this statement:

```
container.Bind<ISessionFactory>().ToConstant(sessionFactory);
```

Note that we've placed our newly created ISessionFactory in our container as a constant. When using NHibernate, it is important to only ever create a single ISessionFactory instance per application. The act of creating the factory is pretty compute intensive, as it is creating all mappings to the database. Further, we only need one, as opposed to one per request, per user, etc.

The statement that follows, where we tell Ninject how to get ISession objects, will be discussed in the next section. For now, just understand that we've configured NHibernate to be able to talk to the database. This is good progress!

Managing the Unit of Work

As discussed in Chapter 3, one of the key benefits of using NHibernate is that it implements a unit of work with its ISession interface. In a service application like the task-management service, we need the database session object—as well as an associated database transaction—to span a complete service call. This provides support for three very important requirements for interacting with persistent data within a web request:

- Keep fetched domain objects in memory so that they are consistent across all operations within a single web request. NHibernate uses the ISession object to keep all fetched data and associated changes in memory. If some code used a different ISession instance, it would not see the same/updated data.

- Use in-memory objects to facilitate caching.

- Track all changes made to domain objects so that saving the changes in an ISession instance will save all changes made during a single web request; this is especially important for updates that involve foreign-key relationships.

In short, it is very important to ensure that every database operation within a given web request uses the same ISession object. This is what we mean by "managing the unit of work."

Fortunately, NHibernate comes equipped with the ability to utilize the ASP.NET HttpContext to manage instances of ISession. In the previous section, when creating the ISessionFactory object, we began leveraging this ability by using the CurrentSessionContext("web") call to tell NHibernate to use its web implementation (which relies on the ASP.NET HttpContext) to manage the current session object. In addition to that, though, we need to use a special class within NHibernate called the CurrentSessionContext. We use this class to manually bind an instance of ISession to the underlying HttpContext, and then turn around and unbind it when the request is complete. It feels like a lot of code. But you only have to do this in one place, and you'll find that it works incredibly well.

It'll be easier to understand if we look at the code, so refer back to the NinjectConfigurator's ConfigureNHibernate method we implemented in the last section. We configured the ISession mapping with Ninject like this:

```
container.Bind<ISession>().ToMethod(CreateSession);
```

This tells Ninject to call the `CreateSession` method whenever an object (e.g., a controller) needs an `ISession` injected into its constructor. Now let's look at the `CreateSession` method.

First, we obtain an instance of the `ISessionFactory` that we configured during application start-up. (This was covered in the previous section.) We then use that `ISessionFactory` object to check whether an existing `ISession` object has already been bound to the `CurrentSessionContext` object. If not, we open a new session and then immediately bind it to the context. (By the way, opening a session in NHibernate is somewhat analogous to opening a connection to the database.) Finally, we return the current/newly context-bound `ISession` object.

This `CreateSession` method will be executed every time any dependent object requests an `ISession` object via Ninject (e.g., through constructor injection). Our implementation ensures that, for a single API request, we only ever create one `ISession` object.

At this point, we have code in place to create and manage a single database session for a given request. To then close and dispose of this `ISession` object, we're going to use an implementation of an `ActionFilterAttribute`. ASP.NET Web API uses these attributes, and derivations thereof, to execute pre and post behaviors around controller methods. Our attribute will decorate the controllers to ensure all controller actions are using a properly managed `ISession` instance. The attribute, and its `IActionTransactionHelper` and `WebContainerManager` dependencies, are implemented as follows. Go ahead and add these to the `WebApi2Book.Web.Common` project, and then we'll discuss them:

WebContainerManager Class

```csharp
using System;
using System.Collections.Generic;
using System.Linq;
using System.Web.Http;
using System.Web.Http.Dependencies;

namespace WebApi2Book.Web.Common
{
    public static class WebContainerManager
    {
        public static IDependencyResolver GetDependencyResolver()
        {
            var dependencyResolver = GlobalConfiguration.Configuration.DependencyResolver;
            if (dependencyResolver != null)
            {
                return dependencyResolver;
            }

            throw new InvalidOperationException("The dependency resolver has not been set.");
        }

        public static T Get<T>()
        {
            var service = GetDependencyResolver().GetService(typeof (T));

            if (service == null)
                throw new NullReferenceException(string.Format(
                    "Requested service of type {0}, but null was found.",
                    typeof (T).FullName));

            return (T) service;
        }
```

```csharp
        public static IEnumerable<T> GetAll<T>()
        {
            var services = GetDependencyResolver().GetServices(typeof (T)).ToList();

            if (!services.Any())
                throw new NullReferenceException(string.Format(
                    "Requested services of type {0}, but none were found.",
                    typeof (T).FullName));

            return services.Cast<T>();
        }
    }
}
```

IActionTransactionHelper Interface

```csharp
using System.Web.Http.Filters;

namespace WebApi2Book.Web.Common
{
    public interface IActionTransactionHelper
    {
        void BeginTransaction();
        void EndTransaction(HttpActionExecutedContext filterContext);
        void CloseSession();
    }
}
```

ActionTransactionHelper Class

```csharp
using System.Web.Http.Filters;
using NHibernate;
using NHibernate.Context;

namespace WebApi2Book.Web.Common
{
    public class ActionTransactionHelper : IActionTransactionHelper
    {
        private readonly ISessionFactory _sessionFactory;

        public ActionTransactionHelper(ISessionFactory sessionFactory)
        {
            _sessionFactory = sessionFactory;
        }

        public bool TransactionHandled { get; private set; }

        public bool SessionClosed { get; private set; }
```

```
public void BeginTransaction()
{
    if (!CurrentSessionContext.HasBind(_sessionFactory)) return;

    var session = _sessionFactory.GetCurrentSession();
    if (session != null)
    {
        session.BeginTransaction();
    }
}

public void EndTransaction(HttpActionExecutedContext filterContext)
{
    if (!CurrentSessionContext.HasBind(_sessionFactory)) return;

    var session = _sessionFactory.GetCurrentSession();

    if (session == null) return;
    if (!session.Transaction.IsActive) return;

    if (filterContext.Exception == null)
    {
        session.Flush();
        session.Transaction.Commit();
    }
    else
    {
        session.Transaction.Rollback();
    }

    TransactionHandled = true;
}

public void CloseSession()
{
    if (!CurrentSessionContext.HasBind(_sessionFactory)) return;

    var session = _sessionFactory.GetCurrentSession();
    session.Close();
    session.Dispose();
    CurrentSessionContext.Unbind(_sessionFactory);
    SessionClosed = true;
}
    }
}
```

UnitOfWorkActionFilterAttribute Class

```
using System.Web.Http.Controllers;
using System.Web.Http.Filters;

namespace WebApi2Book.Web.Common
{
    public class UnitOfWorkActionFilterAttribute : ActionFilterAttribute
    {
        public virtual IActionTransactionHelper ActionTransactionHelper
        {
            get { return WebContainerManager.Get<IActionTransactionHelper>(); }
        }

        public override bool AllowMultiple
        {
            get { return false; }
        }

        public override void OnActionExecuting(HttpActionContext actionContext)
        {
            ActionTransactionHelper.BeginTransaction();
        }

        public override void OnActionExecuted(HttpActionExecutedContext actionExecutedContext)
        {
            ActionTransactionHelper.EndTransaction(actionExecutedContext);
            ActionTransactionHelper.CloseSession();
        }
    }
}
```

And finally, add the following to the bottom of the NinjectConfigurator class' ConfigureNHibernate method so that IActionTransactionHelper instances can be resolved at run time:

```
container.Bind<IActionTransactionHelper>().To<ActionTransactionHelper>().
    InRequestScope();
```

■ **Note**   You'll also need to add a using directive for WebApi2Book.Web.Common.

We'll explore transaction control in the next section, so we won't discuss anything related to that quite yet. Instead, let's look at the attribute's CloseSession method that is called from the OnActionExecuted override. As you can see, the meaningful part of its implementation is in the ActionTransactionHelper class, so let's dive down into that. Once there, note that most of the CloseSession method implementation is similar to the NinjectConfigurator class' CreateSession method we just discussed. It first checks to see if an ISession object is currently bound to the CurrentSessionContext. If so, the method obtains the ISession object with the GetCurrentSession method, and then closes and disposes of it. Finally, it unbinds the ISession object from the current ISessionFactory instance.

To make sure the controller methods take advantage of this "automatic" ISession disposal, you simply need to make sure that they, or the controllers themselves, are decorated with this attribute. We'll apply the attribute at the controller level because we want each action method to participate in a unit of work. So go ahead and add a UnitOfWorkActionFilterAttribute to each controller, like this for the V1 TasksController:

```
[ApiVersion1RoutePrefix("tasks")]
[UnitOfWorkActionFilter]
public class TasksController : ApiController
```

■ **Note**   You'll also need to add a using directive for WebApi2Book.Web.Common.

Great! We've implemented the unit of work. Overall, this implementation provides a nice separation of concerns: the dependent code can use the injected ISession and simply assume it is active and being managed by something outside itself. It doesn't need to worry about session lifetime, database connections, or transactions. It just has to use the ISession to access the database and let other components take care of the rest.

Before we conclude this section, let's circle back and discuss some of the other things—not related to transaction control—that are going on in these classes that we just added:

- The ActionTransactionHelper property in UnitOfWorkActionFilterAttribute provides access to the IActionTransactionHelper dependency. This is necessary because constructor injection isn't possible with an attribute. The runtime creates only a single instance of the attribute for an application, as opposed to one per web request. So we can't store any state or per-request objects.

- We overrode the AllowMultiple method in the attribute to prevent the filter from executing multiple times on the same call.

- We added the WebContainerManager to provide access to dependencies managed by the IDependencyResolver. This is needed to serve areas in code where the resolver cannot automatically reach, such as in an attribute constructor.

Database Transaction Control

The last thing database-related to cover in this chapter is transaction control. Because we have a single ISession instance spanning all operations within a single web request, we also want to wrap all operations within a single database transaction by default.

To make this happen, we're using the custom attribute implemented in the previous section. We overrode both the OnActionExecuting and OnActionExecuted methods. These are called by ASP.NET Web API before and after the controller action method is executed, respectively. The interesting code, though, is in the ActionTransactionHelper class' BeginTransaction and EndTransaction methods, so let's study those.

In BeginTransaction, we first get the current ISession object (if it's available). Thanks to the ISession management code covered in the previous section, it has already been created on-demand and is accessible via the ISessionFactory object. We then use that ISession object to begin a new transaction. Pretty simple.

The EndTransaction method starts by obtaining a reference to the current ISession object, if it's available. It then checks to make sure there is an active transaction, because we don't want to try to commit or roll back a nonexistent transaction. If there is an active transaction, we want to do one of two things: commit it or roll it back. This is dependent on whether an exception occurred somewhere in the execution of the controller action.

We use the `filterContext.Exception` property for this check. If an exception doesn't exist, we flush the session (which forces NHibernate to write all in-memory model changes to the database) and commit the transaction. However, if an exception does exist, we roll back the active transaction.

But why do we have a check for an active session at the start of each `ActionTransactionHelper` method? Shouldn't we always expect an ISession to be available, especially after we've gone to the trouble of adding the `UnitOfWorkActionFilterAttribute` to our controllers? Why even bother with this `CurrentSessionContext.HasBind` test? Well, take a look at our two controllers. At this point, neither requires an ISession. And because neither requires an ISession instance, the framework will never hit our resolver to create one. Therefore, if you were to remove these checks and run the demo that we ran earlier in the "Implementing POST" section, you'd encounter an exception...and we don't like those.

At this point, we have configured everything our task-management service needs in terms of persistence, yet our controller implementations have not advanced beyond a persistence-free, "hello world-ish" state. Hang in there, we'll get to them shortly (really!). First we need to attend to a few more infrastructural items.

Diagnostic Tracing

When you are trying to troubleshoot—or gain deep knowledge of the inner workings of—an application, there is no substitute for a good set of trace logs. Fortunately, enabling tracing in ASP.NET Web API 2 is painless.

Start by installing the tracing package using the NuGet Package Manager console as follows:

```
install-package Microsoft.AspNet.WebApi.Tracing WebApi2Book.Web.Api
```

Then add the following code to the bottom of the `WebApiConfig` class' `Register` method:

```
config.EnableSystemDiagnosticsTracing();
```

And that's it. This code adds the `SystemDiagnosticsTraceWriter` class to the Web API pipeline. Because the `SystemDiagnosticsTraceWriter` class writes traces to `System.Diagnostics.Trace`, if you run the demo from the "Implementing POST" section you'll see trace statements written to Visual Studio's Output window. You can also register additional trace listeners; for example, to write traces to the Windows Event Log, a database, or a text file.

Though we could end this section now (after all, we've accomplished our goal of adding tracing), we want to take things a step further and demonstrate how to implement and register a custom trace writer that plugs into the ASP.NET Web API tracing infrastructure and writes to log4net.

First, we need to provide an `ITraceWriter` implementation. Implement the following `SimpleTraceWriter` class in the root of the `WebApi2Book.Web.Common` project:

SimpleTraceWriter Class

```
using System;
using System.Net.Http;
using System.Web.Http.Tracing;
using log4net;
using WebApi2Book.Common.Logging;

namespace WebApi2Book.Web.Common
{
    public class SimpleTraceWriter : ITraceWriter
    {
        private readonly ILog _log;
```

```csharp
public SimpleTraceWriter(ILogManager logManager)
{
    _log = logManager.GetLog(typeof (SimpleTraceWriter));
}

public void Trace(HttpRequestMessage request, string category, TraceLevel level,
    Action<TraceRecord> traceAction)
{
    var rec = new TraceRecord(request, category, level);
    traceAction(rec);
    WriteTrace(rec);
}

public void WriteTrace(TraceRecord rec)
{
    const string traceFormat =
        "RequestId={0};{1}Kind={2};{3}Status={4};{5}Operation={6};{7}Operator={8};{9}
         Category={10}{11}Request={12}{13}Message={14}";

    var args = new object[]
    {
        rec.RequestId,
        Environment.NewLine,
        rec.Kind,
        Environment.NewLine,
        rec.Status,
        Environment.NewLine,
        rec.Operation,
        Environment.NewLine,
        rec.Operator,
        Environment.NewLine,
        rec.Category,
        Environment.NewLine,
        rec.Request,
        Environment.NewLine,
        rec.Message
    };

    switch (rec.Level)
    {
        case TraceLevel.Debug:
            _log.DebugFormat(traceFormat, args);
            break;
        case TraceLevel.Info:
            _log.InfoFormat(traceFormat, args);
            break;
        case TraceLevel.Warn:
            _log.WarnFormat(traceFormat, args);
            break;
```

```
                    case TraceLevel.Error:
                        _log.ErrorFormat(traceFormat, args);
                        break;
                    case TraceLevel.Fatal:
                        _log.FatalFormat(traceFormat, args);
                        break;
                }
            }
        }
    }
}
```

Finally, add the following code to the bottom of the WebApiConfig class' Register method to register the writer with the framework:

```
//config.EnableSystemDiagnosticsTracing(); // replaced by custom writer
config.Services.Replace(typeof(ITraceWriter),
    new SimpleTraceWriter(WebContainerManager.Get<ILogManager>()));
```

■ **Note**   You'll need to add the following using directives:

- using System.Web.Http.Tracing;

- using WebApi2Book.Common.Logging;

See, wasn't that easy? Now, next time you run the demo from the "Implementing POST" section, you'll find a new log file full of trace information inside of the logs folder of the WebApi2Book root directory that we created back in Chapter 4.

Error handling is next, and it's a little bit more involved.

Error Handling

With the release of ASP.NET Web API 2.1, developers finally have framework support for global handling of unhandled exceptions. The framework also now supports multiple exception loggers, each of which has access to the exception objects themselves and to the contexts in which the exceptions occur. In this section, we'll implement a global exception handler and a custom exception logger, as summarized in Table 5-5.

Table 5-5. *Error-Handling Classes*

Class	Purpose
SimpleExceptionLogger	This simple class' single responsibility is to log exceptions. Although exceptions will also be logged using the tracing we just added in the previous section, this class has access to additional—actually, essential—information not available via the tracing infrastructure.
GlobalExceptionHandler	This is a custom exception handler, which we will use to replace the ASP.NET Web API default exception handler. This allows us to customize the HTTP response that is sent when an unhandled application exception occurs.
SimpleErrorResult	This trivial IHttpActionResult implementation is used to add result information to the exception context. This information is later applied to the HTTP response by ASP.NET Web API.

EXCEPTION LOGGING WITH ELMAH

The ASP.NET Web API team has created a sample demonstrating the logging of all unhandled exceptions with the popular ELMAH framework. It's definitely worth checking out:

http://aspnet.codeplex.com/SourceControl/latest#Samples/WebApi/Elmah/ReadMe.txt

First, add the following class to a new ErrorHandling folder in the WebApi2Book.Web.Common project:

SimpleExceptionLogger Class

```
using System.Web.Http.ExceptionHandling;
using log4net;
using WebApi2Book.Common.Logging;

namespace WebApi2Book.Web.Common.ErrorHandling
{
    public class SimpleExceptionLogger : ExceptionLogger
    {
        private readonly ILog _log;

        public SimpleExceptionLogger(ILogManager logManager)
        {
            _log = logManager.GetLog(typeof (SimpleExceptionLogger));
        }

        public override void Log(ExceptionLoggerContext context)
        {
            _log.Error("Unhandled exception", context.Exception);
        }
    }
}
```

Note that the SimpleExceptionLogger class derives from the framework's ExceptionLogger class. Also note that the exception is obtained from the ExceptionLoggerContext argument. We could do a lot more with this, seeing that we have access to all of the context information, but for the sake of simplicity this will suffice.

To register our exception logger with the framework, add the following to the bottom of the WebApiConfig class' Register method:

```
config.Services.Add(typeof (IExceptionLogger),
    new SimpleExceptionLogger(WebContainerManager.Get<ILogManager>()));
```

■ **Note**   You'll need to add the following using directives:

- using System.Web.Http.ExceptionHandling;
- using WebApi2Book.Web.Common.ErrorHandling;

That's it! However, to help prevent exceptions from escaping without being logged during the application's startup sequence (i.e., before this configuration is fully applied at run time), implement the following method in the WebApiApplication class. This will handle the base HttpApplication class' Error event:

```
protected void Application_Error()
{
    var exception = Server.GetLastError();
    if (exception != null)
    {
        var log = WebContainerManager.Get<ILogManager>().GetLog(typeof (WebApiApplication));
        log.Error("Unhandled exception.", exception);
    }
}
```

■ **Note**   You'll need to add the following using directives:

- using WebApi2Book.Common.Logging;

- using WebApi2Book.Web.Common;

Again, we add this to handle any exceptions that are thrown in the application start-up sequence, before the application has fully initialized the global error handling configuration. As for the implementation, the main thing to note is that the exception that raised the Error event must be accessed by a call to the GetLastError method.

With global exception logging fully in place, let's now focus our efforts on something else made possible with the ASP.NET Web API 2.1 release: globally customizing behavior of unhandled exceptions. To make this more interesting, let's first implement a couple of custom exceptions that we'll need later: RootObjectNotFoundException and ChildObjectNotFoundException. Implement these in a new Exceptions folder in the WebApi2Book.Data project.

RootObjectNotFoundExceptions will be thrown by our various data access objects when the primary, or "aggregate root," data object is not found. Similarly, ChildObjectNotFoundExceptions will be thrown when a required child of a primary data object is not found (for example, a request is made to add a user to a task, but that user doesn't exist). This design allows our data access classes to be free of any concerns about dealing with forming proper HTTP error responses. And, as you'll soon see in our custom ExceptionHandler, it allows us to globally handle these exceptions by creating appropriate HTTP error responses in a class that *is* aware of HTTP.

RootObjectNotFoundException Class

```
using System;

namespace WebApi2Book.Data.Exceptions
{
    [Serializable]
    public class RootObjectNotFoundException : Exception
    {
        public RootObjectNotFoundException(string message) : base(message)
        {
        }
    }
}
```

ChildObjectNotFoundException Class

```
using System;

namespace WebApi2Book.Data.Exceptions
{
    [Serializable]
    public class ChildObjectNotFoundException : Exception
    {
        public ChildObjectNotFoundException(string message) : base(message)
        {
        }
    }
}
```

Next, let's create a simple `IHttpActionResult` implementation to help communicate the error information back to the caller. Add it to the `ErrorHandling` folder in the `WebApi2Book.Web.Common` project:

```
using System.Net;
using System.Net.Http;
using System.Threading;
using System.Threading.Tasks;
using System.Web.Http;

namespace WebApi2Book.Web.Common.ErrorHandling
{
    public class SimpleErrorResult : IHttpActionResult
    {
        private readonly string _errorMessage;
        private readonly HttpRequestMessage _requestMessage;
        private readonly HttpStatusCode _statusCode;

        public SimpleErrorResult(HttpRequestMessage requestMessage, HttpStatusCode statusCode,
            string errorMessage)
        {
            _requestMessage = requestMessage;
            _statusCode = statusCode;
            _errorMessage = errorMessage;
        }

        public Task<HttpResponseMessage> ExecuteAsync(CancellationToken cancellationToken)
        {
            return Task.FromResult(_requestMessage.CreateErrorResponse(_statusCode, _errorMessage));
        }
    }
}
```

It doesn't get much simpler than this! This is an absolutely bare-bones `IHttpActionResult` implementation where we simply use the request message to create a response based on the status code and error message specified in the constructor. (Don't feel cheated; we'll get to a more interesting `IHttpActionResult` in the next section!) But what calls the constructor? You're about to find out.

Now we will replace the default exception handler so that we can fully control the HTTP response message that is sent when an unhandled exception occurs. Start off by referencing System.Web from the WebApi2Book.Web.Common project, and then implement the following custom ExceptionHandler class in the ErrorHandling folder of that same project:

```
using System.Net;
using System.Web;
using System.Web.Http.ExceptionHandling;
using WebApi2Book.Data.Exceptions;

namespace WebApi2Book.Web.Common.ErrorHandling
{
    public class GlobalExceptionHandler : ExceptionHandler
    {
        public override void Handle(ExceptionHandlerContext context)
        {
            var exception = context.Exception;

            var httpException = exception as HttpException;
            if (httpException != null)
            {
                context.Result = new SimpleErrorResult(context.Request,
                    (HttpStatusCode) httpException.GetHttpCode(), httpException.Message);
                return;
            }

            if (exception is RootObjectNotFoundException)
            {
                context.Result = new SimpleErrorResult(context.Request, HttpStatusCode.NotFound,
                    exception.Message);
                return;
            }

            if (exception is ChildObjectNotFoundException)
            {
                context.Result = new SimpleErrorResult(context.Request, HttpStatusCode.Conflict,
                    exception.Message);
                return;
            }

            context.Result = new SimpleErrorResult(context.Request, HttpStatusCode.InternalServerError,
                exception.Message);
        }
    }
}
```

Some items of note:

- The class derives from the framework's ExceptionHandler class.

- The GlobalExceptionHandler is what constructs the SimpleErrorResult instances. By examining the exception available in the framework-provided ExceptionHandlerContext, the GlobalExceptionHandler uses the SimpleErrorResult class to form a response with the proper HttpStatusCode and response message.

- For HttpException objects, the handler creates the response using the exception's status code and message. This ensures the appropriate code is returned in the response, and it ensures that only the exception's message—not its stack trace—is returned as well. Stack trace information is not lost, however. The full exception, including its stack trace, is logged using the SimpleExceptionLogger that we just implemented.

We'll add to this class as we get farther along in our controller implementation and have new types of exceptions that we need to handle at a global level.

To wrap things up, we still need to register our custom exception handler with the framework. Let's do that now, replacing the default exception handler with our custom exception handler. Add the following line to the bottom of the Register method in the WebApiConfig class:

```
config.Services.Replace(typeof (IExceptionHandler), new GlobalExceptionHandler());
```

At this point, with support for routing, dependency injection, persistence, tracing, and error handling in place, we're ready to advance our TasksControllers past their current "hello world-ish" implementation.

Persisting a Task and Returning IHttpActionResult

We're about to embark on another relatively long journey, but at the end of it we'll be able to persist Task objects to the database. We'll also have implemented a custom IHttpActionResult that automatically sets the HttpStatusCode and location header in the response messages. In addition, we'll explore several useful tools, techniques, and architectural patterns along the way. Good stuff! So let's take that first step.

New Service Model Type

The Task service model class we implemented in Chapter 4 contains several properties. Most of these are not necessary, or desired, for adding a new task to the task-management system. Therefore, we will introduce a new service model class, NewTask.

Before we do this, let's remove the Models folder from the WebApi2Book.Web.Api project. We'll remove it for a couple of reasons, the most important one being that it is unnecessary (the other being that it introduces ambiguity to the coding convention we stated at the beginning of the chapter).

Now we can implement NewTask as follows; by now, we assume you can infer where to locate it, based on the namespace:

```
using System;
using System.Collections.Generic;

namespace WebApi2Book.Web.Api.Models
{
    public class NewTask
    {
        public string Subject { get; set; }

        public DateTime? StartDate { get; set; }

        public DateTime? DueDate { get; set; }

        public List<User> Assignees { get; set; }
    }
}
```

Now modify the signature of the AddTask method in the V1 TasksController so that it appears as follows, accepting one of these NewTask objects as a parameter:

```
public Task AddTask(HttpRequestMessage requestMessage, NewTask newTask)
```

And that's it. However, we encourage you to follow along with the book's project code, where you'll see that we also added a NewTaskV2 class to use with the V2 controller. The point of NewTaskV2 is to illustrate that a service model may be changed (in this case simplified) based on user/developer feedback. In V2, the caller only has to provide a single User, not a list of them:

```
using System;

namespace WebApi2Book.Web.Api.Models
{
    public class NewTaskV2
    {
        public string Subject { get; set; }

        public DateTime? StartDate { get; set; }

        public DateTime? DueDate { get; set; }

        public User Assignee { get; set; }
    }
}
```

You can add NewTaskV2 to the project if you'd like, but at this point we're finished discussing things pertaining to V2 in the book. We've got to get on with persisting the task!

SECURITY IMPLICATIONS OF OVERPOSTING

Though we're going to cover the topic of security in the next chapter, we heartily recommend Badrinarayanan Lakshmiraghavan's excellent book, *Pro ASP.NET Web API Security: Securing ASP.NET Web API* (Apress, 2013). It goes into a level of detail that we can't possibly cover in one chapter of our book.

In short, an overposting attack is defined as an HTTP POST or PUT that successfully submits and updates the value of an underlying data property, even though that property wasn't part of the published, visible, or expected request message. For example, a web form in an HR application, or a REST endpoint in an HR-based Web API, might expect a caller to update an employee's first and last names. But if that server-side code is naively binding the incoming POST body to a model object that happens to include a Salary property, and the caller happens to specify a value for that Salary (either maliciously or unintentionally), the code may find itself updating the employee's salary in the database to the specified value.

According to Badrinarayanan, "The best approach to prevent overposting vulnerabilities in ASP.NET Web API is to never use entity classes directly for [service] model binding. Using a subset of the entity class that expects nothing more and nothing less for the scenario at hand is the best approach." And that's exactly what we've done by introducing the NewTask and NewTaskV2 classes.

Persisting the Task

As we said earlier in this chapter, controllers should not be doing much more than simply using the functionality offered by various dependencies. Now it's time to practice what we preach.

Let's begin by creating and configuring several new classes to do the heavy lifting in the AddTask method. First, add the following security-related types to the correct projects in the solution. The IUserSession and related user classes allow us to abstract away from the static HttpContext.Current.User property. Again, by now we assume you can infer where to locate these, based on the namespace (this message will not be repeated):

IUserSession Interface

```
namespace WebApi2Book.Common.Security
{
    public interface IUserSession
    {
        string Firstname { get; }
        string Lastname { get; }
        string Username { get; }
        bool IsInRole(string roleName);
    }
}
```

IWebUserSession Interface

```
using System;
using WebApi2Book.Common.Security;

namespace WebApi2Book.Web.Common.Security
{
    public interface IWebUserSession : IUserSession
    {
        string ApiVersionInUse { get; }
        Uri RequestUri { get; }
        string HttpRequestMethod { get; }
    }
}
```

UserSession Class

```
using System;
using System.Security.Claims;
using System.Web;
using System.Linq;

namespace WebApi2Book.Web.Common.Security
{
    public class UserSession : IWebUserSession
    {
        public string Firstname
        {
            get { return ((ClaimsPrincipal) HttpContext.Current.User).FindFirst(ClaimTypes.
                GivenName).Value; }
        }
```

```
    public string Lastname
    {
        get { return ((ClaimsPrincipal) HttpContext.Current.User).FindFirst(ClaimTypes.Surname).
            Value; }
    }

    public string Username
    {
        get { return ((ClaimsPrincipal) HttpContext.Current.User).FindFirst(ClaimTypes.Name).
            Value; }
    }

    public bool IsInRole(string roleName)
    {
        return HttpContext.Current.User.IsInRole(roleName);
    }

    public Uri RequestUri
    {
        get { return HttpContext.Current.Request.Url; }
    }

    public string HttpRequestMethod
    {
        get { return HttpContext.Current.Request.HttpMethod; }
    }

    public string ApiVersionInUse
    {
        get
        {
            const int versionIndex = 2;
            if (HttpContext.Current.Request.Url.Segments.Count() < versionIndex + 1)
            {
                return string.Empty;
            }

            var apiVersionInUse = HttpContext.Current.Request.Url.Segments[versionIndex].Replace(
                "/", string.Empty);
            return apiVersionInUse;
        }
    }
}
}
```

We'll discuss these further in Chapter 6, "Securing the Service." For now, just understand that these provide convenient access to data describing the current user and request. Before moving on, though, wire this up so that it can be injected as a dependency. This is done first by adding the following method to `NinjectConfigurator`:

```
private void ConfigureUserSession(IKernel container)
{
    var userSession = new UserSession();
    container.Bind<IUserSession>().ToConstant(userSession).InSingletonScope();
    container.Bind<IWebUserSession>().ToConstant(userSession).InSingletonScope();
}
```

Then modify the `AddBindings` method so that it appears as follows:

```
private void AddBindings(IKernel container)
{
    ConfigureLog4net(container);
    ConfigureUserSession(container);
    ConfigureNHibernate(container);

    container.Bind<IDateTime>().To<DateTimeAdapter>().InSingletonScope();
}
```

■ **Note**   You'll need to add the following using directives:

- using `WebApi2Book.Common.Security`;

- using `WebApi2Book.Web.Common.Security`;

Also note that we are configuring an application-wide singleton `UserSession` to be injected for all objects requiring an `IUserSession` or an `IWebUserSession`. This works because `UserSession` implements both interfaces, and because it does not store any state.

Next, add the following types that we'll use to interact with the database via the NHibernate `ISession` object:

IAddTaskQueryProcessor Interface

```
using WebApi2Book.Data.Entities;

namespace WebApi2Book.Data.QueryProcessors
{
    public interface IAddTaskQueryProcessor
    {
        void AddTask(Task task);
    }
}
```

AddTaskQueryProcessor Class

```
using NHibernate;
using NHibernate.Util;
using WebApi2Book.Common;
using WebApi2Book.Common.Security;
```

```
using WebApi2Book.Data.Entities;
using WebApi2Book.Data.Exceptions;
using WebApi2Book.Data.QueryProcessors;

namespace WebApi2Book.Data.SqlServer.QueryProcessors
{
    public class AddTaskQueryProcessor : IAddTaskQueryProcessor
    {
        private readonly IDateTime _dateTime;
        private readonly ISession _session;
        private readonly IUserSession _userSession;

        public AddTaskQueryProcessor(ISession session, IUserSession userSession, IDateTime dateTime)
        {
            _session = session;
            _userSession = userSession;
            _dateTime = dateTime;
        }

        public void AddTask(Task task)
        {
            task.CreatedDate = _dateTime.UtcNow;
            task.Status = _session.QueryOver<Status>().Where(
                x => x.Name == "Not Started").SingleOrDefault();
            task.CreatedBy = _session.QueryOver<User>().Where(
                x => x.Username == _userSession.Username).SingleOrDefault();

            if (task.Users != null && task.Users.Any())
            {
                for (var i = 0; i < task.Users.Count; ++i)
                {
                    var user = task.Users[i];
                    var persistedUser = _session.Get<User>(user.UserId);
                    if (persistedUser == null)
                    {
                        throw new ChildObjectNotFoundException("User not found");
                    }
                    task.Users[i] = persistedUser;
                }
            }

            _session.SaveOrUpdate(task);
        }
    }
}
```

Here we see our new IUserSession being used, along with the ISession and IDateTime we discussed previously. Oh, and note the ChildObjectNotFoundException! Anyway, what's basically happening in AddTask is this:

- The system assigns the task's created date.

- The system assigns a status of Not Started to the task.

- The system uses the user session to indicate the user who created the task.

- The system populates the task's Users collection, forming associations with the User objects fetched from the database. It verifies that all users specified in the new task exist in the system.

- The system persists the task and all its relationships.

Before we move on, we'll wire this up so that it can be injected as a dependency. This is done by adding the following to the bottom of the NinjectConfigurator AddBindings method:

```
container.Bind<IAddTaskQueryProcessor>().To<AddTaskQueryProcessor>().InRequestScope();
```

■ **Note** You'll need to add the following using directives:

- using WebApi2Book.Data.QueryProcessors;

- using WebApi2Book.Data.SqlServer.QueryProcessors;

OK, time for something really cool. We've fallen in love with AutoMapper, a great tool developed by Jimmy Bogard that can be used to easily transfer data from one object to another. As you'll soon see, this comes in handy when mapping between the entity and service model types. We added the AutoMapper NuGet package in Chapter 4, but before we use it we will wrap the primary mapping functions so that we can inject them as dependencies. (Yes, we're a bit disappointed AutoMapper uses static methods.)

Start by adding the following types to the correct projects in the solution:

IAutoMapperTypeConfigurator Interface

```
namespace WebApi2Book.Common.TypeMapping
{
    public interface IAutoMapperTypeConfigurator
    {
        void Configure();
    }
}
```

IAutoMapper Interface

```
namespace WebApi2Book.Common.TypeMapping
{
    public interface IAutoMapper
    {
        T Map<T>(object objectToMap);
    }
}
```

AutoMapperAdapter Class

```
using AutoMapper;

namespace WebApi2Book.Common.TypeMapping
{
    public class AutoMapperAdapter : IAutoMapper
    {
        public T Map<T>(object objectToMap)
        {
            return Mapper.Map<T>(objectToMap);
        }
    }
}
```

To wire it in with Ninject, first add the following method to `NinjectConfigurator`:

```
private void ConfigureAutoMapper(IKernel container)
{
    container.Bind<IAutoMapper>().To<AutoMapperAdapter>().InSingletonScope();
}
```

Then modify the `AddBindings` method so that it appears as follows (adding the call to `ConfigureAutoMapper`):

```
private void AddBindings(IKernel container)
{
    ConfigureLog4net(container);
    ConfigureUserSession(container);
    ConfigureNHibernate(container);
    ConfigureAutoMapper(container);

    container.Bind<IDateTime>().To<DateTimeAdapter>().InSingletonScope();

    container.Bind<IAddTaskQueryProcessor>().To<AddTaskQueryProcessor>().InRequestScope();
}
```

■ **Note** You'll need to add a using directive to `WebApi2Book.Common.TypeMapping` to satisfy the compiler.

Excellent. Now let's configure some mappings. For this, we need to implement IAutoMapperTypeConfigurator for each mapping. Start by implementing the mapping from the NewTask service model type to the Task entity type using AutoMapper's fluent syntax:

```
using AutoMapper;
using WebApi2Book.Common.TypeMapping;
using WebApi2Book.Web.Api.Models;
```

```
namespace WebApi2Book.Web.Api.AutoMappingConfiguration
{
    public class NewTaskToTaskEntityAutoMapperTypeConfigurator : IAutoMapperTypeConfigurator
    {
        public void Configure()
        {
            Mapper.CreateMap<NewTask, Data.Entities.Task>()
                .ForMember(opt => opt.Version, x => x.Ignore())
                .ForMember(opt => opt.CreatedBy, x => x.Ignore())
                .ForMember(opt => opt.TaskId, x => x.Ignore())
                .ForMember(opt => opt.CreatedDate, x => x.Ignore())
                .ForMember(opt => opt.CompletedDate, x => x.Ignore())
                .ForMember(opt => opt.Status, x => x.Ignore())
                .ForMember(opt => opt.Users, x => x.Ignore());
        }
    }
}
```

The `Mapper.CreateMap` method establishes a default mapping between the properties on the `NewTask` class and the properties on the `Task` class. We then fluently tweak this mapping by informing the mapper to ignore several properties on the target class (`Task`) because they aren't available on the source class (`NewTask`). To gain a deeper understanding of AutoMapper, we encourage you to visit the AutoMapper site on GitHub (https://github.com/AutoMapper/AutoMapper); however, this is the gist of what's happening in the code.

Now let's implement the mapping from the `Task` entity to the `Task` service model type. This mapping will be used to return the newly generated `Task` object data to the caller. This is more complicated because it requires an AutoMapper resolver. Add the following:

TaskEntityToTaskAutoMapperTypeConfigurator Class

```
using AutoMapper;
using WebApi2Book.Common.TypeMapping;
using WebApi2Book.Data.Entities;

namespace WebApi2Book.Web.Api.AutoMappingConfiguration
{
    public class TaskEntityToTaskAutoMapperTypeConfigurator : IAutoMapperTypeConfigurator
    {
        public void Configure()
        {
            Mapper.CreateMap<Task, Models.Task>()
                .ForMember(opt => opt.Links, x => x.Ignore())
                .ForMember(opt => opt.Assignees, x => x.ResolveUsing<TaskAssigneesResolver>());
        }
    }
}
```

TaskAssigneesResolver Class

```
using System.Collections.Generic;
using System.Linq;
using AutoMapper;
using WebApi2Book.Common.TypeMapping;
```

```
using WebApi2Book.Data.Entities;
using WebApi2Book.Web.Common;
using User = WebApi2Book.Web.Api.Models.User;

namespace WebApi2Book.Web.Api.AutoMappingConfiguration
{
    public class TaskAssigneesResolver : ValueResolver<Task, List<User>>
    {
        public IAutoMapper AutoMapper
        {
            get { return WebContainerManager.Get<IAutoMapper>(); }
        }

        protected override List<User> ResolveCore(Task source)
        {
            return source.Users.Select(x => AutoMapper.Map<User>(x)).ToList();
        }
    }
}
```

The TaskEntityToTaskAutoMapperTypeConfigurator is fairly straightforward. It ignores the links, because they aren't present on the source (i.e., the entity), and it delegates the Assignees mapping to the resolver.

By examining the resolver's ResolveCore method, we can see that this is mapping users from the source (entity) representation to the target (service model) representation. If you get the sense that something is missing here, you are correct. What's missing is the mapping between entity and service model representations for users, which we'll get to now (please add the following):

UserToUserEntityAutoMapperTypeConfigurator Class

```
using AutoMapper;
using WebApi2Book.Common.TypeMapping;
using WebApi2Book.Web.Api.Models;

namespace WebApi2Book.Web.Api.AutoMappingConfiguration
{
    public class UserToUserEntityAutoMapperTypeConfigurator : IAutoMapperTypeConfigurator
    {
        public void Configure()
        {
            Mapper.CreateMap<User, Data.Entities.User>()
                .ForMember(opt => opt.Version, x => x.Ignore());
        }
    }
}
```

UserEntityToUserAutoMapperTypeConfigurator Class

```
using AutoMapper;
using WebApi2Book.Common.TypeMapping;
using WebApi2Book.Data.Entities;
```

```
namespace WebApi2Book.Web.Api.AutoMappingConfiguration
{
    public class UserEntityToUserAutoMapperTypeConfigurator : IAutoMapperTypeConfigurator
    {
        public void Configure()
        {
            Mapper.CreateMap<User, Models.User>()
                .ForMember(opt => opt.Links, x => x.Ignore());
        }
    }
}
```

Although it's not as obvious as the situation with User types, to complete our mapping we need to map the different Status types. If we don't, AutoMapper will blow up when trying to locate a Status mapping for the different Task class' Status property. Therefore, add the following trivial implementations:

StatusToStatusEntityAutoMapperTypeConfigurator Class

```
using AutoMapper;
using WebApi2Book.Common.TypeMapping;
using WebApi2Book.Web.Api.Models;

namespace WebApi2Book.Web.Api.AutoMappingConfiguration
{
    public class StatusToStatusEntityAutoMapperTypeConfigurator : IAutoMapperTypeConfigurator
    {
        public void Configure()
        {
            Mapper.CreateMap<Status, Data.Entities.Status>()
                .ForMember(opt => opt.Version, x => x.Ignore());
        }
    }
}
```

StatusEntityToStatusAutoMapperTypeConfigurator Class

```
using AutoMapper;
using WebApi2Book.Common.TypeMapping;
using WebApi2Book.Data.Entities;

namespace WebApi2Book.Web.Api.AutoMappingConfiguration
{
    public class StatusEntityToStatusAutoMapperTypeConfigurator : IAutoMapperTypeConfigurator
    {
        public void Configure()
        {
            Mapper.CreateMap<Status, Models.Status>();
        }
    }
}
```

Ah, but there are still some missing pieces regarding this AutoMapper stuff. One, we need a way to make sure the configurators get run somewhere in the application's start-up sequence. Two, we need to configure the IAutoMapperTypeConfigurator classes to be injected in as dependencies. First things first, so implement the following class in the App_Start folder:

```
using System.Collections.Generic;
using System.Linq;
using AutoMapper;
using WebApi2Book.Common.TypeMapping;

namespace WebApi2Book.Web.Api
{
    public class AutoMapperConfigurator
    {
        public void Configure(IEnumerable<IAutoMapperTypeConfigurator> autoMapperTypeConfigurations)
        {
            autoMapperTypeConfigurations.ToList().ForEach(x => x.Configure());

            Mapper.AssertConfigurationIsValid();
        }
    }
}
```

The Configure method, when invoked, will configure each of the IAutoMapperTypeConfigurator instances and then assert that the entire mapping scheme is valid. And how do we integrate this into the application's start-up sequence? Easily, by modifying the WebApiApplication to appear as follows:

```
using System.Web;
using System.Web.Http;
using WebApi2Book.Common.Logging;
using WebApi2Book.Common.TypeMapping;
using WebApi2Book.Web.Common;

namespace WebApi2Book.Web.Api
{
    public class WebApiApplication : HttpApplication
    {
        protected void Application_Start()
        {
            GlobalConfiguration.Configure(WebApiConfig.Register);

            new AutoMapperConfigurator().Configure(
                WebContainerManager.GetAll<IAutoMapperTypeConfigurator>());
        }

        protected void Application_Error()
        {
            var exception = Server.GetLastError();
```

```
            if (exception != null)
            {
                var log = WebContainerManager.Get<ILogManager>().GetLog(typeof(WebApiApplication));
                log.Error("Unhandled exception.", exception);
            }
        }
    }
}
```

Now, to make our IAutoMapperTypeConfigurator instances available for injection, we modify the NinjectConfigurator class' ConfigureAutoMapper method so that it appears as follows:

```
private void ConfigureAutoMapper(IKernel container)
{
    container.Bind<IAutoMapper>().To<AutoMapperAdapter>().InSingletonScope();

    container.Bind<IAutoMapperTypeConfigurator>()
        .To<StatusEntityToStatusAutoMapperTypeConfigurator>()
        .InSingletonScope();
    container.Bind<IAutoMapperTypeConfigurator>()
        .To<StatusToStatusEntityAutoMapperTypeConfigurator>()
        .InSingletonScope();
    container.Bind<IAutoMapperTypeConfigurator>()
        .To<UserEntityToUserAutoMapperTypeConfigurator>()
        .InSingletonScope();
    container.Bind<IAutoMapperTypeConfigurator>()
        .To<UserToUserEntityAutoMapperTypeConfigurator>()
        .InSingletonScope();
    container.Bind<IAutoMapperTypeConfigurator>()
        .To<NewTaskToTaskEntityAutoMapperTypeConfigurator>()
        .InSingletonScope();
    container.Bind<IAutoMapperTypeConfigurator>()
        .To<TaskEntityToTaskAutoMapperTypeConfigurator>()
        .InSingletonScope();
}
```

■ **Note** You'll need to add a using directive to WebApi2Book.Web.Api.AutoMappingConfiguration to satisfy the compiler.

OK, we're in the homestretch! Now we'll add the dependency that the controller will use to add the new task. Implement the following processor (which will in turn use the IAddTaskQueryProcessor we created earlier):

IAddTaskMaintenanceProcessor Interface

```
using WebApi2Book.Web.Api.Models;

namespace WebApi2Book.Web.Api.MaintenanceProcessing
{
    public interface IAddTaskMaintenanceProcessor
```

```
    {
        Task AddTask(NewTask newTask);
    }
}
```

AddTaskMaintenanceProcessor Class

```
using WebApi2Book.Common.TypeMapping;
using WebApi2Book.Data.QueryProcessors;
using WebApi2Book.Web.Api.Models;

namespace WebApi2Book.Web.Api.MaintenanceProcessing
{
    public class AddTaskMaintenanceProcessor : IAddTaskMaintenanceProcessor
    {
        private readonly IAutoMapper _autoMapper;
        private readonly IAddTaskQueryProcessor _queryProcessor;

        public AddTaskMaintenanceProcessor(IAddTaskQueryProcessor queryProcessor,
            IAutoMapper autoMapper)
        {
            _queryProcessor = queryProcessor;
            _autoMapper = autoMapper;
        }

        public Task AddTask(NewTask newTask)
        {
            var taskEntity = _autoMapper.Map<Data.Entities.Task>(newTask);

            _queryProcessor.AddTask(taskEntity);

            var task = _autoMapper.Map<Task>(taskEntity);

            return task;
        }
    }
}
```

This should be pretty easy to figure out. Using injected dependencies that we've implemented, AddTask maps the NewTask service model object to an entity object and then persists it. It then maps the new entity back to a full Task service model object and returns it to the caller.

And now, as you may have guessed, we need to wire it up with Ninject by adding the following to the AddBindings method in NinjectConfigurator:

```
container.Bind<IAddTaskMaintenanceProcessor>().To<AddTaskMaintenanceProcessor>()
        .InRequestScope();
```

■ **Note**   You'll need to add a using directive to WebApi2Book.Web.Api.MaintenanceProcessing to satisfy the compiler.

At this point, we're ready to hook all of this up to the controller so that we can start actually persisting tasks. Reimplement the TasksController as follows:

```
using System.Net.Http;
using System.Web.Http;
using WebApi2Book.Web.Api.Models;
using WebApi2Book.Web.Common;
using WebApi2Book.Web.Common.Routing;
using WebApi2Book.Web.Api.MaintenanceProcessing;

namespace WebApi2Book.Web.Api.Controllers.V1
{
    [ApiVersion1RoutePrefix("tasks")]
    [UnitOfWorkActionFilter]
    public class TasksController : ApiController
    {
        private readonly IAddTaskMaintenanceProcessor _addTaskMaintenanceProcessor;

        public TasksController(IAddTaskMaintenanceProcessor addTaskMaintenanceProcessor)
        {
            _addTaskMaintenanceProcessor = addTaskMaintenanceProcessor;
        }

        [Route("", Name = "AddTaskRoute")]
        [HttpPost]
        public Task AddTask(HttpRequestMessage requestMessage, NewTask newTask)
        {
            var task = _addTaskMaintenanceProcessor.AddTask(newTask);

            return task;
        }
    }
}
```

In this implementation, we see the controller simply delegating its work to the IAddTaskMaintenanceProcessor. Yes, we practice what we preach. The benefits of this will be reemphasized in our discussion of legacy SOAP message support. And you can imagine the benefits this brings to the controller in terms of unit-testability.

Anyway, for now, go ahead and run the demo that we first ran back at the end of the "Implementing POST" section. What do you see? An exception??? Yes, an exception. As a consolation, open the log file and note how well-documented the exception appears! Also note that the client (we're using Fiddler) received a response prepared by our custom GlobalExceptionHandler. At least it's nice to know that our error handling is working!

The cause of the exception, as you may have deduced by examining the log file, is that there is no User in the session. This is because we haven't done any authentication or authorization. Since we won't get to that until the next chapter, and since we really want to see the persistence work, we're going to implement a temporary hack. Change the following line in AddTaskQueryProcessor from this

```
task.CreatedBy = _session.QueryOver<User>().Where(x => x.Username ==
                            _userSession.Username).SingleOrDefault();
```

to this:

```
task.CreatedBy = _session.Get<User>(1L); // HACK: All tasks created by user 1 for now
```

And then re-run the demo. You should see something similar to the following (abbreviated) response:

```
HTTP/1.1 200 OK
Content-Type: text/json; charset=utf-8

{"TaskId":8,"Subject":"Fix something important","StartDate":null,"DueDate":null,
"CreatedDate":"2014-05-03T23:02:53.2704726Z","CompletedDate":null,
"Status":{"StatusId":1,"Name":"Not Started","Ordinal":0},"Assignees":[],"Links":[]}
```

Furthermore, if you examine the task table, you will see that the Task has been persisted to the database. Great! However (isn't there always a "however"?), we've got to do something about the HTTP status code. A web API should be returning a 201 to indicate that a new resource was created, but ours is returning a 200. We should also be populating the response message's Location header. We'll address these functional gaps next by implementing a custom IHttpActionResult.

IHttpActionResult

Before we create the custom IHttpActionResult implementation, we need to implement some prerequisites. First, add the following interface:

```
using System.Collections.Generic;

namespace WebApi2Book.Web.Api.Models
{
    public interface ILinkContaining
    {
        List<Link> Links { get; set; }
        void AddLink(Link link);
    }
}
```

Next, modify the Task service model class to implement the interface. Fortunately, this is trivial, because the interface members are already implemented by Task; the interface just needs to be added to the class declaration:

```
public class Task : ILinkContaining
```

Now add the Constants class. This is just a convenience class aimed at reducing "magic numbers." We only need one of the members for now, but we'll go ahead and add the entire (projected) implementation so that we don't need to revisit it later:

```
namespace WebApi2Book.Common
{
    public static class Constants
    {
        public static class MediaTypeNames
        {
            public const string ApplicationXml = "application/xml";
            public const string TextXml = "text/xml";
            public const string ApplicationJson = "application/json";
            public const string TextJson = "text/json";
        }
```

```csharp
    public static class Paging
    {
        public const int MinPageSize = 1;
        public const int MinPageNumber = 1;
        public const int DefaultPageNumber = 1;
    }

    public static class CommonParameterNames
    {
        public const string PageNumber = "pageNumber";
        public const string PageSize = "pageSize";
    }

    public static class CommonLinkRelValues
    {
        public const string Self = "self";
        public const string All = "all";
        public const string CurrentPage = "currentPage";
        public const string PreviousPage = "previousPage";
        public const string NextPage = "nextPage";
    }

    public static class CommonRoutingDefinitions
    {
        public const string ApiSegmentName = "api";
        public const string ApiVersionSegmentName = "apiVersion";
        public const string CurrentApiVersion = "v1";
    }

    public static class SchemeTypes
    {
        public const string Basic = "basic";
    }

    public static class RoleNames
    {
        public const string Manager = "Manager";
        public const string SeniorWorker = "SeniorWorker";
        public const string JuniorWorker = "JuniorWorker";
    }

    public const string DefaultLegacyNamespace = "http://tempuri.org/";
    }
}
```

The next prerequisite type to add is `LocationLinkCalculator`. This is just a little utility class encapsulating a trivial algorithm that returns the location link from a service model's collection of `Link` objects. Note that it is static (gasp!). While we generally discourage the use of statics because of the tight coupling they introduce, they can be appropriate for trivial utility functions. Does this calculator need to support polymorphism? Does it need to be mocked? No, and probably not, respectively. So implement it as follows:

```
using System;
using System.Linq;
using WebApi2Book.Common;
using WebApi2Book.Web.Api.Models;

namespace WebApi2Book.Web.Api.MaintenanceProcessing
{
    public static class LocationLinkCalculator
    {
        public static Uri GetLocationLink(ILinkContaining linkContaining)
        {
            var locationLink = linkContaining.Links.FirstOrDefault(
                x => x.Rel == Constants.CommonLinkRelValues.Self);
            return locationLink == null ? null : new Uri(locationLink.Href);
        }
    }
}
```

With prerequisites complete, we're now ready to implement the `IHttpActionResult` that indicates a new task has been created. Implement it as follows:

```
using System.Net;
using System.Net.Http;
using System.Threading;
using System.Threading.Tasks;
using System.Web.Http;
using Task = WebApi2Book.Web.Api.Models.Task;

namespace WebApi2Book.Web.Api.MaintenanceProcessing
{
    public class TaskCreatedActionResult : IHttpActionResult
    {
        private readonly Task _createdTask;
        private readonly HttpRequestMessage _requestMessage;

        public TaskCreatedActionResult(HttpRequestMessage requestMessage,
            Task createdTask)
        {
            _requestMessage = requestMessage;
            _createdTask = createdTask;
        }

        public Task<HttpResponseMessage> ExecuteAsync(CancellationToken cancellationToken)
        {
            return System.Threading.Tasks.Task.FromResult(Execute());
        }
```

```
    public HttpResponseMessage Execute()
    {
        var responseMessage = _requestMessage.CreateResponse(
            HttpStatusCode.Created, _createdTask);

        responseMessage.Headers.Location = LocationLinkCalculator.GetLocationLink(_createdTask);

        return responseMessage;
    }
    }
}
```

Looking at the implementation, we see that the constructor accepts an HttpRequestMessage and a Task service model object. It caches those for use in the Execute method, which is invoked from the asynchronous ExecuteAsync method. Execute uses the request message to create a response with the proper HttpStatusCode and Task content. Then it also adds the Location header to the response.

At last, modify the AddTask method of the TasksController to return the custom result:

```
[Route("", Name = "AddTaskRoute")]
[HttpPost]
public IHttpActionResult AddTask(HttpRequestMessage requestMessage, NewTask newTask)
{
    var task = _addTaskMaintenanceProcessor.AddTask(newTask);
    var result = new TaskCreatedActionResult(requestMessage, task);
    return result;
}
```

Though links won't be fully developed until we implement our link services to add the actual links, we will still see the benefit in the response if we hack in a fake link. Therefore, modify the AddTask method of the AddTaskMaintenanceProcessor so that it appears as follows:

```
public Task AddTask(NewTask newTask)
{
    var taskEntity = _autoMapper.Map<Data.Entities.Task>(newTask);

    _queryProcessor.AddTask(taskEntity);

    var task = _autoMapper.Map<Task>(taskEntity);

    // TODO: Implement link service
    task.AddLink(new Link
    {
        Method = HttpMethod.Get.Method,
        Href = "http://localhost:61589/api/v1/tasks/" + task.TaskId,
        Rel = Constants.CommonLinkRelValues.Self
    });

    return task;
}
```

■ **Note** You'll need to add the following `using` directives:

- `using System.Net.Http;`
- `using WebApi2Book.Common;`

And now the moment we've been waiting for…it's demo time! Once again, execute the demo procedures described in the "Implementing POST" section. This time, you should see something similar to the following (abbreviated) response:

```
HTTP/1.1 201 Created
Content-Type: text/json; charset=utf-8
Location: http://localhost:61589/api/v1/tasks/10
```

```
{"TaskId":10,"Subject":"Fix something important","StartDate":null,"DueDate":null,
"CreatedDate":"2014-05-04T02:52:39.9872623Z","CompletedDate":null,
"Status":{"StatusId":1,"Name":"Not Started","Ordinal":0},"Assignees":[],
"Links":[{"Rel":"self","Href":"http://localhost:61589/api/v1/tasks","Method":"GET"}]}
```

Congratulations! But what's the point in returning this `IHttpActionResult`? Why not just return a `Task`? Well, our `IHttpActionResult` class' single responsibility is to encapsulate the logic of setting the response code and `Location` header in the response. We could have put the necessary logic in the controller, but we prefer to keep controllers "thin" and easy to unit test.

Summary

The task-management service we implemented is posting a task, using a message received via a versioned URL, and returning a proper result. We implemented the entire stack, and along the way we dealt with routing, controller selection, dependency management, persistence, type mapping, diagnostic tracing/logging, and error handling. To recap how all of this comes together at runtime, let's summarize it with some pseudo code:

1. Caller makes a web request.

2. ASP.NET Web API starts the activation of the appropriate controller, which is selected using our custom controller selector based on the URL routes registered at application start-up.

3. ASP.NET Web API uses the `NinjectDependencyResolver` to satisfy all of the dependencies of the controller, all of the dependencies each dependency requires, and so on. (It's recursive.)

4. If any object requires an `ISession` object, Ninject calls the `NinjectConfigurator.CreateSession` method to create the `ISession` instance.

5. The `CreateSession` method opens a new session and binds it to the web context so that it will be available for subsequent `ISession` requests.

6. ASP.NET Web API calls the custom unit of work attribute's `OnActionExecuting` override, which in turn starts a new database transaction.

7.   ASP.NET Web API calls the controller action method, which uses dependencies that were injected in during controller activation to execute the actual business logic (i.e., the whole reason the method was called in the first place).

8.   ASP.NET Web API calls the custom unit-of-work attribute's `OnActionExecuted` method, which first ends (either commits or rolls back) the database transaction, and then closes and disposes of the current `ISession` object.

Wow, that's a lot going on for every web request! Yes, and the entire sequence is traced in great detail with the custom diagnostic tracing we configured. In fact, examining the trace log is an excellent way to understand what's going on under the hood!

We also demonstrated some architectural patterns inspired by SOLID design principles. Although all of this will be more meaningful once we add things like security, we've laid a great deal of the groundwork necessary to make much progress going forward.

In the next chapter, we will continue the exploration of "framework things" by examining security. And you'll see again that you can easily pull these concerns into their own classes and wire them up to happen automatically on every web request.

CHAPTER 6

Securing the Service

Ah, security. You knew we'd get here eventually. Security is one of those areas in the architecture that can become wildly complex before you know it. People are counting on you to get it right, with no margin for error. Lawsuits happen and companies end up on the front page, or completely go under, when security is implemented poorly. You simply can't afford to mess it up!

Fortunately, because we are dealing with a RESTful service that is anchored on HTTP, we can leverage widely-used security mechanisms (some of which have been in place for years) for the more complicated and risky parts of the security architecture. In this chapter, we will highlight some of those mechanisms as we add security to our task-management service. Along the way, we'll also highlight some useful design approaches and ASP.NET Web API features that, though not intrinsically tied to security, seem to fit well in the context of this subject.

The Main Idea

In Chapter 5, we implemented a scenario where the user created a task. In this chapter, we are going to return to that scenario and add security to it. We are also going to implement a few more scenarios so that we can more fully illustrate the design and implementation of security in the context of a service built using ASP.NET Web API. Table 6-1 summarizes the service scenarios we will cover in this chapter, including the authorization level required of the user.

Table 6-1. *Scenarios Used to Illustrate Security*

Scenario	Required User Role
Create a task	Manager
Activate, complete, or reactivate a task	Senior Worker
Get a task	Junior Worker

Before we go any further, though, let's agree upon some basic terminology:

- **User**   The end user of the task-management service. This may or may not be an actual human being. We will refer to the user as "he" just for simplicity.

- **Caller**   The application that invokes the task-management service on behalf of the user (e.g., a browser). Fiddler was the caller in Chapter 5.

Now that we've agreed upon that terminology, let's get things started by breaking the security of the service into two parts: authentication and authorization. *Authentication* answers the question, "Is the user of the API service who he claims to be?" And *authorization* answers the question, "Is the user allowed to do what he is trying to do?" In other words, authentication establishes the user's identity, and authorization enforces the user's permissions.

Authentication

The first thing the service must do when it receives a new web request is verify the user's claim of identity. We do this by validating the credentials supplied by the user. Via these credentials, the caller provides two basic pieces of information: who the user claims to be, and how that claim can be verified. You likely do this every day when you log into your computer. You claim to be [your name here], and the password you enter on the login screen provides proof/validation of that claim.

Within the world of HTTP, there are several ways to validate a user's credentials. Table 6-2 lists the more prevalent ones.

Table 6-2. *Types of Authentication in HTTP*

Type	Description
None	You don't need to know the identity of the user, nor do you need to protect any of the site's or service's resources by applying permissions.
Basic	The caller adds an HTTP authorization header containing a user name and password. Those values are essentially plaintext, using only base64 encoding for simple obfuscation.
	This generally requires Secure Sockets Layer (SSL) transport security (i.e., an endpoint that exposes an HTTPS address) to protect the plaintext user name and password.
Digest	Provides a fancier method of putting the user name and password in the HTTP header that provides encryption for those values. This is intended to avoid the need for HTTPS.
Kerberos	Uses an authentication server, such as Windows Active Directory, to provide integrated and seamless credential validation. This is similar to intranet sites on Windows networks that integrate with the domain for user authentication. A lot of internal SharePoint sites use this approach so that a company's users don't have to re-enter their user name and password when they visit the intranet.
Public-Key, Certificates	Relies on caller-provided certificates to identify a user. This is not very useful in a public web site or service, but it is very appropriate for applications where the users or devices are known. An example of this approach is an internal, portable, device-based warehousing application for tracking inventory, or maybe a set of iPads used by the sales team. The group of users is relatively small and well-defined within a company's organizational structure. Each user or device is issued a certificate that identifies him (or it) on every call to your site or service.
Tokens	Largely used when third-party token issuers are involved (e.g., OpenID, OAuth). This relieves your service of the burden of both storing and verifying a user's credentials. Here's how it works (generally speaking):
	The caller first verifies the user name and password using a token issuer that your service trusts. Upon successful verification, the token issuer provides the caller with a token. Once the caller has that token, it uses it to call your service. Since your service trusts the issuer that the caller used for credential verification, your service can trust that the token securely identifies the user, and it therefore doesn't have to bother with verifying the user's credentials itself.

In selecting authentication types to support for the task-management service, we can definitely skip the None option because we actually need to identify the caller and enforce permissions.

We can also eliminate Kerberos and Certificates, because the goal is to keep our examples simple and avoid relying on Active Directory. These particular approaches can be overly complex and impractical when dealing with public-facing Internet applications and services.

Between Basic and Digest, Basic is much easier to implement. With Basic authentication, the service application and its callers have to deal only with plain-text credentials. Basic authentication is actually fairly common, and it is viable even in production environments...provided that transport security is used to protect the credentials. Therefore, we will support Basic authentication in the task-management service. However, SSL transport security configuration is a separate topic, outside the scope of this book. We trust that if you decide to implement Basic authentication on your own ASP.NET Web API services, you will enable support for HTTPS.

Finally, we will also support a form of token-based security in the task-management service, because token-based security has become so common these days that it is impossible to ignore (e.g., you've probably heard of OpenID and/or OAuth). It's also a lot easier to implement than it was just a few years ago, thanks to increasing standardization and availability of open-source libraries. Speaking of which, we'll use one of our own libraries to make implementing token-based security as painless as possible.

Authorization

Once the service has securely identified the user, it needs to enforce some basic permissions. The task-management service will have three levels of users, as indicated earlier in Table 6-1.

These days, the concept of *claims* has finally caught on. The main idea is to associate a list of key-value string pairs with an authenticated user, where the key-value pairs provide all kinds of information about the user. This information includes things the user is claiming to have or to be able to do, roles the user is claiming to belong to, and so on. And because a specific type of claim can support more than one instance, the structure can be used for assigning roles. For example, Table 6-3 demonstrates what a set of claims for "Bob" might look like. Note that the Role claim type has more than one value (i.e., Bob belongs to more than one role).

Table 6-3. *An Example User's Claims*

Claim type	Example claim value
Email	bob@gmail.com
UserId	BSmith
Surname	Smith
Givenname	Bob
SID	Bob's security identifier; usually something issued by the system: C73832EE-3191-4DC7-A3D4-25ADDDD5496B
Role	Manager
Role	Senior Worker

Strictly speaking, claims aren't limited to values dealing only with authorization. They do, however, provide a nice structure for indicating the roles a user belongs to, which is of primary interest when it comes to authorization.

Overview of the Authentication and Authorization Process

Before we start coding, let's take a high-level look at what's involved in the authentication and authorization process. Each time a request comes into the task-management service, the following things happen (in this order):

1. A web request arrives that includes an HTTP authorization header containing information about the user and how that information can be verified.

2. The service verifies the user information. Note, however, in the case of token-based authentication, the trusted token issuer has already verified the user information; all the service needs to do is verify that the token was actually issued by the trusted token issuer.

3. The service sets up a security principal object on the current HTTP context that contains the current user's identity and associated claims (e.g., userId, email, firstname, lastname, and roles). Each web request executes in its own HTTP context, so each request will execute within the context of the user's principal.

4. All "downstream" code checks the current context's principal to determine if/how processing is allowed to continue. If processing is not allowed to continue, the service will communicate this to the caller via a response message containing the appropriate HTTP status code (i.e., 401 - Unauthorized).

Now let's get into the implementation so that we can see all of this in action!

■ **Note**   As in previous chapters, unless otherwise noted, we implement one public type per file. The file name should match the type name, and the file location should match the namespace name. For example, the WebApi2Book.Web.Common.Routing.ApiVersionConstraint class is in a file named "ApiVersionConstraint.cs", which is located in a project folder named "Routing" in the WebApi2Book.Web.Common project.

Securing the POST

We implemented the TasksController class' AddTask action method in Chapter 5, but we did it without securing it in any way. Let's return to that method and get some security around it.

The Authorization Filter

Let's secure the AddTask method in the V1 controller (remember, we are finished with the V2 controller) by adding the Authorize attribute (i.e., an "authorization filter") to it as follows. Be sure to use the Web API version of the attribute (found in the System.Web.Http namespace), and not the MVC version. Also, be sure to add a using directive for WebApi2Book.Common to satisfy the compiler. Note that we are using the attribute to specify that the user must have a manager role:

```
[Route("", Name = "AddTaskRoute")]
[HttpPost]
[Authorize(Roles = Constants.RoleNames.Manager)]
```

```
public IHttpActionResult AddTask(HttpRequestMessage requestMessage, NewTask newTask)
{
    var task = _addTaskMaintenanceProcessor.AddTask(newTask);
    var result = new TaskCreatedActionResult(requestMessage, task);
    return result;
}
```

Now, we'll repeat the POST demo from Chapter 5, just to see if anything has changed:

POST Request (abbreviated)

```
POST http://localhost:61589/api/v1/tasks HTTP/1.1
Content-Type: text/json

{"Subject":"Fix something important"}
```

You should see the following response:

POST Response (abbreviated)

```
HTTP/1.1 401 Unauthorized
Content-Type: text/json; charset=utf-8

{"Message":"Authorization has been denied for this request."}
```

Isn't that great? We have secured the POST by simply applying an attribute to the appropriate controller action method! But why was this so easy? The reason is because ASP.NET Web API is doing the heavy lifting for us. First, the framework's message-processing infrastructure detects the presence of the Authorize action filter attribute on the AddTask method. This causes it to ensure that a security principal containing a manager role has been established on the current HTTP context before invoking the action method. The framework rightly detects that there is no such principal available, and therefore, without ever invoking the target AddTask method, it creates an error response (complete with the correct HTTP status code), which it returns to the caller.

So now we've secured our action method, but these POST requests will always fail until 1) they contain information necessary to establish a principal with the manager role, and 2) until we implement the code that actually uses that information to build a principal and associate it with the current context. Let's address this next.

A Message Handler to Support HTTP Basic Authentication

If you review the simplified ASP.NET Web API processing pipeline diagram from the previous chapter (Figure 5-1), you'll notice that message handlers are invoked before filters and controller actions. This makes message handlers well suited to take on the responsibility of building a principal and associating it with the current context. Remember, the principal must be established on the current context before the authorization filter is hit, or else the request will be rejected.

Before we implement our message handler (this first one will support Basic authentication), we need to add the security service to which it delegates some of its principal-building responsibilities. Therefore, add the following types:

IBasicSecurityService Interface

```
namespace WebApi2Book.Web.Api.Security
{
    public interface IBasicSecurityService
    {
        bool SetPrincipal(string username, string password);
    }
}
```

BasicSecurityService Class

```
using System.Security.Claims;
using System.Security.Principal;
using System.Threading;
using System.Web;
using log4net;
using NHibernate;
using WebApi2Book.Common;
using WebApi2Book.Common.Logging;
using WebApi2Book.Data.Entities;
using WebApi2Book.Web.Common;

namespace WebApi2Book.Web.Api.Security
{
    public class BasicSecurityService : IBasicSecurityService
    {
        private readonly ILog _log;

        public BasicSecurityService(ILogManager logManager)
        {
            _log = logManager.GetLog(typeof(BasicSecurityService));
        }

        public virtual ISession Session
        {
            get { return WebContainerManager.Get<ISession>(); }
        }

        public bool SetPrincipal(string username, string password)
        {
            var user = GetUser(username);

            IPrincipal principal = null;
            if (user == null || (principal = GetPrincipal(user)) == null)
            {
                _log.DebugFormat("System could not validate user {0}", username);
                return false;
            }

            Thread.CurrentPrincipal = principal;
            if (HttpContext.Current != null)
            {
                HttpContext.Current.User = principal;
            }

            return true;
        }
```

```
public virtual IPrincipal GetPrincipal(User user)
{
    var identity = new GenericIdentity(user.Username, Constants.SchemeTypes.Basic);

    identity.AddClaim(new Claim(ClaimTypes.GivenName, user.Firstname));
    identity.AddClaim(new Claim(ClaimTypes.Surname, user.Lastname));

    var username = user.Username.ToLowerInvariant();
    switch (username)
    {
        case "bhogg":
            identity.AddClaim(new Claim(ClaimTypes.Role, Constants.RoleNames.Manager));
            identity.AddClaim(new Claim(ClaimTypes.Role, Constants.RoleNames.SeniorWorker));
            identity.AddClaim(new Claim(ClaimTypes.Role, Constants.RoleNames.JuniorWorker));
            break;
        case "jbob":
            identity.AddClaim(new Claim(ClaimTypes.Role, Constants.RoleNames.SeniorWorker));
            identity.AddClaim(new Claim(ClaimTypes.Role, Constants.RoleNames.JuniorWorker));
            break;
        case "jdoe":
            identity.AddClaim(new Claim(ClaimTypes.Role, Constants.RoleNames.JuniorWorker));
            break;
        default:
            return null;
    }

    return new ClaimsPrincipal(identity);
}

public virtual User GetUser(string username)
{
    username = username.ToLowerInvariant();
    return
        Session.QueryOver<User>().Where(x => x.Username == username).SingleOrDefault();
}
    }
}
```

Then wire this up so that it can be used as a dependency. This is done by adding the following to the NinjectConfigurator AddBindings method:

```
container.Bind<IBasicSecurityService>().To<BasicSecurityService>().InSingletonScope();
```

■ **Note** You'll need to add a using directive for WebApi2Book.Web.Api.Security to satisfy the compiler.

Let's review. The first thing to note in this security service is that the ISession dependency is not constructor-injected. This is because the BasicSecurityService is constructed in the application's startup sequence, before the application has prepared an ISession instance. (We'll see this when we configure the message handler.) The Session property provides the BasicSecurityService with "lazy" access to the ISession managed by the Ninject container; by the time it accesses it, the ISession is available as a dependency. On a related note, the fact that the BasicSecurityService stores no state itself (other than the ILog instance, which is safe for multithread access) allows us to configure it as a singleton, as you can see in the code snippet just shown.

The next method, SetPrincipal, uses the GetPrincipal method to construct a security principal. If a valid principal can be constructed, it associates the principal with the current thread. This is mostly for legacy purposes (e.g., by convention, some third-party libraries look for a principal on the current thread). More importantly, however, SetPrincipal also places the principal on the current HttpContext. *This is vitally important to do in ASP.NET Web API applications, because while multiple threads may be used to process a single request (and therefore some threads may not automatically have access to the principal via* Thread.CurrentPrincipal*), the current HttpContext and the principal associated with it will be—and will need to be—accessible throughout an entire call.* Fortunately, NuGet security packages for Web API, including the one we're going to use later for token-based security, typically take care of this important detail.

The last method, GetPrincipal, is an extremely simplified approach to constructing a principal from user credentials. In this case, we're only using part of the user's credential, username (used to fetch the User); we're not even verifying the password. Why is this so incredibly simplified? Well, because at this level we're dealing with concerns not unique to ASP.NET Web API. Verifying user credentials at this level should be concerns of a credential management and verification package, like ASP.NET Membership (used the previous edition of this book) or ASP.NET Identity (which is Microsoft's latest approach to membership). As our focus is on ASP.NET Web API, not credential management and verification, we will move on to our custom handler. Go ahead and implement the handler now as follows:

```
using System;
using System.Net;
using System.Net.Http;
using System.Net.Http.Headers;
using System.Text;
using System.Threading;
using System.Threading.Tasks;
using System.Web;
using log4net;
using WebApi2Book.Common;
using WebApi2Book.Common.Logging;

namespace WebApi2Book.Web.Api.Security
{
    public class BasicAuthenticationMessageHandler : DelegatingHandler
    {
        public const char AuthorizationHeaderSeparator = ':';
        private const int UsernameIndex = 0;
        private const int PasswordIndex = 1;
        private const int ExpectedCredentialCount = 2;

        private readonly ILog _log;
        private readonly IBasicSecurityService _basicSecurityService;

        public BasicAuthenticationMessageHandler(ILogManager logManager,
            IBasicSecurityService basicSecurityService)
        {
            _basicSecurityService = basicSecurityService;
            _log = logManager.GetLog(typeof (BasicAuthenticationMessageHandler));
        }
```

```
protected override async Task<HttpResponseMessage> SendAsync(
    HttpRequestMessage request,
    CancellationToken cancellationToken)
{
    if (HttpContext.Current.User.Identity.IsAuthenticated)
    {
        _log.Debug("Already authenticated; passing on to next handler...");
        return await base.SendAsync(request, cancellationToken);
    }

    if (!CanHandleAuthentication(request))
    {
        _log.Debug("Not a basic auth request; passing on to next handler...");
        return await base.SendAsync(request, cancellationToken);
    }

    bool isAuthenticated;
    try
    {
        isAuthenticated = Authenticate(request);
    }
    catch (Exception e)
    {
        _log.Error("Failure in auth processing", e);
        return CreateUnauthorizedResponse();
    }

    if (isAuthenticated)
    {
        var response = await base.SendAsync(request, cancellationToken);
        return response.StatusCode == HttpStatusCode.Unauthorized ? CreateUnauthorizedResponse():
            response;
    }

    return CreateUnauthorizedResponse();
}

public bool CanHandleAuthentication(HttpRequestMessage request)
{
    return (request.Headers != null
            && request.Headers.Authorization != null
            && request.Headers.Authorization.Scheme.ToLowerInvariant() ==
                Constants.SchemeTypes.Basic);
}

public bool Authenticate(HttpRequestMessage request)
{
    _log.Debug("Attempting to authenticate...");
```

```
            var authHeader = request.Headers.Authorization;
            if (authHeader == null)
            {
                return false;
            }

            var credentialParts = GetCredentialParts(authHeader);
            if (credentialParts.Length != ExpectedCredentialCount)
            {
                return false;
            }

            return _basicSecurityService.SetPrincipal(credentialParts[UsernameIndex],
                credentialParts[PasswordIndex]);
        }

        public string[] GetCredentialParts(AuthenticationHeaderValue authHeader)
        {
            var encodedCredentials = authHeader.Parameter;
            var credentialBytes = Convert.FromBase64String(encodedCredentials);
            var credentials = Encoding.ASCII.GetString(credentialBytes);
            var credentialParts = credentials.Split(AuthorizationHeaderSeparator);
            return credentialParts;
        }

        public HttpResponseMessage CreateUnauthorizedResponse()
        {
            var response = new HttpResponseMessage(HttpStatusCode.Unauthorized);
            response.Headers.WwwAuthenticate.Add(
                new AuthenticationHeaderValue(Constants.SchemeTypes.Basic));
            return response;
        }
    }
}
```

The first thing to note is that BasicAuthenticationMessageHandler derives from DelegatingHandler, an ASP.NET Web API base class. The handler overrides the SendAsync method. This allows it to pass a request to the next handler in the ASP.NET Web API processing pipeline, in cases where processing is allowed to continue, by calling base.SendAsync. It also allows it to return an error response, in cases where processing is not allowed to continue, by calling CreateUnauthorizedResponse.

The value added by CreateUnauthorizedResponse is seen in the second line of the method, where it adds the Basic scheme to the response's WwwAuthenticate header. A response with the Unauthorized (401) HTTP status code together with the Basic scheme in the header will trigger most browsers to prompt for Username and Password.

Next, let's take a look at the following code, which is executed if the user was successfully authenticated:

```
var response = await base.SendAsync(request, cancellationToken);
return response;
```

The first line passes processing along to the next handler and waits for the response. The next line simply returns the response. The rest of the methods are also fairly straightforward:

- CanHandleAuthentication examines the request and returns true if it contains an HTTP header indicating the Basic authorization scheme.

- Authenticate uses GetCredentials to extract the credentials from the request, and then it delegates the actual work of setting the principal to the security service we implemented earlier.

- GetCredentials parses the credentials from the request. The thing to remember here is that the credentials arrive base64-encoded and separated by a delimiter (":").

Now that we've implemented the handler, the last step is to configure it to be added to the application's message-handler pipeline. This is configured during application startup, so let's return to the WebApiApplication class and modify it so that it appears as follows:

```
using System.Web;
using System.Web.Http;
using WebApi2Book.Common.Logging;
using WebApi2Book.Common.TypeMapping;
using WebApi2Book.Web.Api.Security;
using WebApi2Book.Web.Common;

namespace WebApi2Book.Web.Api
{
    public class WebApiApplication : HttpApplication
    {
        protected void Application_Start()
        {
            GlobalConfiguration.Configure(WebApiConfig.Register);

            RegisterHandlers();

            new AutoMapperConfigurator().Configure(
                WebContainerManager.GetAll<IAutoMapperTypeConfigurator>());
        }

        private void RegisterHandlers()
        {
            var logManager = WebContainerManager.Get<ILogManager>();

            GlobalConfiguration.Configuration.MessageHandlers.Add(
                new BasicAuthenticationMessageHandler(logManager,
                    WebContainerManager.Get<IBasicSecurityService>()));
        }

        protected void Application_Error()
        {
            var exception = Server.GetLastError();
```

```
        if (exception != null)
        {
            var log = WebContainerManager.Get<ILogManager>().GetLog(typeof (WebApiApplication));
            log.Error("Unhandled exception.", exception);
        }
    }
  }
}
}
```

Note the new method, RegisterHandlers. We're going to be adding more handlers later, so we figured it would be good to break this configuration out into a separate method. Looking at the implementation, this adds the handler to the MessageHandlers collection of the Web API global configuration object, and with this in place, all requests to the task-management service will be intercepted by the BasicAuthenticationMessageHandler. For requests decorated with the Basic scheme, the handler will verify the user's credentials and set up a corresponding principal using the trivial implementation in the BasicSecurityService. To prove that all of this is working properly, let's now revisit the demo and see this in action!

First, we need to add the Basic authentication information to the request message. Here we see the encoded information for "bhogg", who, as you may recall from the BasicSecurityService implementation, is a manager. Note the second line; YmhvZ2c6aWdub3J1ZA== represents bhogg's base64-encoded credentials:

POST Request - Manager (abbreviated)

```
POST http://localhost:61589/api/v1/tasks HTTP/1.1
Authorization: Basic YmhvZ2c6aWdub3J1ZA==
Content-Type: text/json

{"Subject":"Fix something important"}
```

Now we'll send the request (we're using Fiddler) and examine the response:

POST Response - Manager (abbreviated)

```
HTTP/1.1 201 Created
Content-Type: text/json; charset=utf-8

{"TaskId":17,"Subject":"Fix something important","StartDate":null,"DueDate":null,
"CreatedDate":"2014-05-10T19:02:52.2408621Z","CompletedDate":null,
"Status":{"StatusId":1,"Name":"Not Started","Ordinal":0},"Assignees":[],
"Links":[{"Rel":"self","Href":"http://localhost:61589/api/v1/tasks/17","Method":"GET"}]}
```

Excellent! Our credentials for manager bhogg have been accepted. We've created a task, only this time we've done it securely. Let's make sure the security we've put in place is actually working by sending another request—this time, with the credentials of a user in a junior worker role. This request should be denied, because the AddTask controller action requires the user be in the Manager role. Note that amRvZTppZ25vcmVk represents the credentials for jdoe, the junior worker:

POST Request - Junior Worker (abbreviated)

```
POST http://localhost:61589/api/v1/tasks HTTP/1.1
Authorization: Basic amRvZTppZ25vcmVk
Content-Type: text/json

{"Subject":"Fix something important"}
```

POST Response - Junior Worker (abbreviated)

```
HTTP/1.1 401 Unauthorized
WWW-Authenticate: basic
```

Perfect. This demonstrates that we have secured our "Add a Task" scenario; only managers can create a task in our task-management service. The next thing we'll do is implement the remaining scenarios from Table 6-1 leveraging the security infrastructure we've put in place. After that, we'll show how we can add support for token-based security...without having to modify any of our existing code! This is due to ASP.NET Web API's excellent extensibility support related to message handlers.

Securing Non-Resource API Operations

In Chapter 3, we designed the API for non-resource API operations. The design is summarized in Table 3-4. What's missing from the design is the security aspect, so let's extend the design now by taking security into account, as shown in Table 6-4.

Table 6-4. *A List of Task Status Operations*

URI	Verb	Description	Security
/api/tasks/123/activations	POST	Starts, or "activates," a task; returns the updated task in the response	Requires Senior Worker role
/api/tasks/123/completions	POST	Completes a task; returns the updated task in the response	Requires Senior Worker role
/api/tasks/123/reactivations	POST	Reopens, or "re-activates," a task; returns the updated task in the response	Requires Senior Worker role; all reactivations will be audited

Activate a Task

With that as an introduction, let's start by adding support to activate a task. We'll follow our usual bottom-up approach of adding dependencies first, and the first dependency we'll add is a query processor. Remember that the ITaskByIdQueryProcessor interface is in the WebApi2Book.Data project, while its implementation is in the WebApi2Book.Data.SqlServer project (within the QueryProcessors folder).

ITaskByIdQueryProcessor Interface

```
using WebApi2Book.Data.Entities;

namespace WebApi2Book.Data.QueryProcessors
{
    public interface ITaskByIdQueryProcessor
    {
        Task GetTask(long taskId);
    }
}
```

TaskByIdQueryProcessor Class

```
using NHibernate;
using WebApi2Book.Data.Entities;
using WebApi2Book.Data.QueryProcessors;

namespace WebApi2Book.Data.SqlServer.QueryProcessors
{
    public class TaskByIdQueryProcessor : ITaskByIdQueryProcessor
    {
        private readonly ISession _session;

        public TaskByIdQueryProcessor(ISession session)
        {
            _session = session;
        }

        public Task GetTask(long taskId)
        {
            var task = _session.Get<Task>(taskId);
            return task;
        }
    }
}
```

Dependency Configuration (add to NinjectConfigurator.AddBindings)

```
container.Bind<ITaskByIdQueryProcessor>().To<TaskByIdQueryProcessor>().InRequestScope();
```

We introduced the concept of using query processors back in Chapter 5. Basically, query processors are part of a Strategy Pattern implementation to provide access to persistent data. The TaskByIdQueryProcessor implementation is fairly trivial, performing a simple "get" against the database by taskId.

Our next dependency to add is also a query processor. The query processor we just added is responsible for fetching data, but this one is responsible for updating data. Implement it as follows:

IUpdateTaskStatusQueryProcessor Interface

```
using WebApi2Book.Data.Entities;

namespace WebApi2Book.Data.QueryProcessors
{
    public interface IUpdateTaskStatusQueryProcessor
    {
        void UpdateTaskStatus(Task taskToUpdate, string statusName);
    }
}
```

UpdateTaskStatusQueryProcessor Class

```
using NHibernate;
using WebApi2Book.Data.Entities;
using WebApi2Book.Data.QueryProcessors;

namespace WebApi2Book.Data.SqlServer.QueryProcessors
{
    public class UpdateTaskStatusQueryProcessor : IUpdateTaskStatusQueryProcessor
    {
        private readonly ISession _session;

        public UpdateTaskStatusQueryProcessor(ISession session)
        {
            _session = session;
        }

        public void UpdateTaskStatus(Task taskToUpdate, string statusName)
        {
            var status = _session.QueryOver<Status>().Where(x => x.Name == statusName).SingleOrDefault();

            taskToUpdate.Status = status;

            _session.SaveOrUpdate(taskToUpdate);
        }
    }
}
```

Dependency Configuration (add to NinjectConfigurator.AddBindings)

```
container.Bind<IUpdateTaskStatusQueryProcessor>().To<UpdateTaskStatusQueryProcessor>()
        .InRequestScope();
```

The UpdateTaskStatusQueryProcessor implementation is similarly unremarkable. It's just finding the appropriate status object and associating it with the task.

The next dependency is slightly more interesting. It performs all of the "business logic" required to activate a task. Implement it as follows:

IStartTaskWorkflowProcessor Interface

```
using WebApi2Book.Web.Api.Models;

namespace WebApi2Book.Web.Api.MaintenanceProcessing
{
    public interface IStartTaskWorkflowProcessor
    {
        Task StartTask(long taskId);
    }
}
```

StartTaskWorkflowProcessor Class

```
using WebApi2Book.Common;
using WebApi2Book.Common.TypeMapping;
using WebApi2Book.Data.Exceptions;
using WebApi2Book.Data.QueryProcessors;
using WebApi2Book.Web.Api.Models;

namespace WebApi2Book.Web.Api.MaintenanceProcessing
{
    public class StartTaskWorkflowProcessor : IStartTaskWorkflowProcessor
    {
        private readonly IAutoMapper _autoMapper;
        private readonly ITaskByIdQueryProcessor _taskByIdQueryProcessor;
        private readonly IDateTime _dateTime;
        private readonly IUpdateTaskStatusQueryProcessor _updateTaskStatusQueryProcessor;

        public StartTaskWorkflowProcessor(ITaskByIdQueryProcessor taskByIdQueryProcessor,
            IUpdateTaskStatusQueryProcessor updateTaskStatusQueryProcessor, IAutoMapper autoMapper,
             IDateTime dateTime)
        {
            _taskByIdQueryProcessor = taskByIdQueryProcessor;
            _updateTaskStatusQueryProcessor = updateTaskStatusQueryProcessor;
            _autoMapper = autoMapper;
            _dateTime = dateTime;
        }

        public Task StartTask(long taskId)
        {
            var taskEntity = _taskByIdQueryProcessor.GetTask(taskId);
            if (taskEntity == null)
            {
                throw new RootObjectNotFoundException("Task not found");
            }

            // Simulate some workflow logic...
            if (taskEntity.Status.Name != "Not Started")
            {
                throw new BusinessRuleViolationException(
                    "Incorrect task status. Expected status of 'Not Started'.");
            }

            taskEntity.StartDate = _dateTime.UtcNow;
            _updateTaskStatusQueryProcessor.UpdateTaskStatus(taskEntity, "In Progress");

            var task = _autoMapper.Map<Task>(taskEntity);

            return task;
        }
    }
}
```

Dependency Configuration (add to NinjectConfigurator.AddBindings)

```
container.Bind<IStartTaskWorkflowProcessor>().To<StartTaskWorkflowProcessor>().InRequestScope();
```

We'll explain this next, but first we have to add one more dependency to satisfy the compiler: BusinessRuleViolationException. Instances of this trivial exception type are thrown to indicate an attempted violation of the business logic. Implement it as follows:

BusinessRuleViolationException Class

```
using System;

namespace WebApi2Book.Common
{
    public class BusinessRuleViolationException : Exception
    {
        public BusinessRuleViolationException(string incorrectTaskStatus) :
            base(incorrectTaskStatus)
        {
        }
    }
}
```

Now that we've made the compiler happy, let's review the StartTaskWorkflowProcessor class' StartTask method. It begins by delegating to ITaskByIdQueryProcessor to find a Task entity with the specified taskId. An instance of the RootObjectNotFoundException class, which was introduced in Chapter 5, is thrown if no such Task can be found.

Next, we encounter some "business logic", which enforces a business rule requiring a task to have a status of Not Started in order to be activated. If that condition is satisfied, the ITaskByIdQueryProcessor sets the task's StartDate, and then delegates the job of actually updating the Status to the IUpdateTaskStatusQueryProcessor. Last, the injected IAutoMapper dependency converts the task from an entity representation to a service model representation, which is then returned to the invoker of the StartTask method.

And now it's finally time to implement that invoker of the StartTask method, which is the TaskWorkflowController. (Remember, these are "conceptual resources," as we discussed in Chapter 3, which is why this method is not on the TasksController.) Implement it as follows:

```
using System.Web.Http;
using WebApi2Book.Common;
using WebApi2Book.Web.Api.MaintenanceProcessing;
using WebApi2Book.Web.Api.Models;
using WebApi2Book.Web.Common;
using WebApi2Book.Web.Common.Routing;

namespace WebApi2Book.Web.Api.Controllers.V1
{
    [ApiVersion1RoutePrefix("")]
    [UnitOfWorkActionFilter]
    public class TaskWorkflowController : ApiController
    {
        private readonly IStartTaskWorkflowProcessor _startTaskWorkflowProcessor;
```

```
        public TaskWorkflowController(IStartTaskWorkflowProcessor startTaskWorkflowProcessor)
        {
            _startTaskWorkflowProcessor = startTaskWorkflowProcessor;
        }

        [HttpPost]
        [Authorize(Roles = Constants.RoleNames.SeniorWorker)]
        [Route("tasks/{taskId:long}/activations", Name = "StartTaskRoute")]
        public Task StartTask(long taskId)
        {
            var task = _startTaskWorkflowProcessor.StartTask(taskId);
            return task;
        }
    }
}
```

And that's it; we have implemented the ability to activate a task! Note that we've leveraged several attributes with this implementation. However, we've discussed all of these before, so we will press onward.

Before we can rightly claim victory and move on to the next scenario, though, we should prove that what we've implemented actually works. We'll send the following request to activate task #17, which we created at the end of the previous section. *Be sure to substitute the actual number of the task you created if it wasn't 17.* Note that we're providing bhogg's credentials to ensure that the request is authorized (because he's a member of the Senior Worker role):

Activate Task Request (abbreviated)

```
POST http://localhost:61589/api/v1/tasks/17/activations HTTP/1.1
Authorization: Basic YmhvZ2c6aWdub3JlZA==
```

Activate Task Response (abbreviated)

```
HTTP/1.1 200 OK
Content-Type: application/json; charset=utf-8

{"TaskId":17,"Subject":"Fix something important","StartDate":"2014-05-13T00:52:34.2373052Z",
"DueDate":null,"CreatedDate":"2014-05-10T19:02:52","CompletedDate":null,
"Status":{"StatusId":2,"Name":"In Progress","Ordinal":1},"Assignees":[],"Links":[]}
```

This is correct so far. The task is now In Progress, and we have a non-null value for StartDate. Now let's test our business logic requiring tasks to have a Not Started status in order to be activated. To do so, send the request again... and the result is

```
HTTP/1.1 500 Internal Server Error
Content-Type: application/json; charset=utf-8

{"Message":"Incorrect task status. Expected status of 'Not Started'."}
```

Well, the message looks OK, but the status code is incorrect. We should be returning a status code of 402 to indicate a custom business rule violation, not 500, which indicates a server error. Fortunately, we have the GlobalExceptionHandler, and this status-code translation is a perfect job for it. Add the highlighted code to its Handle method, add a using directive for WebApi2Book.Common, and then retry the request:

```
...
if (exception is ChildObjectNotFoundException)
{
    context.Result = new SimpleErrorResult(context.Request, HttpStatusCode.Conflict, exception.Message);
    return;
}

if (exception is BusinessRuleViolationException)
{
    context.Result = new SimpleErrorResult(context.Request, HttpStatusCode.PaymentRequired,
        exception.Message);
    return;
}

context.Result = new SimpleErrorResult(context.Request, HttpStatusCode.InternalServerError,
    exception.Message);
...
```

You should see something similar to the following (note the change in the response code):

```
HTTP/1.1 402 Payment Required
Content-Type: application/json; charset=utf-8

{"Message":"Incorrect task status. Expected status of 'Not Started'."}
```

This is exactly what we wanted to see! Now we can rightly claim victory and move on to the next scenario.

Complete a Task

This section will go quickly, because we've already implemented most of the dependencies we need to complete a task. The first, and only, new dependency we need to add is ICompleteTaskWorkflowProcessor. Go ahead and implement it now:

ICompleteTaskWorkflowProcessor Interface

```
using WebApi2Book.Web.Api.Models;

namespace WebApi2Book.Web.Api.MaintenanceProcessing
{
    public interface ICompleteTaskWorkflowProcessor
    {
        Task CompleteTask(long taskId);
    }
}
```

CompleteTaskWorkflowProcessor Class

```
using WebApi2Book.Common;
using WebApi2Book.Common.TypeMapping;
using WebApi2Book.Data.Exceptions;
using WebApi2Book.Data.QueryProcessors;
using WebApi2Book.Web.Api.Models;

namespace WebApi2Book.Web.Api.MaintenanceProcessing
{
    public class CompleteTaskWorkflowProcessor : ICompleteTaskWorkflowProcessor
    {
        private readonly IAutoMapper _autoMapper;
        private readonly ITaskByIdQueryProcessor _taskByIdQueryProcessor;
        private readonly IDateTime _dateTime;
        private readonly IUpdateTaskStatusQueryProcessor _updateTaskStatusQueryProcessor;

        public CompleteTaskWorkflowProcessor(ITaskByIdQueryProcessor taskByIdQueryProcessor,
            IUpdateTaskStatusQueryProcessor updateTaskStatusQueryProcessor, IAutoMapper autoMapper,
            IDateTime dateTime)
        {
            _taskByIdQueryProcessor = taskByIdQueryProcessor;
            _updateTaskStatusQueryProcessor = updateTaskStatusQueryProcessor;
            _autoMapper = autoMapper;
            _dateTime = dateTime;
        }

        public Task CompleteTask(long taskId)
        {
            var taskEntity = _taskByIdQueryProcessor.GetTask(taskId);
            if (taskEntity == null)
            {
                throw new RootObjectNotFoundException("Task not found");
            }

            // Simulate some workflow logic...
            if (taskEntity.Status.Name != "In Progress")
            {
                throw new BusinessRuleViolationException(
                    "Incorrect task status. Expected status of 'In Progress'.");
            }

            taskEntity.CompletedDate = _dateTime.UtcNow;
            _updateTaskStatusQueryProcessor.UpdateTaskStatus(taskEntity, "Completed");

            var task = _autoMapper.Map<Task>(taskEntity);

            return task;
        }
    }
}
```

Dependency Configuration (add to NinjectConfigurator.AddBindings)

```
container.Bind<ICompleteTaskWorkflowProcessor>().To<CompleteTaskWorkflowProcessor>()
    .InRequestScope();
```

This class is similar to the StartTaskWorkflowProcessor, only this time we are requiring a status of In Progress in order to complete the processing, and we are updating the task's CompletedDate rather than the StartDate.

Now, let's hook it up to the controller, which should appear as follows:

```
using System.Web.Http;
using WebApi2Book.Common;
using WebApi2Book.Web.Api.MaintenanceProcessing;
using WebApi2Book.Web.Api.Models;
using WebApi2Book.Web.Common;
using WebApi2Book.Web.Common.Routing;

namespace WebApi2Book.Web.Api.Controllers.V1
{
    [ApiVersion1RoutePrefix("")]
    [UnitOfWorkActionFilter]
    [Authorize(Roles = Constants.RoleNames.SeniorWorker)]
    public class TaskWorkflowController : ApiController
    {
        private readonly IStartTaskWorkflowProcessor _startTaskWorkflowProcessor;
        private readonly ICompleteTaskWorkflowProcessor _completeTaskWorkflowProcessor;

        public TaskWorkflowController(IStartTaskWorkflowProcessor startTaskWorkflowProcessor,
            ICompleteTaskWorkflowProcessor completeTaskWorkflowProcessor)
        {
            _startTaskWorkflowProcessor = startTaskWorkflowProcessor;
            _completeTaskWorkflowProcessor = completeTaskWorkflowProcessor;
        }

        [HttpPost]
        [Route("tasks/{taskId:long}/activations", Name = "StartTaskRoute")]
        public Task StartTask(long taskId)
        {
            var task = _startTaskWorkflowProcessor.StartTask(taskId);
            return task;
        }

        [HttpPost]
        [Route("tasks/{taskId:long}/completions", Name = "CompleteTaskRoute")]
        public Task CompleteTask(long taskId)
        {
            var task = _completeTaskWorkflowProcessor.CompleteTask(taskId);
            return task;
        }
    }
}
```

As you can see, the controller is still quite simple. However, note that we've moved the `Authorize` attribute from the `StartTask` method and placed it on the controller class itself. As a result, we've broadened its scope of influence. Instead of restricting `StartTask` to users with a Senior Worker role, it is now requiring a Senior Worker role for every action method in the controller. This is exactly what we want, and it sure cuts down on clutter that would otherwise be introduced by copy|paste. We could even apply the `Authorize` attribute at the global configuration level—ASP. NET Web API supports this kind of global application of attributes—but we won't because it doesn't meet our security requirements from a "business" perspective. Still, it's good to know the capability exists.

Before wrapping up this section, let's send a couple of requests to ensure everything is working properly. First, let's close task #17:

Complete Task Request (abbreviated)

```
POST http://localhost:61589/api/v1/tasks/17/completions HTTP/1.1
Authorization: Basic YmhvZ2c6aWdub3J1ZA==
```

Complete Task Response (abbreviated)

```
HTTP/1.1 200 OK
Content-Type: application/json; charset=utf-8

{"TaskId":17,"Subject":"Fix something important","StartDate":"2014-05-13T00:52:34","DueDate":null,
"CreatedDate":"2014-05-10T19:02:52","CompletedDate":"2014-05-13T02:13:08.9855782Z",
"Status":{"StatusId":3,"Name":"Completed","Ordinal":2},"Assignees":[],"Links":[]}
```

So far, so good. We see the Status and CompletedDate are being assigned properly. Now let's retry the message so that we can see if our business rule is being enforced:

```
HTTP/1.1 402 Payment Required
Content-Type: application/json; charset=utf-8

{"Message":"Incorrect task status. Expected status of 'In Progress'."}
```

It is, indeed! Just what we wanted to see. Now on to the final scenario in this section.

Reactivate a Task

This section will be much like the previous one. We'll throw in a little twist, though: in this section, we're going to audit task reactivations using a custom async filter. With the release of ASP.NET Web API 2.1, async filter implementation is greatly simplified because the framework now provides virtual `On*Async` methods to override. We'll show just how simple it is...after we implement the controller method.

The first dependency we need to add is `IReactivateTaskWorkflowProcessor`. Go ahead and implement it now:

IReactivateTaskWorkflowProcessor Interface

```
using WebApi2Book.Web.Api.Models;

namespace WebApi2Book.Web.Api.MaintenanceProcessing
{
    public interface IReactivateTaskWorkflowProcessor
    {
        Task ReactivateTask(long taskId);
    }
}
```

```csharp
using WebApi2Book.Common;
using WebApi2Book.Common.TypeMapping;
using WebApi2Book.Data.Exceptions;
using WebApi2Book.Data.QueryProcessors;
using WebApi2Book.Web.Api.Models;

namespace WebApi2Book.Web.Api.MaintenanceProcessing
{
    public class ReactivateTaskWorkflowProcessor : IReactivateTaskWorkflowProcessor
    {
        private readonly IAutoMapper _autoMapper;
        private readonly ITaskByIdQueryProcessor _taskByIdQueryProcessor;
        private readonly IUpdateTaskStatusQueryProcessor _updateTaskStatusQueryProcessor;

        public ReactivateTaskWorkflowProcessor(ITaskByIdQueryProcessor taskByIdQueryProcessor,
            IUpdateTaskStatusQueryProcessor updateTaskStatusQueryProcessor, IAutoMapper autoMapper)
        {
            _taskByIdQueryProcessor = taskByIdQueryProcessor;
            _updateTaskStatusQueryProcessor = updateTaskStatusQueryProcessor;
            _autoMapper = autoMapper;
        }

        public Task ReactivateTask(long taskId)
        {
            var taskEntity = _taskByIdQueryProcessor.GetTask(taskId);
            if (taskEntity == null)
            {
                throw new RootObjectNotFoundException("Task not found");
            }

            // Simulate some workflow logic...
            if (taskEntity.Status.Name != "Completed")
            {
                throw new BusinessRuleViolationException(
                    "Incorrect task status. Expected status of 'Completed'.");
            }

            taskEntity.CompletedDate = null;
            _updateTaskStatusQueryProcessor.UpdateTaskStatus(taskEntity, "In Progress");

            var task = _autoMapper.Map<Task>(taskEntity);

            return task;
        }
    }
}
```

Dependency Configuration (add to NinjectConfigurator.AddBindings)

```csharp
container.Bind<IReactivateTaskWorkflowProcessor>().To<ReactivateTaskWorkflowProcessor>()
    .InRequestScope();
```

This class is similar to the CompleteTaskWorkflowProcessor, only this time we are requiring a status of Completed in order to complete the processing, and we are updating the task's CompletedDate by resetting it to null.

Now, let's hook it up to the controller, which should appear as follows:

```
using System.Web.Http;
using WebApi2Book.Common;
using WebApi2Book.Web.Api.MaintenanceProcessing;
using WebApi2Book.Web.Api.Models;
using WebApi2Book.Web.Common;
using WebApi2Book.Web.Common.Routing;

namespace WebApi2Book.Web.Api.Controllers.V1
{
    [ApiVersion1RoutePrefix("")]
    [UnitOfWorkActionFilter]
    [Authorize(Roles = Constants.RoleNames.SeniorWorker)]
    public class TaskWorkflowController : ApiController
    {
        private readonly IStartTaskWorkflowProcessor _startTaskWorkflowProcessor;
        private readonly ICompleteTaskWorkflowProcessor _completeTaskWorkflowProcessor;
        private readonly IReactivateTaskWorkflowProcessor _reactivateTaskWorkflowProcessor;

        public TaskWorkflowController(IStartTaskWorkflowProcessor startTaskWorkflowProcessor,
            ICompleteTaskWorkflowProcessor completeTaskWorkflowProcessor,
            IReactivateTaskWorkflowProcessor reactivateTaskWorkflowProcessor)
        {
            _startTaskWorkflowProcessor = startTaskWorkflowProcessor;
            _completeTaskWorkflowProcessor = completeTaskWorkflowProcessor;
            _reactivateTaskWorkflowProcessor = reactivateTaskWorkflowProcessor;
        }

        [HttpPost]
        [Route("tasks/{taskId:long}/activations", Name = "StartTaskRoute")]
        public Task StartTask(long taskId)
        {
            var task = _startTaskWorkflowProcessor.StartTask(taskId);
            return task;
        }

        [HttpPost]
        [Route("tasks/{taskId:long}/completions", Name = "CompleteTaskRoute")]
        public Task CompleteTask(long taskId)
        {
            var task = _completeTaskWorkflowProcessor.CompleteTask(taskId);
            return task;
        }
```

```
        [HttpPost]
        [Route("tasks/{taskId:long}/reactivations", Name = "ReactivateTaskRoute")]
        public Task ReactivateTask(long taskId)
        {
            var task = _reactivateTaskWorkflowProcessor.ReactivateTask(taskId);
            return task;
        }
    }
}
```

Again, the controller is still quite simple. Let's send a couple of requests to ensure everything is working properly. First, let's reactivate task #17 using bhogg's credentials:

Reactivate Task Request (abbreviated)

```
POST http://localhost:61589/api/v1/tasks/17/reactivations HTTP/1.1
Authorization: Basic YmhvZ2c6aWdub3JlZA==
```

Reactivate Task Response (abbreviated)

```
HTTP/1.1 200 OK
Content-Type: application/json; charset=utf-8

{"TaskId":17,"Subject":"Fix something important","StartDate":"2014-05-13T00:52:34","DueDate":null,
"CreatedDate":"2014-05-10T19:02:52","CompletedDate":null,
"Status":{"StatusId":2,"Name":"In Progress","Ordinal":1},"Assignees":[],"Links":[]}
```

So far, so good. We see that Status and CompletedDate are being updated properly. Now let's retry the message so that we can see if our business rule is being enforced:

```
HTTP/1.1 402 Payment Required
Content-Type: application/json; charset=utf-8

{"Message":"Incorrect task status. Expected status of 'Completed'."}
```

Perfect! It's not allowing us to reactivate a task that is already active, and the response looks correct.

Auditing

So now let's get to the auditing. The first thing to do is implement the custom attribute (implement it as follows):

```
using System.Threading;
using System.Threading.Tasks;
using System.Web.Http.Controllers;
using System.Web.Http.Filters;
using log4net;
using WebApi2Book.Common.Logging;
using WebApi2Book.Common.Security;
```

```csharp
namespace WebApi2Book.Web.Common.Security
{
    public class UserAuditAttribute : ActionFilterAttribute
    {
        private readonly ILog _log;
        private readonly IUserSession _userSession;

        public UserAuditAttribute()
            : this(WebContainerManager.Get<ILogManager>(), WebContainerManager.Get<IUserSession>())
        {
        }

        public UserAuditAttribute(ILogManager logManager, IUserSession userSession)
        {
            _userSession = userSession;
            _log = logManager.GetLog(typeof (UserAuditAttribute));
        }

        public override bool AllowMultiple
        {
            get { return false; }
        }

        public override Task OnActionExecutingAsync(HttpActionContext actionContext,
            CancellationToken cancellationToken)
        {
            _log.Debug("Starting execution...");
            var userName = _userSession.Username;
            return Task.Run(() => AuditCurrentUser(userName), cancellationToken);
        }

        public void AuditCurrentUser(string username)
        {
            // Simulate long auditing process
            _log.InfoFormat("Action being executed by user={0}", username);
            Thread.Sleep(3000);
        }

        public override void OnActionExecuted(HttpActionExecutedContext actionExecutedContext)
        {
            _log.InfoFormat("Action executed by user={0}", _userSession.Username);
        }
    }
}
```

And now apply the attribute to the controller's ReactivateTask method:

```
[HttpPost]
[UserAudit]
[Route("tasks/{taskId:long}/reactivations", Name = "ReactivateTaskRoute")]
public Task ReactivateTask(long taskId)
{
    var task = _reactivateTaskWorkflowProcessor.ReactivateTask(taskId);
    return task;
}
```

■ **Note** You'll also need to add a using directive for WebApi2Book.Web.Common.Security to satisfy the compiler.

Although most of its implementation consists of writing debug messages and sleeping, this attribute demonstrates the ability to do something useful in terms of security; specifically, the ability to noninvasively audit user actions. By simply applying this attribute to a controller action method, to an entire controller, or even to the global configuration, we have added auditing.

The attribute's implementation is straightforward, with a couple of items to note: First, in an actual production application, you will probably be writing auditing information to a database, not to a log file. Second, notice how we capture the user name in OnActionExecutingAsync prior to performing the actual audit. This is because the HttpContext.Current.User object that our IUserSession implementation relies upon is not available in the AuditCurrentUser method, so we need to first capture this information from IUserSession and then pass it into AuditCurrentUser.

Now let's see the auditing attribute in action. At this point, task #17 needs to be "completed" before we can reactivate it. So go ahead and send a completion request to get it into the correct state for reactivating:

```
POST http://localhost:61589/api/v1/tasks/17/completions HTTP/1.1
Authorization: Basic YmhvZ2c6aWdub3JlZA==
```

Assuming this was successful, send a request to reactivate the task:

```
POST http://localhost:61589/api/v1/tasks/17/reactivations HTTP/1.1
Authorization: Basic YmhvZ2c6aWdub3JlZA==
```

Nothing new to see here; you should have received a response similar to the response from the first reactivation, shown earlier. But now let's look in the application's log file to verify that we are, indeed, auditing the reactivation. Amidst the many lines of SimpleTraceWriter-generated information, you should see something similar to the following:

```
2014-05-13 12:52:38,990 DEBUG [81] WebApi2Book.Web.Common.Security.UserAuditAttribute
  - Starting execution...
2014-05-13 12:52:38,990 INFO  [82] WebApi2Book.Web.Common.Security.UserAuditAttribute
  - Action being executed by user=bhogg
2014-05-13 12:52:42,068 INFO  [82] WebApi2Book.Web.Common.Security.UserAuditAttribute
  - Action executed by user=bhogg
```

And that's it. By leveraging ASP.NET Web API's improved async filter support, we have easily and noninvasively provided auditing for task reactivation. Before we conclude this section, note how processing switched from thread #81 to thread #82. This helps illustrate why we always need to ensure that the principal is associated with the HttpContext, as mentioned earlier in the "A Message Handler to Support HTTP Basic Authentication" section, and not just the thread principal.

GET a Task

The last scenario we'll implement (described in Table 6-5) in this chapter involves retrieving data for a particular task.

Table 6-5. *Get a Task*

URI	Verb	Description
/api/tasks/123	GET	Gets the details for a single task

We'll restrict the operation itself to users who are at least junior workers through the use of an authorization filter, and we'll also implement a message handler to remove sensitive data from the response for users who are not members of the Senior Worker role. So much to do—let's get started!

Keeping with our bottom-up, thin-controller approach, we'll begin by adding the class that the controller delegates its work to:

ITaskByIdInquiryProcessor Interface

```
using WebApi2Book.Web.Api.Models;

namespace WebApi2Book.Web.Api.InquiryProcessing
{
    public interface ITaskByIdInquiryProcessor
    {
        Task GetTask(long taskId);
    }
}
```

TaskByIdInquiryProcessor Class

```
using WebApi2Book.Common.TypeMapping;
using WebApi2Book.Data.QueryProcessors;
using WebApi2Book.Data.Exceptions;
using WebApi2Book.Web.Api.Models;

namespace WebApi2Book.Web.Api.InquiryProcessing
{
    public class TaskByIdInquiryProcessor : ITaskByIdInquiryProcessor
    {
        private readonly IAutoMapper _autoMapper;
        private readonly ITaskByIdQueryProcessor _queryProcessor;

        public TaskByIdInquiryProcessor(ITaskByIdQueryProcessor queryProcessor,
            IAutoMapper autoMapper)
        {
            _queryProcessor = queryProcessor;
            _autoMapper = autoMapper;
        }

        public Task GetTask(long taskId)
        {
            var taskEntity = _queryProcessor.GetTask(taskId);
```

```
            if (taskEntity == null)
            {
                throw new RootObjectNotFoundException("Task not found");
            }

            var task = _autoMapper.Map<Task>(taskEntity);

            return task;
        }
    }
}
```

Dependency Configuration (add to NinjectConfigurator.AddBindings)

```
container.Bind<ITaskByIdInquiryProcessor>().To<TaskByIdInquiryProcessor>().InRequestScope();
```

■ **Note**   You'll also need to add a `using` directive for `WebApi2Book.Web.Api.InquiryProcessing` to satisfy the compiler.

It doesn't get much easier than that. GetTask uses the ITaskByIdQueryProcessor (which we added earlier in the "Activate a Task" section) to fetch the entity. Then it uses the IAutoMapper to transfer the data to a service model object that can be returned in the response.

To complete the basic scenario, add the new GetTask method to the TasksController, which should now appear as follows:

```
using System.Net.Http;
using System.Web.Http;
using WebApi2Book.Common;
using WebApi2Book.Web.Api.InquiryProcessing;
using WebApi2Book.Web.Api.MaintenanceProcessing;
using WebApi2Book.Web.Api.Models;
using WebApi2Book.Web.Common;
using WebApi2Book.Web.Common.Routing;

namespace WebApi2Book.Web.Api.Controllers.V1
{
    [ApiVersion1RoutePrefix("tasks")]
    [UnitOfWorkActionFilter]
    public class TasksController : ApiController
    {
        private readonly IAddTaskMaintenanceProcessor _addTaskMaintenanceProcessor;
        private readonly ITaskByIdInquiryProcessor _taskByIdInquiryProcessor;

        public TasksController(IAddTaskMaintenanceProcessor addTaskMaintenanceProcessor,
            ITaskByIdInquiryProcessor taskByIdInquiryProcessor)
        {
            _addTaskMaintenanceProcessor = addTaskMaintenanceProcessor;
            _taskByIdInquiryProcessor = taskByIdInquiryProcessor;
        }
```

```
        [Route("", Name = "AddTaskRoute")]
        [HttpPost]
        [Authorize(Roles = Constants.RoleNames.Manager)]
        public IHttpActionResult AddTask(HttpRequestMessage requestMessage, NewTask newTask)
        {
            var task = _addTaskMaintenanceProcessor.AddTask(newTask);
            var result = new TaskCreatedActionResult(requestMessage, task);
            return result;
        }

        [Route("{id:long}", Name = "GetTaskRoute")]
                public Task GetTask(long id)
                {
                    var task = _taskByIdInquiryProcessor.GetTask(id);
                    return task;
                }
    }
}
```

Also add an authorization filter to the controller to ensure that users are members of the Junior Worker role as a minimum requirement to perform any task operation:

```
[ApiVersion1RoutePrefix("tasks")]
[UnitOfWorkActionFilter]
[Authorize(Roles = Constants.RoleNames.JuniorWorker)]
public class TasksController : ApiController
```

At this point, [Authorize(Roles = Constants.RoleNames.Manager)] is still decorating the AddTask method, because adding a task requires a manager role. This illustrates how the authorization requirements of the filter with the narrower scope (the one on the method) are combined with the requirements of the one with the broader scope (the one on the class). As a result, the user has to satisfy all of the authorization requirements in the entire chain.

Now let's send a request to prove that this is working properly:

Get Task Request (abbreviated)

```
GET http://localhost:61589/api/v1/tasks/17 HTTP/1.1
Authorization: Basic YmhvZ2c6aWdub3JlZA==
```

Get Task Response (abbreviated)

```
HTTP/1.1 200 OK
Content-Type: application/json; charset=utf-8

{"TaskId":17,"Subject":"Fix something important","StartDate":"2014-05-13T00:52:34","DueDate":null,
"CreatedDate":"2014-05-10T19:02:52","CompletedDate":null,
"Status":{"StatusId":2,"Name":"In Progress","Ordinal":1},"Assignees":[],"Links":[]}
```

Yes, it looks like our Get operation is working properly, so we will move on to implementing a message handler that can conditionally remove sensitive data from the response. Before we do that, though, we need to add some members to the Task service model class for the message handler to use to remove sensitive data. Add the following members to WebApi2Book.Web.Api.Models.Task:

```
private bool _shouldSerializeAssignees;

public void SetShouldSerializeAssignees(bool shouldSerialize)
{
    _shouldSerializeAssignees = shouldSerialize;
}

public bool ShouldSerializeAssignees()
{
    return _shouldSerializeAssignees;
}
```

By convention, ASP.NET Web API uses reflection to call ShouldSerialize* methods to determine if specific public properties should be serialized. We leverage this behavior by pairing ShouldSerializeAssignees with the SetShouldSerializeAssignees method to control the serialization of assignees. In doing so, we have provided a mechanism for the message handler to dynamically control whether a task's assignees should be serialized.

Now it's time to implement the message handler, so implement it as follows:

```
using System.Net.Http;
using System.Threading;
using System.Threading.Tasks;
using log4net;
using WebApi2Book.Common;
using WebApi2Book.Common.Logging;
using WebApi2Book.Common.Security;
using Task = WebApi2Book.Web.Api.Models.Task;

namespace WebApi2Book.Web.Api.Security
{
    public class TaskDataSecurityMessageHandler : DelegatingHandler
    {
        private readonly ILog _log;
        private readonly IUserSession _userSession;

        public TaskDataSecurityMessageHandler(ILogManager logManager, IUserSession userSession)
        {
            _userSession = userSession;
            _log = logManager.GetLog(typeof (TaskDataSecurityMessageHandler));
        }

        protected override async Task<HttpResponseMessage> SendAsync(
            HttpRequestMessage request,
            CancellationToken cancellationToken)
        {
            var response = await base.SendAsync(request, cancellationToken);
```

```
        if (CanHandleResponse(response))
        {
            ApplySecurityToResponseData((ObjectContent) response.Content);
        }

        return response;
    }

    public bool CanHandleResponse(HttpResponseMessage response)
    {
        var objectContent = response.Content as ObjectContent;
        var canHandleResponse = objectContent != null && objectContent.ObjectType == typeof (Task);
        return canHandleResponse;
    }

    public void ApplySecurityToResponseData(ObjectContent responseObjectContent)
    {
        var removeSensitiveData = !_userSession.IsInRole(Constants.RoleNames.SeniorWorker);

        if (removeSensitiveData)
        {
            _log.DebugFormat("Applying security data masking for user {0}", _userSession.Username);
        }

        ((Task) responseObjectContent.Value).SetShouldSerializeAssignees
            (!removeSensitiveData);
    }
}

}
```

We'll review the handler code shortly, but first we need to write the code to configure it at run time. The handler is configured during application startup, so let's return to the WebApiApplication class and modify the RegisterHandlers method so that it appears as follows:

```
private void RegisterHandlers()
{
    var logManager = WebContainerManager.Get<ILogManager>();
    var userSession = WebContainerManager.Get<IUserSession>();

    GlobalConfiguration.Configuration.MessageHandlers.Add(
        new BasicAuthenticationMessageHandler(logManager,
            WebContainerManager.Get<IBasicSecurityService>()));

    GlobalConfiguration.Configuration.MessageHandlers.Add(
        new TaskDataSecurityMessageHandler(logManager, userSession));
}
```

■ **Note**   You'll also need to add a using directive for WebApi2Book.Common.Security to satisfy the compiler.

Looking back at the TaskDataSecurityMessageHandler implementation, we see that it, like BasicAuthenticationMessageHandler, derives from the ASP.NET Web API's DelegatingHandler base class. As with BasicAuthenticationMessageHandler, it overrides SendAsync. However, this time the implementation passes the request on down the chain with a call to base.SendAsync without inspecting it first. That's because this handler is interested only in the response, and it's going to act upon the response only if CanHandleResponse returns true, indicating that the response contains a Task service model object.

If CanHandleResponse indicates that the response contains task data, SendAsync invokes ApplySecurityToResponseData. It is here that the assignees are removed from the response if the user does not have a Senior Worker role. ApplySecurityToResponseData also logs the removal, for debugging purposes.

With this is in place, let's do a demo to make sure this sensitive data-removal functionality is working. The demo won't be terribly dramatic, because at this point we haven't associated any users (or "assignees") with any tasks. However, we can at least verify that the Assignees property is being removed from the response for users who lack a Senior Worker role.

First, we'll test the functionality with bhogg's credentials. We can do this by repeating the request we sent at the beginning of this section. You should see something similar to the following:

Get Task Request (abbreviated)

```
GET http://localhost:61589/api/v1/tasks/17 HTTP/1.1
Authorization: Basic YmhvZ2c6aWdub3JlZA==
```

Get Task Response (abbreviated)

```
HTTP/1.1 200 OK
Content-Type: application/json; charset=utf-8

{"TaskId":17,"Subject":"Fix something important","StartDate":"2014-05-13T00:52:34","DueDate":null,
"CreatedDate":"2014-05-10T19:02:52","CompletedDate":null,
"Status":{"StatusId":2,"Name":"In Progress","Ordinal":1},"Assignees":[],"Links":[]}
```

Note that the Assignees property appears in the response, as expected. Now repeat the test, this time with jdoe's credentials:

Get Task Request (abbreviated)

```
GET http://localhost:61589/api/v1/tasks/17 HTTP/1.1
Authorization: Basic amRvZTppZ25vcmVk
```

Get Task Response (abbreviated)

```
HTTP/1.1 200 OK
Content-Type: application/json; charset=utf-8

{"TaskId":17,"Subject":"Fix something important","StartDate":"2014-05-13T00:52:34","DueDate":null,
"CreatedDate":"2014-05-10T19:02:52","CompletedDate":null,
"Status":{"StatusId":2,"Name":"In Progress","Ordinal":1},"Links":[]}
```

Correct! User jdoe is only a junior worker, so the handler stripped the Assignees property from the response. Our security is working perfectly!

In the next section, we will bring token-based security into the picture and demonstrate how noninvasive the process of adding new authentication schemes can be with ASP.NET Web API.

Applying Token-Based Security

In the previous section, we demonstrated two important concepts. One, utilizing the extensibility of ASP.NET Web API to build a message handler that deals with a service-level concern (i.e., authentication). And two, the simple strategy and mechanics behind HTTP Basic authentication. Now we'd like to cover the basics of token-based security, as well as securing your ASP.NET Web API service with a token-based authentication library.

Token Basics

The most important concept to understand when it comes to token security is this: your service doesn't validate the user's credentials. In fact, your service doesn't even receive the user's credentials, at least in the traditional sense. In place of the user's user name and password, you receive a token that was created and signed by a trusted issuer. And because your service trusts the token issuer, you can merely accept the token as-is, without having to separately validate any credentials from the caller. In the context of securing your service, a token

- Identifies the user

- Contains contents that can be trusted (signed)

- Can be used in place of credentials (user name and password)

- Can contain other attributes

Your driver's license is an example of a "token" you use on a regular basis. Similar to the preceding list, a driver's license

- Identifies the holder

- Is generally trusted

- Requires no other secrets or proof

- Contains other attributes (or, "claims") of the holder

First, your driver's license is used to identify you. Pretty simple! Next, most people checking your driver's license will trust that it is valid. This is because the license is issued by a government entity and is usually signed in some fashion (e.g., water mark). And because it is trusted, the person checking your license doesn't need to ask for a password or PIN or any other proof of identity. And finally, your license includes other attributes beyond just your identity. In application security vernacular, the identity and other attributes are often referred to as "claims" (as discussed at the beginning of this chapter). That is, you are claiming various things about yourself with your license. You can see a sample driver's license in Figure 6-1.

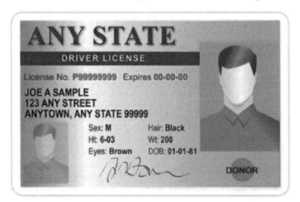

Figure 6-1. *Sample driver's license showing the holder's "claims" (Patrimonio Designs LTD/Shutterstock.com)*

For example, your license shows your claims of name (identity), address, gender, weight, height, eye color, and more. And again, because your license is created and signed by your state of residence, anyone reading it will trust the claims to be valid.

In short, a token is just a pile of claims that happens to be signed by a trusted issuer, thus removing the need for your service to store user names and passwords. This is huge, of course, as not having to store passwords greatly reduces the risk of your users' passwords being exposed.

The JSON Web Token

There are various formats of software security tokens available, and the current prevailing format is the JSON Web Token (*JWT*, for short). This format contains some header information, a signature, and the token's claims. In plain text, the token's claims might look like this:

```
{
    "Givenname":"Boss",
    "Surname":"Hogg",
    "UserId":"bhogg",
    "Email":"bhogg@example.com",
    "Height":"180cm",
    "Role":"Manager"
}
```

The token's header is used to specify some other things like signature algorithm, expiration date, name of the issue, and a few other attributes.

TOKENS WITH OAUTH2 AND OPENID CONNECT

In this book, we aren't going to cover the implementation details of OAuth integration with identity providers such as Facebook, Twitter, and Google. However, the OAuth2 and OpenId Connect specifications utilize the JWT token format. So as long as you're accepting JWTs, your service will easily accept access tokens generated and signed by these services. In fact, accepting these tokens is really all you need to do in order to support integration with such OAuth providers. Of course, we're skipping over some details, but that's essentially it. Most of the code required to support OAuth is actually found in the client or calling application, not the service.

Since the information in the token is really all we need in order to authorize the user (bhogg is a Manager, for example), our main job here is to validate the token's signature and convert the JWT to a .NET IPrincipal object. As you recall from the section on HTTP Basic authentication, we can utilize a message handler to perform this work. Then, once the HttpContext's user is set, the Authorize attribute already on our controllers and methods will protect us.

For this particular message handler, we're going to leverage an existing NuGet package instead of implementing it ourselves. You can read about the package here: https://www.nuget.org/packages/JwtAuthForWebAPI. Let's dive into the code that leverages this package for our task-management service!

Configuring the JwtAuthForWebAPI Package

With the solution open, run the following command in the Package Manager console:

```
install-package JwtAuthForWebAPI -Pre WebApi2Book.Web.Api
```

This will install our JWT-based NuGet package into the web project. Note that we're using a pre-release version of the package. This is needed because at the time of this writing the underlying JWT library from Microsoft is also still in pre-release. By the time you read this, though, you may need to remove the "-Pre" argument. The JwtAuthForWebAPI page on nuget.org will indicate the appropriate command to execute.

Once the package is installed, add the following to the configSections element in the web.config file:

```
<section name="JwtAuthForWebAPI" type="JwtAuthForWebAPI.JwtAuthForWebApiConfigurationSection"/>
```

Then add the following section, below the configSections element:

```
<JwtAuthForWebAPI
    AllowedAudience="http://www.example.com"
    Issuer="corp"
    SymmetricKey="cXdlcnR5dWlvcGFzZGZnaGprbHp4Y3bimOxMjMONTY=" />
```

In a minute, we will add the code that reads these configuration values. But first, a few words about the SymmetricKey property.

You can sign JWTs by using either a private key (of a public/private key pair) or a shared symmetric key. An example of using a public/private key pair is utilizing an X.509 certificate. Certificates have been around for a number of years, and mechanisms are in place for ensuring their authenticity and for storing and managing them securely. In the configuration code just shown, if we wanted to use a certificate instead of a symmetric key, we would use the SubjectCertificateName property instead, like this (replacing the SymmetricKey property):

```
SubjectCertificateName="CN=JwtAuthForWebAPI Example"
```

One could argue that using certificates for signing these tokens is more secure. Regardless, using a shared symmetric key is easier to demonstrate, so that's what we're doing here. You can create your own symmetric key by running the following statements within PowerShell:

```
$keyBytes=[System.Text.Encoding]::UTF8.GetBytes("qwertyuiopasdfghjklzxcvbnm123456")
[System.Convert]::ToBase64String($keyBytes)
```

The first line creates a byte array from a 32-character string. The second line then converts the array to a base64 encoded string. This method of signing is called "shared key" because, unlike public/private key pairs, the issuer and the service must both have a copy of the same key (i.e., the base64 string).

You are free to use the symmetric key shown earlier, or you can generate your own. You should definitely generate your own if you plan to use a symmetric key in a production environment, though!

Next we need to add the code that configures the associated message handler. Add the following to the bottom of the RegisterHandlers method in the WebApiApplication class:

```
var builder = new SecurityTokenBuilder();
var reader = new ConfigurationReader();
GlobalConfiguration.Configuration.MessageHandlers.Add(
    new JwtAuthenticationMessageHandler
    {
        AllowedAudience = reader.AllowedAudience,
        Issuer = reader.Issuer,
        SigningToken = builder.CreateFromKey(reader.SymmetricKey)
    });
```

■ **Note** You'll also need to add a using directive for JwtAuthForWebAPI to satisfy the compiler.

The SecurityTokenBuilder object is used to create a SecurityToken from a symmetric key. *Note that you can use the same builder to create a* SecurityToken *from a certificate subject name.* And the ConfigurationReader object is used to read the configuration values we added to the web.config file.

And that's it! The JWT-based handler is now configured and added to the ASP.NET Web API message handlers collection. At this point, your service can accept JWTs that are signed with the specific symmetric key, intended for the specified audience, and issued by the specific issuer. The rest of the security-related code we've already added (i.e., the Authorize attribute and IUserSession) will work exactly as they did before. And because we've added to the handlers collection, our service can now accept either HTTP Basic authentication or JWTs.

Let's make a few JWT-based calls to our service using Fiddler.

Getting a Task Using a JWT

Before we can make a call with Fiddler, we need to first create a valid JWT. If you look in the code associated with this book, you will find a small Console application called CreateJwt. The code is very simple, the guts of which look like this:

```
using System;
using System.Diagnostics;
using System.IdentityModel.Protocols.WSTrust;
using System.IdentityModel.Tokens;
using System.Security.Claims;

namespace CreateJwt
{
    internal class Program
    {
        private const string SymmetricKey = "cXdlcnR5dWlvcGFzZGZnaGprbHp4Y3Zibm0xMjM0NTY=";

        private static void Main(string[] args)
        {
            var key = Convert.FromBase64String(SymmetricKey);
            var credentials = new SigningCredentials(
                new InMemorySymmetricSecurityKey(key),
                "http://www.w3.org/2001/04/xmldsig-more#hmac-sha256",
                "http://www.w3.org/2001/04/xmlenc#sha256");

            var tokenDescriptor = new SecurityTokenDescriptor
            {
                Subject = new ClaimsIdentity(new[]
                {
                    new Claim(ClaimTypes.Name, "bhogg"),
                    new Claim(ClaimTypes.GivenName, "Boss"),
                    new Claim(ClaimTypes.Surname, "Hogg"),
                    new Claim(ClaimTypes.Role, "Manager"),
                    new Claim(ClaimTypes.Role, "SeniorWorker"),
                    new Claim(ClaimTypes.Role, "JuniorWorker")
                }),
```

```
                TokenIssuerName = "corp",
                AppliesToAddress = "http://www.example.com",
                SigningCredentials = credentials,
                Lifetime = new Lifetime(DateTime.UtcNow, DateTime.UtcNow.AddYears(10))
            };

            var tokenHandler = new JwtSecurityTokenHandler();
            var token = tokenHandler.CreateToken(tokenDescriptor);
            var tokenString = tokenHandler.WriteToken(token);

            Console.WriteLine(tokenString);
            Debug.WriteLine(tokenString);

            Console.ReadLine();
        }
    }
}
```

Note first that the symmetric key matches that which we placed in the web.config file in the previous section. Second, we are specifying a few claims—the roles being the most relevant for our discussion at this point. And third, we are setting the expiration date to 10 years from the current date. Obviously, a production-ready lifetime might be a little shorter!

And finally, the console app writes the generated JWT to the console (and debug window). The token generated when writing this book was

```
eyJ0eXAiOiJKV1QiLCJhbGciOiJIUzI1NiJ9.eyJpc3MiOiJjb3JwIiwiYXVkIjoiaHR0cDovL3d3dy
5leGFtcGxlLmNvbSIsIm5iZiI6MTQwMDU1Mzc1NywiZXhwIjoxNzE2MTcyOTU3LCJ1bmlxdWVfbmFtZ
SI6ImJob2dnIiwiZ2l2ZW5fbmFtZSI6IkJvc3MiLCJmYW1pbHlfbmFtZSI6IkhvZ2ciLCJyb2xlIjpb
Ik1hbmFnZXIiLCJkdW5pb3JJXb3JrZXIiXX0.Ls73kz8OrCaCNqzc3K32BVO9_LnJDL8c1g5AXKIzn8w
```

We will need to alter our API call by changing the Authorization header a bit. First, change the authorization scheme to Bearer. And then replace the base64-encoded user name and password with the generated JWT string. The resulting request looks like this:

```
GET http://localhost:52975/api/v1/tasks/2 HTTP/1.1
Authorization: Bearer
eyJ0eXAiOiJKV1QiLCJhbGciOiJIUzI1NiJ9.eyJpc3MiOiJjb3JwIiwiYXVkIjoiaHR0cD
ovL3d3dy5leGFtcGxlLmNvbSIsIm5iZiI6MTQwMDU1Mzc1NywiZXhwIjoxNzE2MTcyOTU3LCJ1bmlxdWVfbmFtZSI6Im
Job2dnIiwiZ2l2ZW5fbmFtZSI6IkJvc3MiLCJmYW1pbHlfbmFtZSI6IkhvZ2ciLCJyb2xlIjpbIk1hbmFnZXIiLCJkdW5pb3JJX
b3JrZXIiXX0.Ls73kz8OrCaCNqzc3K32BVO9_LnJDL8c1g5AXKIzn8w
```

■ **Note** The formatting here places the JWT on a separate line, but in reality there is only a space between "Bearer" and the JWT value, not a new line.

You can experiment with the token generation code in the CreateJwt console application, removing a role or two. In doing so, you will get the same unauthorized responses that we showed earlier in this chapter.

SSL, XSS, CORS, and CSRF

We would be remiss if we didn't at least acknowledge some of the security concerns within web applications today. Vulnerabilities dealing with cross-site scripting and cross-site request forgery, and supporting things like cross-origin requests and SSL, are most certainly at the top of web site architecture concerns. But given that we're talking about a REST service in this book, these concerns take on a slightly different meaning. In truth, most of them are more related to HTTP requests coming from web pages (i.e., web forms and AJAX calls) than they are API calls originating from non-web clients.

As such, we will cover topics like these in Chapter 9, when we demonstrate the consumption of our new task-management service by a couple different web pages.

Summary

In this chapter, you learned how to leverage the power of ASP.NET Web API message handlers to implement a service-wide feature: authentication. You built a handler for supporting HTTP Basic authentication by hand. And then, with just a few lines of code, you configured a NuGet package to provide support for JSON Web Token based security. Then you utilized the Authorize attribute at both the controller and controller action level to protect your service.

You also learned how to implement auditing using the new ASP.NET Web API async filter feature, as well as global handling of our own custom exceptions.

In the next chapter, we will explore how to support some miscellaneous service features like partial resource updates, resource relationships, and a few others.

CHAPTER 7

■ ■ ■

Dealing with Relationships, Partial Updates, and Other Complexities

In the previous chapter, after a brief introduction to the concepts of authentication and authorization, we added security to the task-management service. We began by applying an authorization filter to secure the AddTask method, and we complemented this by implementing a custom message handler supporting Basic authentication. After that, we implemented several scenarios (continuing with the theme of security) to further develop our application's functional capabilities and to demonstrate various ASP.NET Web API features (e.g., global exception handling of custom exceptions, scoping of filter attributes, serialization control, async filters). We wrapped things up by adding support for token-based security.

In this chapter, we will continue building out the RESTful API we designed in Chapter 3. We will deal with the following topics:

- **Relationships** We'll manage task assignees.

- **Partial updates** We'll update an existing task.

- **Input validation** We'll validate the request to update an existing task.

- **Paging of results** We'll get all tasks and use a query string to control the paging of results.

- **Context-sensitive hypermedia** We'll add links to the response.

And, naturally, we will highlight several great ASP.NET Web API features along the way. Now let's get started.

■ **Note** As in previous chapters, unless otherwise noted, we implement one public type per file. The file name should match the type name, and the file location should match the namespace name. For example, the WebApi2Book.Web.Common.Routing.ApiVersionConstraint class is in a file named "ApiVersionConstraint.cs", which is located in a project folder named "Routing" in the WebApi2Book.Web.Common project.

Task and User Relationships

We dealt with a simple relationship in the "Securing Non-Resource API Operations" section of Chapter 6—namely, the relationship between Task and Status. Now we will add support for a more complicated relationship—namely, the relationship between Task and User. Table 7-1, which is excerpted from Table 3-3 in Chapter 3, summarizes what we will implement in this section.

Table 7-1. *A List of Task Operations*

URI	Verb	Description
/api/tasks/123/users	PUT	Replaces all users on the specified task; returns the updated task in the response
/api/tasks/123/users	DELETE	Deletes all users from the specified task; returns the updated task in the response
/api/tasks/123/users/456	PUT	Adds the specified user (e.g., 456) as an assignee on the task; returns the updated task in the response
/api/tasks/123/users/456	DELETE	Deletes the specified user from the assignee list; returns the updated task in the response

We'll stick with our bottom-up approach of adding dependencies first, and the first dependency we'll implement is a query processor, as follows:

IUpdateTaskQueryProcessor Interface

```
using System.Collections.Generic;
using WebApi2Book.Data.Entities;

namespace WebApi2Book.Data.QueryProcessors
{
    public interface IUpdateTaskQueryProcessor
    {
        Task ReplaceTaskUsers(long taskId, IEnumerable<long> userIds);
        Task DeleteTaskUsers(long taskId);
        Task AddTaskUser(long taskId, long userId);
        Task DeleteTaskUser(long taskId, long userId);
    }
}
```

UpdateTaskQueryProcessor Class

```
using System.Collections.Generic;
using System.Linq;
using NHibernate;
using WebApi2Book.Data.Entities;
using WebApi2Book.Data.Exceptions;
using WebApi2Book.Data.QueryProcessors;

namespace WebApi2Book.Data.SqlServer.QueryProcessors
{
    public class UpdateTaskQueryProcessor : IUpdateTaskQueryProcessor
    {
        private readonly ISession _session;

        public UpdateTaskQueryProcessor(ISession session)
        {
            _session = session;
        }
```

```
public Task ReplaceTaskUsers(long taskId, IEnumerable<long> userIds)
{
    var task = GetValidTask(taskId);

    UpdateTaskUsers(task, userIds, false);

    _session.SaveOrUpdate(task);

    return task;
}

public Task DeleteTaskUsers(long taskId)
{
    var task = GetValidTask(taskId);

    UpdateTaskUsers(task, null, false);

    _session.SaveOrUpdate(task);

    return task;
}

public Task AddTaskUser(long taskId, long userId)
{
    var task = GetValidTask(taskId);

    UpdateTaskUsers(task, new[] {userId}, true);

    _session.SaveOrUpdate(task);

    return task;
}

public Task DeleteTaskUser(long taskId, long userId)
{
    var task = GetValidTask(taskId);

    var user = task.Users.FirstOrDefault(x => x.UserId == userId);
    if (user != null)
    {
        task.Users.Remove(user);
        _session.SaveOrUpdate(task);
    }

    return task;
}
```

```csharp
        public virtual Task GetValidTask(long taskId)
        {
            var task = _session.Get<Task>(taskId);
            if (task == null)
            {
                throw new RootObjectNotFoundException("Task not found");
            }

            return task;
        }

        public virtual User GetValidUser(long userId)
        {
            var user = _session.Get<User>(userId);
            if (user == null)
            {
                throw new ChildObjectNotFoundException("User not found");
            }

            return user;
        }

        public virtual void UpdateTaskUsers(Task task, IEnumerable<long> userIds, bool
                                            appendToExisting)
        {
            if (!appendToExisting)
            {
                task.Users.Clear();
            }

            if (userIds != null)
            {
                foreach (var user in userIds.Select(GetValidUser))
                {
                    if (!task.Users.Contains(user))
                    {
                        task.Users.Add(user);
                    }
                }
            }
        }
    }
}
```

Dependency Configuration (add to NinjectConfigurator.AddBindings)

```csharp
container.Bind<IUpdateTaskQueryProcessor>().To<UpdateTaskQueryProcessor>().InRequestScope();
```

Note that three of the four interface methods (ReplaceTaskUsers, DeleteTaskUsers, and AddTaskUser) have a similar pattern of implementation. First, a Task is fetched from the database. Then the Users collection is updated appropriately via the UpdateTaskUsers method. Finally, the updated Task is persisted back to the database with its updated Users associations.

UpdateTaskUsers is a helper method that either replaces the existing Users collection in its entirety or appends something to it, as directed by the calling method to produce the desired result. The foreach loop ensures that duplicate users aren't added to the specified task. This protects the *idempotence* (remember that term from Chapter 2?) of the operations that rely upon this method.

The only other nontrivial method is DeleteTaskUser. This method supports the idempotence of the "remove the user from the task" operation by first ensuring that the specified user is still associated with the task before trying to break the association.

The next dependency to implement is also simple; in fact, it's simpler than the query processor we just discussed. Implement it as follows:

ITaskUsersMaintenanceProcessor Interface

```
using System.Collections.Generic;
using WebApi2Book.Web.Api.Models;

namespace WebApi2Book.Web.Api.MaintenanceProcessing
{
    public interface ITaskUsersMaintenanceProcessor
    {
        Task ReplaceTaskUsers(long taskId, IEnumerable<long> userIds);
        Task DeleteTaskUsers(long taskId);
        Task AddTaskUser(long taskId, long userId);
        Task DeleteTaskUser(long taskId, long userId);
    }
}
```

TaskUsersMaintenanceProcessor Class

```
using System.Collections.Generic;
using WebApi2Book.Common.TypeMapping;
using WebApi2Book.Data.QueryProcessors;
using WebApi2Book.Web.Api.Models;

namespace WebApi2Book.Web.Api.MaintenanceProcessing
{
    public class TaskUsersMaintenanceProcessor : ITaskUsersMaintenanceProcessor
    {
        private readonly IAutoMapper _autoMapper;
        private readonly IUpdateTaskQueryProcessor _queryProcessor;

        public TaskUsersMaintenanceProcessor(IUpdateTaskQueryProcessor queryProcessor,
            IAutoMapper autoMapper)
        {
            _queryProcessor = queryProcessor;
            _autoMapper = autoMapper;
        }
```

```
    public Task ReplaceTaskUsers(long taskId, IEnumerable<long> userIds)
    {
        var taskEntity = _queryProcessor.ReplaceTaskUsers(taskId, userIds);
        return CreateTaskResponse(taskEntity);
    }

    public Task DeleteTaskUsers(long taskId)
    {
        var taskEntity = _queryProcessor.DeleteTaskUsers(taskId);
        return CreateTaskResponse(taskEntity);
    }

    public Task AddTaskUser(long taskId, long userId)
    {
        var taskEntity = _queryProcessor.AddTaskUser(taskId, userId);
        return CreateTaskResponse(taskEntity);
    }

    public Task DeleteTaskUser(long taskId, long userId)
    {
        var taskEntity = _queryProcessor.DeleteTaskUser(taskId, userId);
        return CreateTaskResponse(taskEntity);
    }

    public virtual Task CreateTaskResponse(Data.Entities.Task taskEntity)
    {
        var task = _autoMapper.Map<Task>(taskEntity);
        return task;
    }
  }
}
```

Dependency Configuration (add to NinjectConfigurator.AddBindings)

```
container.Bind<ITaskUsersMaintenanceProcessor>().To<TaskUsersMaintenanceProcessor>()
    .InRequestScope();
```

TaskUsersMaintenanceProcessor is so trivial that it requires little discussion. Here are some items to note before moving on:

- The implementation is necessarily dependent upon the WebApi2Book2.Data and WebApi2Book.Web.Api.Models projects. Therefore, it would have been inappropriate to push its logic down into the query processor, which should have no knowledge of WebApi2Book.Web.Api.Models.

- The full implementation, available in our GitHub repository, includes logic in CreateTaskResponse that adds hypermedia links to the Task response. This is the main reason why CreateTaskResponse was broken out into a separate method. In this section, we're focusing on relationships, so that detail was omitted here. We'll get to links later in the chapter.

And now to bring it all together, implement the TaskUsersController class as follows:

```
using System.Collections.Generic;
using System.Web.Http;
using WebApi2Book.Common;
using WebApi2Book.Web.Api.MaintenanceProcessing;
using WebApi2Book.Web.Api.Models;
using WebApi2Book.Web.Common;
using WebApi2Book.Web.Common.Routing;

namespace WebApi2Book.Web.Api.Controllers.V1
{
    [ApiVersion1RoutePrefix("tasks")]
    [UnitOfWorkActionFilter]
    [Authorize(Roles = Constants.RoleNames.SeniorWorker)]
    public class TaskUsersController : ApiController
    {
        private readonly ITaskUsersMaintenanceProcessor _taskUsersMaintenanceProcessor;

        public TaskUsersController(ITaskUsersMaintenanceProcessor taskUsersMaintenanceProcessor)
        {
            _taskUsersMaintenanceProcessor = taskUsersMaintenanceProcessor;
        }

        [Route("{taskId:long}/users", Name = "ReplaceTaskUsersRoute")]
        [HttpPut]
        public Task ReplaceTaskUsers(long taskId, [FromBody] IEnumerable<long> userIds)
        {
            var task = _taskUsersMaintenanceProcessor.ReplaceTaskUsers(taskId, userIds);
            return task;
        }

        [Route("{taskId:long}/users", Name = "DeleteTaskUsersRoute")]
        [HttpDelete]
        public Task DeleteTaskUsers(long taskId)
        {
            var task = _taskUsersMaintenanceProcessor.DeleteTaskUsers(taskId);
            return task;
        }

        [Route("{taskId:long}/users/{userId:long}", Name = "AddTaskUserRoute")]
        [HttpPut]
        public Task AddTaskUser(long taskId, long userId)
        {
            var task = _taskUsersMaintenanceProcessor.AddTaskUser(taskId, userId);
            return task;
        }
```

```
[Route("{taskId:long}/users/{userId:long}", Name = "DeleteTaskUserRoute")]
[HttpDelete]
public Task DeleteTaskUser(long taskId, long userId)
{
    var task = _taskUsersMaintenanceProcessor.DeleteTaskUser(taskId, userId);
    return task;
}
    }
}
```

Again, it's another very simple class, at least at first glance. However, note the route prefix attribute, the various route attributes, the HttpPut and HttpDelete attributes, the authorization filter, and the unit-of-work attribute. Through the use of these declarative attributes (which we've discussed in previous chapters), a lot of cross-cutting concerns are taken care of for us so that we don't need to clutter the controller code with them. These ensure that the request gets routed to the correct controller and action method, is restricted to users with the required role, and is processed in the context of a unit of work to ensure database updates are handled properly. It turns that there's a lot more going on in here than one would think by a simple line count!

Let's test it out to ensure it's working properly. We'll follow the order of operations listed in Table 7-1, so let's start by assigning a couple of users to a task. We'll use our favorite task (#17), and we'll use bhogg's credentials because we know he's authorized (because he's a senior worker). *As always, be sure to substitute the actual number of the task you created back in Chapter 5—and have been working with ever since—if it wasn't 17:*

Replace Task Users Request (abbreviated)

```
PUT http://localhost:61589/api/v1/tasks/17/users/ HTTP/1.1
Content-Type: application/json; charset=utf-8
Authorization: Basic YmhvZ2c6aWdub3J1lZA==

[2,3]
```

Note how we need to specify only the user IDs, not entire users, in the request message body to add them as assignees. And now for the response:

Replace Task Users Response (abbreviated)

```
HTTP/1.1 200 OK
Content-Type: application/json; charset=utf-8

{"TaskId":17,"Subject":"Fix something important","StartDate":"2014-05-13T00:52:34","DueDate":null,
"CreatedDate":"2014-05-10T19:02:52","CompletedDate":null,
"Status":{"StatusId":2,"Name":"In Progress","Ordinal":1},
"Assignees":[{"UserId":2,"Username":"jbob","Firstname":"Jim","Lastname":"Bob",
"Links":[]},{"UserId":3,"Username":"jdoe","Firstname":"John","Lastname":"Doe","Links":[]}],
"Links":[]}
```

Excellent—Jim Bob and John Doe have been added as assignees to the task! We have finally associated User objects with Task objects. Because the operation is idempotent, you should be able to send the request multiple times and get the same response; in fact, this applies to all operations in this section.

Now let's remove all assignees from the task:

Remove Task Users Request (abbreviated)

```
DELETE http://localhost:61589/api/v1/tasks/17/users HTTP/1.1
Content-Type: application/json; charset=utf-8
Authorization: Basic YmhvZ2c6aWdub3J1ZA==
```

Remove Task Users Response (abbreviated)

```
HTTP/1.1 200 OK
Content-Type: application/json; charset=utf-8
```

```
{"TaskId":17,"Subject":"Fix something important","StartDate":"2014-05-13T00:52:34","DueDate":null,
"CreatedDate":"2014-05-10T19:02:52","CompletedDate":null,
"Status":{"StatusId":2,"Name":"In Progress","Ordinal":1},"Assignees":[],"Links":[]}
```

As expected, we're back to the situation where task #17 has no assignees. Next, let's assign a single user to the task. Note the assignee's ID is in the URL instead of the message body this time:

Add Task User Request (abbreviated)

```
PUT http://localhost:61589/api/v1/tasks/17/users/2 HTTP/1.1
Content-Type: application/json; charset=utf-8
Authorization: Basic YmhvZ2c6aWdub3J1ZA==
```

Add Task User Response (abbreviated)

```
HTTP/1.1 200 OK
Content-Type: application/json; charset=utf-8
```

```
{"TaskId":17,"Subject":"Fix something important","StartDate":"2014-05-13T00:52:34","DueDate":null,
"CreatedDate":"2014-05-10T19:02:52","CompletedDate":null,
"Status":{"StatusId":2,"Name":"In Progress","Ordinal":1},
"Assignees":[{"UserId":2,"Username":"jbob","Firstname":"Jim","Lastname":"Bob","Links":[]}],
"Links":[]}
```

This looks good; user #2 (Jim Bob) is back on the task. However, to complete our testing, go ahead and remove him as follows by specifying his ID in the URL:

Remove Task User Request (abbreviated)

```
DELETE http://localhost:61589/api/v1/tasks/17/users/2 HTTP/1.1
Content-Type: application/json; charset=utf-8
Authorization: Basic YmhvZ2c6aWdub3J1ZA==
```

Remove Task User Response (abbreviated)

```
HTTP/1.1 200 OK
Content-Type: application/json; charset=utf-8
```

```
{"TaskId":17,"Subject":"Fix something important","StartDate":"2014-05-13T00:52:34","DueDate":null,
"CreatedDate":"2014-05-10T19:02:52","CompletedDate":null,
"Status":{"StatusId":2,"Name":"In Progress","Ordinal":1},"Assignees":[],"Links":[]}
```

And it looks like everything is working properly. Jim Bob is no longer assigned to the task.

We're ready to move on to the topic of partial updates, but before we do, please re-send the "Replace Task Users" request so that the task data is a little bit more interesting going forward!

Partial Update of a Task Using PUT/PATCH

Recalling our discussion of HTTP verbs from Chapter 2, we know that, by convention, a PUT operation is used to replace the corresponding resource in its entirety. This is why we designed our operation to update a task as shown in Table 7-2 (which is excerpted from Table 3-3 in Chapter 3).

Table 7-2. *Update a Task*

URI	Verb	Description
/api/tasks/123	PUT	Updates the specified task; returns the updated task in the response

However, often there are times when it is more desirable to apply a partial modification to a resource rather than replace the entire resource. It is for this reason the PATCH method was created, and in this section we will implement the ability to partially (or fully, as it turns out) update a task.

Let's begin with the query processor, and this one should look familiar: it's the UpdateTaskQueryProcessor. Add the highlighted lines to the interface and class as shown:

IUpdateTaskQueryProcessor Interface Modifications

```
using System.Collections.Generic;
using WebApi2Book.Data.Entities;
using PropertyValueMapType = System.Collections.Generic.Dictionary<string, object>;

namespace WebApi2Book.Data.QueryProcessors
{
    public interface IUpdateTaskQueryProcessor
    {
        Task GetUpdatedTask(long taskId, PropertyValueMapType updatedPropertyValueMap);
...
```

UpdateTaskQueryProcessor Class Modifications

```
using System.Collections.Generic;
using System.Linq;
using NHibernate;
using WebApi2Book.Data.Entities;
using WebApi2Book.Data.Exceptions;
using WebApi2Book.Data.QueryProcessors;
using PropertyValueMapType = System.Collections.Generic.Dictionary<string, object>;

namespace WebApi2Book.Data.SqlServer.QueryProcessors
{
    public class UpdateTaskQueryProcessor : IUpdateTaskQueryProcessor
    {
        private readonly ISession _session;
```

```
        public UpdateTaskQueryProcessor(ISession session)
        {
            _session = session;
        }

        public Task GetUpdatedTask(long taskId, PropertyValueMapType updatedPropertyValueMap)
        {
            var task = GetValidTask(taskId);

            var propertyInfos = typeof(Task).GetProperties();
            foreach (var propertyValuePair in updatedPropertyValueMap)
            {
                propertyInfos.Single(x => x.Name == propertyValuePair.Key)
                    .SetValue(task, propertyValuePair.Value);
            }

            _session.SaveOrUpdate(task);

            return task;
        }
...
```

The using directive is used to define an alias to the Dictionary<string,object> type. It is syntactic sugar and nothing more. Each element in an instance of the PropertyValueMapType is used to map a property name (string) to a corresponding property value (object). Note that the scope of a using directive is limited to the file in which it appears, which is why it appears in both files.

The real work is done in the GetUpdatedTask method. This method accepts two parameters: taskId, which uniquely identifies the Task to update, and updatedPropertyValueMap, which contains one element per property to be modified. Note that in an extreme case, the updatedPropertyValueMap could contain an element for every updateable Task property, and in this case the operation would function more like a PUT than a PATCH. Keep this in mind; we'll revisit it once we get to the controller.

Now let's analyze the GetUpdatedTask logic. First, the Task is fetched from the database. Next, each property on the Task that is represented by an element in the updatedPropertyValueMap is updated using reflection. Finally, the updated Task is persisted.

Gee, that was fairly easy. It seems like the hard part would be computing the updatedPropertyValueMap, so where does that logic appear? Well, we'll get to that in a little while. First, we're going to deviate from our usual bottom-up approach and implement the controller. The code will be in a noncompilable state for a while because we will be referencing an undefined dependency, but this approach will make things easier to explain in the long run. Go ahead and add the following method to TasksController:

```
[Route("{id:long}", Name = "UpdateTaskRoute")]
[HttpPut]
[HttpPatch]
[Authorize(Roles = Constants.RoleNames.SeniorWorker)]
public Task UpdateTask(long id, [FromBody] object updatedTask)
{
    var task = _updateTaskMaintenanceProcessor.UpdateTask(id, updatedTask);
    return task;
}
```

Then modify the constructor to accept a new (currently undefined) dependency, as shown in the highlighted code:

```
...
private readonly ITaskByIdInquiryProcessor _taskByIdInquiryProcessor;
private readonly IUpdateTaskMaintenanceProcessor _updateTaskMaintenanceProcessor;

public TasksController(IAddTaskMaintenanceProcessor addTaskMaintenanceProcessor,
    ITaskByIdInquiryProcessor taskByIdInquiryProcessor,
    IUpdateTaskMaintenanceProcessor updateTaskMaintenanceProcessor)
{
    _addTaskMaintenanceProcessor = addTaskMaintenanceProcessor;
    _taskByIdInquiryProcessor = taskByIdInquiryProcessor;
    _updateTaskMaintenanceProcessor = updateTaskMaintenanceProcessor;
}
...
```

The UpdateTask method appears deceptively simple. But, as we discussed in the previous section, a lot of things are happening behind the scenes. One of those things is the routing; the framework will route PUT *and* PATCH requests to this method. This is appropriate, as we recently mentioned, because sometimes a user will actually want to replace the targeted resource (i.e., the Task identified by the id parameter) with an entirely new representation. Also, some callers are not even able to send a request containing the PATCH verb (e.g., Flash-based callers have this restriction). So, even though we're blurring the lines somewhat between PUT and PATCH, this is one of those cases where a bit of pragmatism, rather than stubborn adherence to every detail of the HTTP specification, will make things more usable for the callers.

Another thing to note is that the updatedTask parameter is of type object. With the model-binding capabilities of ASP.NET Web API available, why would we want the method to accept the parsed request body as an object? For one thing, this makes partial updates possible. If the method accepted a Task containing data that the user wanted to *partially* update, it would also have to accept a list of property names to update. Otherwise, for example, how would the application know how to interpret a null Subject property? Would null indicate that the user wants to clear the subject, or would it indicate that he simply doesn't want to modify it? So, rather than requiring the caller to also provide a list of property names, the implementation accepts a potentially sparse representation of the Task.

Another reason for the updatedTask parameter's object type is that the framework will parse the task data from the message body and deliver it to UpdateTask in the form of JSON or XML, as determined by the request message's Content-Type header. The common type between these two representations is object; hence, the current signature.

At this point, we're ready to move on to implementing the IUpdateTaskMaintenanceProcessor and one of its dependencies, IUpdateablePropertyDetector. This pair of dependencies works together to compute the updatedPropertyValueMap that we discussed earlier. IUpdateablePropertyDetector determines which properties to update, and IUpdateTaskMaintenanceProcessor uses this information to populate the updatedPropertyValueMap. We'll also need to modify the Task service model class so that it can be inspected by the IUpdateablePropertyDetector. So much to do!

Let's start by adding the IUpdateablePropertyDetector as follows:

IUpdateablePropertyDetector Interface

```
using System.Collections.Generic;

namespace WebApi2Book.Web.Common
{
    public interface IUpdateablePropertyDetector
```

```
    {
        IEnumerable<string> GetNamesOfPropertiesToUpdate<TTargetType>(
            object objectContainingUpdatedData);
    }
}
```

JObjectUpdateablePropertyDetector Class

```
using System;
using System.Collections.Generic;
using System.ComponentModel.DataAnnotations;
using System.Linq;
using System.Reflection;
using Newtonsoft.Json.Linq;

namespace WebApi2Book.Web.Common
{
    public class JObjectUpdateablePropertyDetector : IUpdateablePropertyDetector
    {
        public IEnumerable<string> GetNamesOfPropertiesToUpdate<TTargetType>(
            object objectContainingUpdatedData)
        {
            var objectDataAsJObject = (JObject)objectContainingUpdatedData;

            var propertyInfos = typeof(TTargetType).GetProperties();

            var modifiablePropertyInfos = propertyInfos
                .Where(x =>
                {
                    var editableAttribute =
                        x.GetCustomAttributes(typeof(EditableAttribute)).FirstOrDefault() as
                            EditableAttribute;
                    return editableAttribute != null && editableAttribute.AllowEdit;
                }
                );

            var namesOfSuppliedProperties =
                objectDataAsJObject.Properties().Select(x => x.Name);

            return
                modifiablePropertyInfos.Select(x => x.Name)
                    .Where(x => namesOfSuppliedProperties.Contains(
                        x, StringComparer.InvariantCultureIgnoreCase));
        }
    }
}
```

Note that you will need to reference System.ComponentModel.DataAnnotations in the WebApi2Book.Web.Common project after implementing the preceding class.

Dependency Configuration (add to NinjectConfigurator.AddBindings)

```
container.Bind<IUpdateablePropertyDetector>().To<JObjectUpdateablePropertyDetector>()
    .InSingletonScope();
```

The first thing you may have noted, from the class name if nothing else, is that some of this implementation is JSON-specific. We could have provided an implementation to handle both JSON and XML (hint: by examining the Content-Type header of the request message and delegating to the appropriate code), but we figured it would be a better use of our time together to try to keep the focus on ASP.NET Web API and avoid getting bogged down in those sorts of details. Besides, the basic algorithms are the same regardless of content type.

As you can see, the parsed task object enters the GetNamesOfPropertiesToUpdate method and is immediately cast to a JObject, one of the many useful types in the powerful Json.NET package—which, by the way, was automatically added when you created the project back in Chapter 4. We'll return to it in a minute.

The next thing that happens is the property metadata is calculated based on the generic parameter type (which, in this scenario, means TTargetType is going to arrive as Task). Then, inspecting this property metadata one property at a time, we build a list of PropertyInfo instances. Each element in the list corresponds to a property in the target class decorated with an EditableAttribute and having an AllowEdit value of true. This is important, because we want the user to be able to update only editable properties. (This is a guard against overposting.)

Next, we return to the JObject, from which we extracted the names of the properties represented in the task fragment. We then filter this list (namesOfSuppliedProperties) against the list of modifiable properties (modifiablePropertyInfos) and return the result as a list of names of the properties to update. In this way, we have provided a flexible mechanism that can support full or partial updates in a way that is not vulnerable to overposting attacks.

Now let's decorate Task with attributes to indicate which properties are modifiable. The class should appear as follows:

```
using System;
using System.Collections.Generic;
using System.ComponentModel.DataAnnotations;

namespace WebApi2Book.Web.Api.Models
{
    public class Task : ILinkContaining
    {
        private List<Link> _links;
        private bool _shouldSerializeAssignees;

        [Key]
        public long? TaskId { get; set; }

        [Editable(true)]
        public string Subject { get; set; }

        [Editable(true)]
        public DateTime? StartDate { get; set; }

        [Editable(true)]
        public DateTime? DueDate { get; set; }

        [Editable(false)]
        public DateTime? CreatedDate { get; set; }
```

```
    [Editable(false)]
    public DateTime? CompletedDate { get; set; }

    [Editable(false)]
    public Status Status { get; set; }

    [Editable(false)]
    public List<User> Assignees { get; set; }

    [Editable(false)]
    public List<Link> Links
    {
        get { return _links ?? (_links = new List<Link>()); }
        set { _links = value; }
    }

    public void AddLink(Link link)
    {
        Links.Add(link);
    }

    public void SetShouldSerializeAssignees(bool shouldSerialize)
    {
        _shouldSerializeAssignees = shouldSerialize;
    }

    public bool ShouldSerializeAssignees()
    {
        return _shouldSerializeAssignees;
    }
    }
}
```

You need to reference System.ComponentModel.DataAnnotations from the WebApi2Book.Web.Api.Models project to satisfy the compiler.

Note the Key attribute, which identifies the property that uniquely identifies each instance. Also, note that certain properties are not user-editable. For example, CreatedDate is set by the application; it is not user-editable. Also, Assignees is not user-editable because we want users to modify a task's assignees via the relationships API we implemented in the previous section.

Now we are ready to add the missing piece that sits between the controller and the query processor: the IUpdateTaskMaintenanceProcessor. Implement it as follows:

IUpdateTaskMaintenanceProcessor Interface

```
using WebApi2Book.Web.Api.Models;

namespace WebApi2Book.Web.Api.MaintenanceProcessing
{
    public interface IUpdateTaskMaintenanceProcessor
    {
        Task UpdateTask(long taskId, object taskFragment);
    }
}
```

UpdateTaskMaintenanceProcessor Class

```
using System.Linq;
using Newtonsoft.Json.Linq;
using WebApi2Book.Common.TypeMapping;
using WebApi2Book.Data.QueryProcessors;
using WebApi2Book.Web.Api.Models;
using WebApi2Book.Web.Common;
using PropertyValueMapType = System.Collections.Generic.Dictionary<string, object>;

namespace WebApi2Book.Web.Api.MaintenanceProcessing
{
    public class UpdateTaskMaintenanceProcessor : IUpdateTaskMaintenanceProcessor
    {
        private readonly IAutoMapper _autoMapper;
        private readonly IUpdateTaskQueryProcessor _queryProcessor;
        private readonly IUpdateablePropertyDetector _updateablePropertyDetector;

        public UpdateTaskMaintenanceProcessor(IUpdateTaskQueryProcessor queryProcessor,
            IAutoMapper autoMapper,
            IUpdateablePropertyDetector updateablePropertyDetector)
        {
            _queryProcessor = queryProcessor;
            _autoMapper = autoMapper;
            _updateablePropertyDetector = updateablePropertyDetector;
        }

        public Task UpdateTask(long taskId, object taskFragment)
        {
            var taskFragmentAsJObject = (JObject) taskFragment;
            var taskContainingUpdateData = taskFragmentAsJObject.ToObject<Task>();

            var updatedPropertyValueMap = GetPropertyValueMap(
                taskFragmentAsJObject, taskContainingUpdateData);

            var updatedTaskEntity = _queryProcessor.GetUpdatedTask(taskId, updatedPropertyValueMap);

            var task = _autoMapper.Map<Task>(updatedTaskEntity);

            return task;
        }

        public virtual PropertyValueMapType GetPropertyValueMap(
            JObject taskFragment, Task taskContainingUpdateData)
        {
            var namesOfModifiedProperties = _updateablePropertyDetector
                .GetNamesOfPropertiesToUpdate<Task>(taskFragment).ToList();

            var propertyInfos = typeof (Task).GetProperties();
            var updatedPropertyValueMap = new PropertyValueMapType();
```

```
        foreach (var propertyName in namesOfModifiedProperties)
        {
            var propertyValue = propertyInfos.Single(
                x => x.Name == propertyName).GetValue(taskContainingUpdateData);
            updatedPropertyValueMap.Add(propertyName, propertyValue);
        }

        return updatedPropertyValueMap;
    }
  }
}
```

Dependency Configuration (add to NinjectConfigurator.AddBindings)

```
container.Bind<IUpdateTaskMaintenanceProcessor>().To<UpdateTaskMaintenanceProcessor>()
    .InRequestScope();
```

As with JObjectUpdateablePropertyDetector, you can see that parts of this implementation are JSON-specific. As with JObjectUpdateablePropertyDetector, we could have also supported XML; however, for similar reasons as stated previously, we chose to leave that as an exercise for the motivated reader.

Let's analyze the current implementation, starting with UpdateTask. UpdateTask begins by using JObject to parse the task fragment into an actual Task instance. Next, it invokes GetPropertyValueMap, which uses the task fragment and the parsed Task instance to compute the updatedPropertyValueMap that gets passed to the query processor. As we discussed earlier, the updates actually get applied in the query processor. Finally, the automapper maps the task entity returned by the query processor into a service model object, which is then returned to the method caller (which is, in this case, the controller).

Diving down into GetPropertyValueMap, we see it first uses the IUpdateablePropertyDetector to determine the names of properties that need to be updated. Then, for each of those properties, it gets the corresponding value from the Task instance and adds the property name and value pair to the map. Finally, it returns the map to the method caller.

Now that we've completed the implementation and answered the question about the origin of the updatedPropertyValueMap (which was asked when we were discussing UpdateTaskQueryProcessor), it's time to prove that this actually works! We'll start with a PUT, using bhogg's credentials (he's a senior worker, so he's authorized) and our favorite task (#17):

Update Task Request - PUT (abbreviated)

```
PUT http://localhost:61589/api/v1/tasks/17 HTTP/1.1
Content-Type: application/json; charset=utf-8
Authorization: Basic YmhvZ2c6aWdub3JlZA==

{"Subject":"Get a new HDMI cable",
  "CreatedDate":"2011-01-01"
}
```

Update Task Response - PUT (abbreviated)

```
HTTP/1.1 200 OK
Content-Type: application/json; charset=utf-8

{"TaskId":17,"Subject":"Get a new HDMI cable","StartDate":"2014-05-13T00:52:34","DueDate":null,
"CreatedDate":"2014-05-10T19:02:52","CompletedDate":null,
"Status":{"StatusId":2,"Name":"In Progress","Ordinal":1},
"Assignees":[{"UserId":2,"Username":"jbob","Firstname":"Jim","Lastname":"Bob",
"Links":[]},{"UserId":3,"Username":"jdoe","Firstname":"John","Lastname":"Doe","Links":[]}],
"Links":[]}
```

Very nice! Notice how the `Subject` was updated but the `CreatedDate` was not. It looks like our overpost-proof update functionality is working correctly. We'll conclude by doing something similar, only this time with a PATCH:

Update Task Request - PATCH (abbreviated)

```
PATCH http://localhost:61589/api/v1/tasks/17 HTTP/1.1
Content-Type: application/json; charset=utf-8
Authorization: Basic YmhvZ2c6aWdub3JlZA==

{"Subject":"Fix the compile error that broke the build",
  "CompletedDate":"2011-01-01"
}
```

Update Task Response - PATCH (abbreviated)

```
HTTP/1.1 200 OK
Content-Type: application/json; charset=utf-8

{"TaskId":17,"Subject":"Fix the compile error that broke the build",
"StartDate":"2014-05-13T00:52:34","DueDate":null,
"CreatedDate":"2014-05-10T19:02:52","CompletedDate":null,
"Status":{"StatusId":2,"Name":"In Progress","Ordinal":1},
"Assignees":[{"UserId":2,"Username":"jbob","Firstname":"Jim","Lastname":"Bob","Links":[]},
{"UserId":3,"Username":"jdoe","Firstname":"John","Lastname":"Doe","Links":[]}],"Links":[]}
```

Great, it's working perfectly; `Subject` was updated but `CompletedDate` was not. But how do we guard against callers passing in garbage via the message body? As a matter of fact, that's our next topic!

Validation Using an Action Filter

We've made great progress, but we're still lacking input validation. What if the contents of updatedTask parameter in the TasksController class' UpdateTask method were gibberish, having nothing to do with a task? We'd be wasting valuable server resources by beginning to process such a request, only to have it fail with an exception. What we need is a way to validate the request before it even gets to the action method. Fortunately, ASP.NET Web API provides support for such validation, through the use of custom action filters.

Specialized Action Filter to Validate Task Updates

We've implemented action filters before (e.g., the `UnitOfWorkActionFilterAttribute` and `UserAuditAttribute` classes), so some of this should look familiar. Let's begin by implementing the attribute (adding it as follows), and then we'll analyze it and apply it to the `UpdateTask` action method:

```
using System.Net;
using System.Net.Http;
using System.Web.Http.Controllers;
using System.Web.Http.Filters;
using log4net;
using Newtonsoft.Json;
using Newtonsoft.Json.Linq;
using WebApi2Book.Common.Logging;
using WebApi2Book.Web.Api.Models;
using WebApi2Book.Web.Common;

namespace WebApi2Book.Web.Api.MaintenanceProcessing
{
    public class ValidateTaskUpdateRequestAttribute : ActionFilterAttribute
    {
        private readonly ILog _log;

        public ValidateTaskUpdateRequestAttribute()
            : this(WebContainerManager.Get<ILogManager>())
        {
        }

        public ValidateTaskUpdateRequestAttribute(ILogManager logManager)
        {
            _log = logManager.GetLog(typeof (ValidateTaskUpdateRequestAttribute));
        }

        public override bool AllowMultiple
        {
            get { return false; }
        }

        public override void OnActionExecuting(HttpActionContext actionContext)
        {
            var taskId = (long) actionContext.ActionArguments[ActionParameterNames.TaskId];
            var taskFragment =
                (JObject) actionContext.ActionArguments[ActionParameterNames.TaskFragment];
            _log.DebugFormat("{0} = {1}", ActionParameterNames.TaskFragment, taskFragment);

            if (taskFragment == null)
            {
                const string errorMessage = "Malformed or null request.";
                _log.Debug(errorMessage);
                actionContext.Response = actionContext.Request.CreateErrorResponse(
                    HttpStatusCode.BadRequest, errorMessage);
                return;
            }
```

```
        try
        {
            var task = taskFragment.ToObject<Task>();
            if (task.TaskId.HasValue && task.TaskId != taskId)
            {
                const string errorMessage = "Task ids do not match.";
                _log.Debug(errorMessage);
                actionContext.Response = actionContext.Request.CreateErrorResponse(
                    HttpStatusCode.BadRequest, errorMessage);
            }
        }
        catch (JsonException ex)
        {
            _log.Debug(ex.Message);
            actionContext.Response = actionContext.Request.CreateErrorResponse(
                HttpStatusCode.BadRequest, ex.Message);
        }
    }

    public static class ActionParameterNames
    {
        public const string TaskFragment = "updatedTask";
        public const string TaskId = "id";
    }
    }
}
```

Only the OnActionExecuting method contains logic that we haven't explained previously when analyzing other action filters, so we'll focus on it. It begins by accessing the task's id from the HttpActionContext. We know this is safe to do because, by this point in the request processing pipeline, the controller's UpdateTask action method has already been selected by ASP.NET Web API as the target of the request, and UpdateTask has a route constraint requiring a parameter named id of type long. ASP.NET Web API uses routing information, including constraints, to automatically populate the HttpActionContext, so we can therefore be certain that an action argument named id of type long is available for us in actionContext.

Next, the data to be bound to the updatedTask parameter (i.e., taskFragment) is examined. If no JSON-compatible data is available, we create an error response using the action context's Request object and assign it to the action context's Response property. This prevents processing from reaching the controller action method.

After that, taskFragment, a JObject instance, is parsed into an actual Task. If this parsing fails (resulting in an exception), again, we create an error response and assign it to the action context's Response property to prevent processing from reaching the controller method.

Finally, the task identifiers from the URL and the message body are compared. If they differ, again—you guessed it—we create an error response and assign it to the action context's Response property to prevent processing from reaching the controller method. The request is considered valid if the action context has not been assigned a response by the time OnActionExecuting ends, and ASP.NET Web API will invoke the controller action method.

Note that this is again a JSON-specific implementation. This helps ensure that the JSON-specific processing described in the previous "Partial Update of a Task Using PUT/PATCH" section will be successful. As mentioned in that section, support for XML could have been provided—hint: by examining the (actionContext.Request.Content).Headers.ContentType. However, for reasons stated previously, we decided to forgo that exercise.

At this point, we've implemented the action filter, but for this to be effective, we need to apply the attribute to the controller method. Therefore, update the UpdateTask method so that it appears as follows:

```
[Route("{id:long}", Name = "UpdateTaskRoute")]
[HttpPut]
[HttpPatch]
[ValidateTaskUpdateRequest]
[Authorize(Roles = Constants.RoleNames.SeniorWorker)]
public Task UpdateTask(long id, [FromBody] object updatedTask)
{
    var task = _updateTaskMaintenanceProcessor.UpdateTask(id, updatedTask);
    return task;
}
```

Now let's see this in action. First send a valid request (using senior worker bhogg's credentials) to ensure we didn't break any of the update functionality we implemented previously:

Update Task Request (abbreviated)

```
PATCH http://localhost:61589/api/v1/tasks/17 HTTP/1.1
Content-Type: application/json; charset=utf-8
Authorization: Basic YmhvZ2c6aWdub3JlZA==

{"DueDate":"2014-05-20"}
```

Update Task Response (abbreviated)

```
HTTP/1.1 200 OK
Content-Type: application/json; charset=utf-8

{"TaskId":17,"Subject":"Fix the compile error that broke the build","StartDate":"2014-05-
13T00:52:34",
"DueDate":"2014-05-20T00:00:00","CreatedDate":"2014-05-10T19:02:52","CompletedDate":null,
"Status":{"StatusId":2,"Name":"In Progress","Ordinal":1},
"Assignees":[{"UserId":2,"Username":"jbob","Firstname":"Jim","Lastname":"Bob",
"Links":[]},{"UserId":3,"Username":"jdoe","Firstname":"John","Lastname":"Doe","Links":[]}],
"Links":[]}
```

Looks good. We successfully updated the due date. Next, let's send an invalid request (note the invalid DueDate) to ensure we're getting the proper response:

Update Task Request (abbreviated)

```
PATCH http://localhost:61589/api/v1/tasks/17 HTTP/1.1
Content-Type: application/json; charset=utf-8
Authorization: Basic YmhvZ2c6aWdub3JlZA==

{"DueDate":"2015-02-30"}
```

Update Task Response (abbreviated)

```
HTTP/1.1 400 Bad Request
Content-Type: application/json; charset=utf-8

{"Message":"Could not convert string to DateTime: 2015-02-30. Path 'DueDate'."}
```

This is exactly what we wanted to see. Our implementation filtered out the bad request before it ever reached the controller action method, and it returned an appropriate response by means of the HttpResponseException. There are some gaps in this implementation (for example, the action filter is not requiring a non-empty subject, and Subject is a required field in the database), but we trust we've provided a sufficient foundation for you to build upon as you add validation to your own projects. Therefore, instead of continuing to dwell on this very specialized action filter example, let's implement another action filter—one that is more general purpose.

Generalized Action Filter to Validate New Tasks

The action filter we built in the last section is suited only for the TaskController class' UpdateTask action method. Though it removes the cross-cutting concern of validation from the method, which is good, it is not suited for general use.

In this section, however, we will implement an action filter that may be used to decorate virtually any controller action method. There are three things required to make this particular approach effective:

1. Implement the action filter.

2. Use standard .NET data annotations to decorate the validation target class(es).

3. Apply the action filter attribute to the appropriate controller action method(s).

The action filter and the overall approach we are going to implement are general; however, our example will be to enforce a non-empty Subject for new tasks.

Let's get started by implementing the action filter. Add it as follows:

```
using System.Net;
using System.Net.Http;
using System.Web.Http.Controllers;
using System.Web.Http.Filters;

namespace WebApi2Book.Web.Common.Validation
{
    public class ValidateModelAttribute : ActionFilterAttribute
    {
        public override void OnActionExecuting(HttpActionContext actionContext)
        {
            if (actionContext.ModelState.IsValid == false)
            {
                actionContext.Response = actionContext.Request.CreateErrorResponse(
                    HttpStatusCode.BadRequest, actionContext.ModelState);
            }
        }
    }
```

```
        public override bool AllowMultiple
        {
            get { return false; }
        }
    }
}
```

As with ValidateTaskUpdateRequestAttribute, the only logic we need to discuss is in OnActionExecuting. This override leverages ASP.NET Web API's model-binding process, which performs validation, so we essentially get validation for free! By the time this method is invoked, the framework has performed the model binding and validation, and the results are available in the HttpActionContext. All we need to do is examine the action context's ModelState property and, if it returns false, create an error response using the action context's Request object and assign it to the action context's Response property. This prevents processing from reaching the controller action method.

Next, we need to decorate a class that will be the validation target. We'll use the NewTask service model class that is used to add new tasks. Modify it by decorating the Subject property so that it appears as follows:

```
using System;
using System.Collections.Generic;
using System.ComponentModel.DataAnnotations;

namespace WebApi2Book.Web.Api.Models
{
    public class NewTask
    {
        [Required(AllowEmptyStrings = false)]
        public string Subject { get; set; }

        public DateTime? StartDate { get; set; }

        public DateTime? DueDate { get; set; }

        public List<User> Assignees { get; set; }
    }
}
```

Finally, we need to apply the action filter attribute to the appropriate controller action method; therefore, modify the TasksController class' AddTask method so that it appears as follows:

```
[Route("", Name = "AddTaskRoute")]
[HttpPost]
[ValidateModel]
[Authorize(Roles = Constants.RoleNames.Manager)]
public IHttpActionResult AddTask(HttpRequestMessage requestMessage, NewTask newTask)
{
    var task = _addTaskMaintenanceProcessor.AddTask(newTask);
    var result = new TaskCreatedActionResult(requestMessage, task);
    return result;
}
```

■ **Note**   You'll need to add a `using` directive for `WebApi2Book.Web.Common.Validation` to satisfy the compiler.

And now it's demo time. We'll begin by submitting a valid request to demonstrate that we haven't broken anything (using bhogg's credentials, as usual):

Create Task Request (abbreviated)

```
POST http://localhost:61589/api/v1/tasks HTTP/1.1
Authorization: Basic YmhvZ2c6aWdub3JlZA==
Content-Type: text/json

{"Subject":"Clean the keyboard",
"DueDate":"2014-06-01"}
```

Create Task Response - (abbreviated)

```
HTTP/1.1 201 Created
Content-Type: text/json; charset=utf-8

{"TaskId":18,"Subject":"Clean the keyboard","StartDate":null,"DueDate":"2014-06-01T00:00:00",
"CreatedDate":"2014-05-19T19:10:40.4724304Z","CompletedDate":null,
"Status":{"StatusId":1,"Name":"Not Started","Ordinal":0},
"Assignees":[],"Links":[{"Rel":"self","Href":"http://localhost:61589/api/v1/
tasks/18","Method":"GET"}]}
```

This is looking good so far. Now submit a request with no subject (this should be rejected):

Create Task Request (abbreviated)

```
POST http://localhost:61589/api/v1/tasks HTTP/1.1
Authorization: Basic YmhvZ2c6aWdub3JlZA==
Content-Type: text/json

{"DueDate":"2014-06-01"}
```

Create Task Response (abbreviated)

```
HTTP/1.1 400 Bad Request
Content-Type: text/json; charset=utf-8

{"Message":"The request is invalid.","ModelState":{"newTask.Subject":["The Subject field is
required."]}}
```

Excellent! With so much support from ASP.NET Web API, we've easily added generalized request validation to our task-management service. The framework is doing most of the work for us, by validating the data in the request against the data annotations in the target type. All we really had to do was put the pieces together.

Now let's move on to implementing paging, which is necessary when dealing with potentially large response messages.

Paging of Results

At this point, our task–management service database contains, at most, a couple dozen tasks. Processing a request message to return all tasks at this point would not be a big deal in terms of performance, network traffic, etc. However, consider a situation where the number of tasks was in the thousands or millions. Returning data for all tasks in this case would be foolish at best, impossible at worst. So we need to provide a mechanism that calling applications can use to page through results, much the same way Internet search engines (Google, Bing, etc.) provide a way to page through search results.

To illustrate paging of results, we will implement the operation described in Table 7-3, which we designed in Chapter 3 (and is excerpted from Table 3-3).

Table 7-3. *A List of Task Operations*

URI	Verb	Description
/api/tasks	GET	Gets the full list of all tasks; optionally, specify a filter

At a high level, our implementation consists of two basic concerns:

1. Construct a filter based on the request's query string.

2. Apply the filter to produce the response.

Later, we'll show how these basic concerns map to dependencies used by TasksController to provide the desired functionality, but first let's build them.

Constructing the Filter with a Data Request Factory

Our implementation will use the query parameters in the incoming URI to support filtering. We will allow the user to specify a page number and a page size for the results. So, for example, the URI used to request page #3, with a page size of 30, would be as follows:

/api/tasks?pageNumber=3&pageSize=30

Let's get started by implementing a class that encapsulates these parameters. Add it as follows:

```
namespace WebApi2Book.Data
{
    public class PagedDataRequest
    {
        public PagedDataRequest(int pageNumber, int pageSize)
        {
            PageNumber = pageNumber;
            PageSize = pageSize;
        }

        public int PageNumber { get; private set; }
        public int PageSize { get; private set; }
        public bool ExcludeLinks { get; set; }
    }
}
```

Now we can implement the factory, which will create a PagedDataRequest from a request URI. Add it as follows. Note, the code will not be buildable until we later add in some additional dependencies.

IPagedDataRequestFactory Interface

```
using System;
using WebApi2Book.Data;

namespace WebApi2Book.Web.Api.InquiryProcessing
{
    public interface IPagedDataRequestFactory
    {
        PagedDataRequest Create(Uri requestUri);
    }
}
```

PagedDataRequestFactory Class

```
using System;
using System.Net;
using System.Net.Http;
using System.Web;
using log4net;
using WebApi2Book.Common;
using WebApi2Book.Common.Extensions;
using WebApi2Book.Common.Logging;
using WebApi2Book.Data;

namespace WebApi2Book.Web.Api.InquiryProcessing
{
    public class PagedDataRequestFactory : IPagedDataRequestFactory
    {
        public const int DefaultPageSize = 25;

        public const int MaxPageSize = 50;

        private readonly ILog _log;

        public PagedDataRequestFactory(ILogManager logManager)
        {
            _log = logManager.GetLog(typeof (PagedDataRequestFactory));
        }

        public PagedDataRequest Create(Uri requestUri)
        {
            int? pageNumber;
            int? pageSize;
```

```
            try
            {
                var valueCollection = requestUri.ParseQueryString();

                pageNumber =
                    PrimitiveTypeParser.Parse<int?>(valueCollection[Constants.CommonParameterNames.
                                        PageNumber]);
                pageSize = PrimitiveTypeParser.Parse<int?>(
                    valueCollection[Constants.CommonParameterNames.PageSize]);
            }
            catch (Exception e)
            {
                _log.Error("Error parsing input", e);
                throw new HttpException((int) HttpStatusCode.BadRequest, e.Message);
            }

            pageNumber = pageNumber.GetBoundedValue(Constants.Paging.DefaultPageNumber,
                Constants.Paging.MinPageNumber);
            pageSize = pageSize.GetBoundedValue(DefaultPageSize,
                Constants.Paging.MinPageSize, MaxPageSize);

            return new PagedDataRequest(pageNumber.Value, pageSize.Value);
        }
    }
}
```

Dependency Configuration (add to NinjectConfigurator.AddBindings)

```
container.Bind<IPagedDataRequestFactory>().To<PagedDataRequestFactory>().InSingletonScope();
```

The Create method begins by using the Uri class' ParseQueryString method to parse the query string into a standard .NET NameValueCollection. The page number and page size are then parsed from this collection using a custom parser (which we'll examine soon). Note the use of the nullable type (int?), because we can't guarantee the caller will provide these values in the query string. Also note that the parsing logic is wrapped in a try-catch, because it is possible that the query string contains bogus data (e.g., alpha characters for the pageNumber).

Next, the page number and page size are coerced into reasonable values using the GetBoundedValue extension method. (We'll add that soon, too.)

Finally, the method returns a new PagedDataRequest containing correct (and possibly default) values for the page number and page size.

Now let's add in those missing dependencies used by Create. Start by adding in the PrimitiveTypeParser class:

```
using System.ComponentModel;

namespace WebApi2Book.Common
{
    public static class PrimitiveTypeParser
    {
```

```
    public static T Parse<T>(string valueAsString)
    {
        var converter = TypeDescriptor.GetConverter(typeof (T));
        var result = converter.ConvertFromString(valueAsString);
        return (T) result;
    }
  }
}
```

Though we could have used int.TryParse in this case, this is a class we use in some of our other projects to conveniently parse just about any type of data, including nullable value type data; it's nice to not have to deal with the TryParse method's out parameter. Yes, it's static, like the LocationLinkCalculator. Does this parser need to support polymorphism? Does it need to be mocked? No and no. So it's fine as a simple, static, utility method.

Now add in the extension methods:

```
using System;

namespace WebApi2Book.Common.Extensions
{
    public static class IntExtensions
    {
        public static int GetBoundedValue(this int value, int min, int max)
        {
            var boundedValue = Math.Min(Math.Max(value, min), max);
            return boundedValue;
        }

        public static int GetBoundedValue(this int? value, int defaultValue, int min)
        {
            var valToBound = value ?? defaultValue;
            var boundedValue = Math.Max(valToBound, min);
            return boundedValue;
        }

        public static int GetBoundedValue(this int? value, int defaultValue, int min, int max)
        {
            var valToBound = value ?? defaultValue;
            var boundedValue = GetBoundedValue(valToBound, min, max);
            return boundedValue;
        }
    }
}
```

These extension methods provide a convenient, general-purpose way to apply floor, ceiling, and default values to nullable integers. Nothing web-specific here; just a collection of handy utility methods we included for completeness.

At this point, we've finished constructing the filter from the URI, and the code should once again be in a buildable state. Let's move on to processing the filtered request.

Filtering the Results

Now we need to apply the filter to produce the response. We'll continue our bottom-up approach, starting with some utility types and ultimately reaching the controller. Let's begin by implementing the ResultsPagingUtility class as follows (you will need add a reference in the WebApi2Book.Data project to the WebApi2Book.Common project):

ResultsPagingUtility Class

```
using System;
using WebApi2Book.Common;

namespace WebApi2Book.Data
{
    public static class ResultsPagingUtility
    {
        private const string ValueLessThanOneErrorMessage = "Value may not be less than 1.";
        private const string ValueLessThanZeroErrorMessage = "Value may not be less than 0.";

        public static int CalculatePageSize(int requestedValue, int maxValue)
        {
            if (requestedValue < 1)
                throw new ArgumentOutOfRangeException(
                    "requestedValue", requestedValue, ValueLessThanOneErrorMessage);
            if (maxValue < 1)
                throw new ArgumentOutOfRangeException(
                    "maxValue", maxValue, ValueLessThanOneErrorMessage);

            var boundedPageSize = Math.Min(requestedValue, maxValue);
            return boundedPageSize;
        }

        public static int CalculateStartIndex(int pageNumber, int pageSize)
        {
            if (pageNumber < 1)
                throw new ArgumentOutOfRangeException(
                    Constants.CommonParameterNames.PageNumber, pageNumber,
                        ValueLessThanOneErrorMessage);
            if (pageSize < 1)
                throw new ArgumentOutOfRangeException(
                    Constants.CommonParameterNames.PageSize, pageSize,
                        ValueLessThanOneErrorMessage);

            var startIndex = (pageNumber - 1)*pageSize;
            return startIndex;
        }

        public static int CalculatePageCount(int totalItemCount, int pageSize)
        {
            if (totalItemCount < 0)
                throw new ArgumentOutOfRangeException("totalItemCount", totalItemCount,
                    ValueLessThanZeroErrorMessage);
```

```
            if (pageSize < 1)
                throw new ArgumentOutOfRangeException(Constants.CommonParameterNames.PageSize,
                    pageSize, ValueLessThanOneErrorMessage);

            var totalPageCount = (totalItemCount + pageSize - 1)/pageSize;
            return totalPageCount;
        }
    }
}
```

This encapsulates logic to restrict page numbers and sizes to reasonable values. Unlike the PagedDataRequestFactory, this class will throw ArgumentOutOfRangeException exceptions because, by this point in the processing, all invalid user input should have been corrected or rejected as appropriate. The only interesting method is CalculatePageCount, which implements a formula that ensures a correct page count based on the total number of items and the page size. Note the protection for divide-by-zero exceptions!

Next, let's implement the QueryResult class as follows:

```
using System.Collections.Generic;

namespace WebApi2Book.Data
{
    public class QueryResult<T>
    {
        public QueryResult(IEnumerable<T> queriedItems, int totalItemCount, int pageSize)
        {
            PageSize = pageSize;
            TotalItemCount = totalItemCount;
            QueriedItems = queriedItems ?? new List<T>();
        }

        public int TotalItemCount { get; private set; }

        public int TotalPageCount
        {
            get { return ResultsPagingUtility.CalculatePageCount(TotalItemCount, PageSize); }
        }

        public IEnumerable<T> QueriedItems { get; private set; }

        public int PageSize { get; private set; }
    }
}
```

The QueryResult class serves as a paging-enhanced data-transfer object (DTO) that is used to encapsulate data returned by the query processor. The TotalItemCount is meant to represent the total number of items, unrestricted by paging logic. Also note that QueryResult uses the ResultsPagingUtility class that we just implemented to compute the TotalPageCount derived property.

With those utility types now available, we are now ready to implement the query processor. Implement it as follows:

IAllTasksQueryProcessor Interface

```
using WebApi2Book.Data.Entities;

namespace WebApi2Book.Data.QueryProcessors
{
    public interface IAllTasksQueryProcessor
    {
        QueryResult<Task> GetTasks(PagedDataRequest requestInfo);
    }
}
```

AllTasksQueryProcessor Class

```
using NHibernate;
using WebApi2Book.Data.Entities;
using WebApi2Book.Data.QueryProcessors;

namespace WebApi2Book.Data.SqlServer.QueryProcessors
{
    public class AllTasksQueryProcessor : IAllTasksQueryProcessor
    {
        private readonly ISession _session;

        public AllTasksQueryProcessor(ISession session)
        {
            _session = session;
        }

        public QueryResult<Task> GetTasks(PagedDataRequest requestInfo)
        {
            var query = _session.QueryOver<Task>();

            var totalItemCount = query.ToRowCountQuery().RowCount();

            var startIndex = ResultsPagingUtility.CalculateStartIndex(requestInfo.PageNumber,
                requestInfo.PageSize);

            var tasks = query.Skip(startIndex).Take(requestInfo.PageSize).List();

            var queryResult = new QueryResult<Task>(tasks, totalItemCount, requestInfo.PageSize);

            return queryResult;
        }
    }
}
```

Dependency Configuration (add to NinjectConfigurator.AddBindings)

```
container.Bind<IAllTasksQueryProcessor>().To<AllTasksQueryProcessor>().InRequestScope();
```

There's only one method in this query processor, and it looks rather simple. Don't be fooled; there's a lot going on in this little method! First, we obtain an NHibernate IQueryOver instance from our NHibernate session. Think of this as queryable access to the entire Task table; we haven't fetched any data, we have just established queryable access to it.

Next, we use the IQueryOver RowCount method to calculate the total item count. This does hit the database; it returns the total number of rows in the Task table. Then we calculate the start index, based on the page number and page size. We use that calculated start index value in the next statement, where we jump to the first record in the page and fetch the corresponding page of data by employing the Skip and Take Linq methods. This in and of itself doesn't hit the database, but the List method invocation at the end of the statement does.

At this point, the method has fetched all of the requested data from the database. The only thing left to do is package it all up in a QueryResult and return it to the invoker, which just so happens to be an IAllTasksInquiryProcessor.

We will implement IAllTasksInquiryProcessor soon, but first we need to take care of some more utility types that it uses. First, add IPageLinkContaining as follows:

```
namespace WebApi2Book.Web.Api.Models
{
    public interface IPageLinkContaining : ILinkContaining
    {
        int PageNumber { get; set; }
        int PageCount { get; set; }
    }
}
```

Next, implement PagedDataInquiryResponse, which implements ILinkContaining, as follows:

```
using System.Collections.Generic;

namespace WebApi2Book.Web.Api.Models
{
    public class PagedDataInquiryResponse<T> : IPageLinkContaining
    {
        private List<T> _items;
        private List<Link> _links;

        public List<T> Items
        {
            get { return _items ?? (_items = new List<T>()); }
            set { _items = value; }
        }

        public int PageSize { get; set; }

        public List<Link> Links
        {
            get { return _links ?? (_links = new List<Link>()); }
            set { _links = value; }
        }
```

```
        public void AddLink(Link link)
        {
            Links.Add(link);
        }

        public int PageNumber { get; set; }
        public int PageCount { get; set; }
    }
}
```

PagedDataInquiryResponse is a DTO that can be used to return type-safe paged data (thanks to generics) and relevant hypermedia links. We'll get to the links in the next section. The other members should be self-explanatory.

Now it's time to go ahead and implement IAllTasksInquiryProcessor as follows:

IAllTasksInquiryProcessor Interface

```
using WebApi2Book.Data;
using WebApi2Book.Web.Api.Models;

namespace WebApi2Book.Web.Api.InquiryProcessing
{
    public interface IAllTasksInquiryProcessor
    {
        PagedDataInquiryResponse<Task> GetTasks(PagedDataRequest requestInfo);
    }
}
```

AllTasksInquiryProcessor Class

```
using System.Collections.Generic;
using System.Linq;
using WebApi2Book.Common.TypeMapping;
using WebApi2Book.Data;
using WebApi2Book.Data.QueryProcessors;
using WebApi2Book.Web.Api.Models;
using PagedTaskDataInquiryResponse =
WebApi2Book.Web.Api.Models.PagedDataInquiryResponse<WebApi2Book.Web.Api.Models.Task>;

namespace WebApi2Book.Web.Api.InquiryProcessing
{
    public class AllTasksInquiryProcessor : IAllTasksInquiryProcessor
    {
        private readonly IAutoMapper _autoMapper;
        private readonly IAllTasksQueryProcessor _queryProcessor;

        public AllTasksInquiryProcessor(IAllTasksQueryProcessor queryProcessor, IAutoMapper autoMapper)
        {
            _queryProcessor = queryProcessor;
            _autoMapper = autoMapper;
        }
```

```
    public PagedTaskDataInquiryResponse GetTasks(PagedDataRequest requestInfo)
    {
        var queryResult = _queryProcessor.GetTasks(requestInfo);

        var tasks = GetTasks(queryResult.QueriedItems).ToList();

        var inquiryResponse = new PagedTaskDataInquiryResponse
        {
            Items = tasks,
            PageCount = queryResult.TotalPageCount,
            PageNumber = requestInfo.PageNumber,
            PageSize = requestInfo.PageSize
        };

        return inquiryResponse;
    }

    public virtual IEnumerable<Task> GetTasks(IEnumerable<Data.Entities.Task> taskEntities)
    {
        var tasks = taskEntities.Select(x => _autoMapper.Map<Task>(x)).ToList();

        return tasks;
    }
  }
}
```

Dependency Configuration (add to NinjectConfigurator.AddBindings)

```
container.Bind<IAllTasksInquiryProcessor>().To<AllTasksInquiryProcessor>().InRequestScope();
```

The GetTasks overload that implements the IAllTasksInquiryProcessor interface is where the main logic is; the other overload simply uses the IAutoMapper to map the retrieved task entities to service-model representations. Even so, the main logic is fairly simple: use the query processor to fetch the task entities, convert those to service-model representations, and then package up all of the results into a PagedTaskDataInquiryResponse and return it to the invoker.

The invoker happens to be . . . the TasksController class' GetTasks action method. Implement the method as follows:

```
[Route("", Name = "GetTasksRoute")]
public PagedDataInquiryResponse<Task> GetTasks(HttpRequestMessage requestMessage)
{
    var request = _pagedDataRequestFactory.Create(requestMessage.RequestUri);

    var tasks = _allTasksInquiryProcessor.GetTasks(request);
    return tasks;
}
```

Then add the dependencies required by the GetTasks method:

```
public class TasksController : ApiController
{
    private readonly IAddTaskMaintenanceProcessor _addTaskMaintenanceProcessor;
    private readonly ITaskByIdInquiryProcessor _taskByIdInquiryProcessor;
    private readonly IUpdateTaskMaintenanceProcessor _updateTaskMaintenanceProcessor;
    private readonly IPagedDataRequestFactory _pagedDataRequestFactory;
    private readonly IAllTasksInquiryProcessor _allTasksInquiryProcessor;

    public TasksController(IAddTaskMaintenanceProcessor addTaskMaintenanceProcessor,
        ITaskByIdInquiryProcessor taskByIdInquiryProcessor,
        IUpdateTaskMaintenanceProcessor updateTaskMaintenanceProcessor,
        IPagedDataRequestFactory pagedDataRequestFactory,
         IAllTasksInquiryProcessor allTasksInquiryProcessor)
    {
        _addTaskMaintenanceProcessor = addTaskMaintenanceProcessor;
        _taskByIdInquiryProcessor = taskByIdInquiryProcessor;
        _updateTaskMaintenanceProcessor = updateTaskMaintenanceProcessor;
        _pagedDataRequestFactory = pagedDataRequestFactory;
        _allTasksInquiryProcessor = allTasksInquiryProcessor;
    }
...
```

GetTasks is yet another simple action method, but as we've seen before, these action methods are supported by heavy lifting being done in the dependencies and attributes. All GetTasks does is delegate its work to the IAllTasksInquiryProcessor, passing it a custom request that it obtained from the IPagedDataRequestFactory. This is what we like: "thin" controllers that are easy to test!

Speaking of testing, it's time to test this paging functionality. If you've been following along, you should now have at least 18 tasks in your database. Let's fetch the second page, specifying a page size of 10 and using bhogg's highly-privileged credentials (adjusting the page number and size as needed based on the number of tasks in your database):

Paged Tasks Request (abbreviated)

```
GET http://localhost:61589/api/v1/tasks?pageNumber=2&pageSize=10 HTTP/1.1
Content-Type: text/json
Authorization: Basic YmhvZ2c6aWdub3JlZA==
```

This time we depicted the result using the Fiddler JSON viewer, because showing the raw result, as we did previously, buried the significant portions of what we're trying to demonstrate in too much detail. From Figure 7-1, you can see our familiar task #17. It appears on the correct page (i.e., 2), with a correct page count (i.e., 2) and correct page size (i.e., 10) based on the query string we provided in the request. However, something is missing: the assignees! What happened?

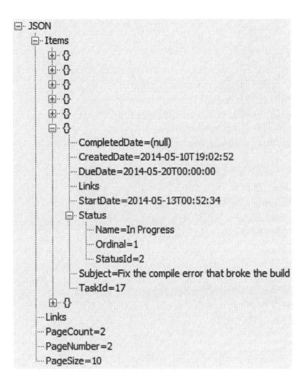

Figure 7-1. *Paged tasks response (abbreviated)*

In the "GET a Task" section of Chapter 6, we implemented a message handler to control whether a task's assignees should appear in the response message based on the user's permissions. That handler, TaskDataSecurityMessageHandler, was designed to handle simple Task content but not PagedDataInquiryResponse<Task> content. We are returning the latter type of content in this scenario, so the handler is not operating on the response. As a result, each Task object's ShouldSerializeAssignees method is returning the default value of false, and we are therefore not seeing any assignees.

To solve the problem, we could modify TaskDataSecurityMessageHandler to handle both response types. However, this would violate the Open/Closed Principle that we mentioned in Chapter 5. Instead, we'll add a new handler and leave the existing functionality that operates on responses with simple Task content undisturbed. Implement the new handler as follows:

```
using System.Net.Http;
using System.Threading;
using System.Threading.Tasks;
using log4net;
using WebApi2Book.Common;
using WebApi2Book.Common.Logging;
using WebApi2Book.Common.Security;
using WebApi2Book.Web.Api.Models;
using Task = WebApi2Book.Web.Api.Models.Task;

namespace WebApi2Book.Web.Api.Security
{
    public class PagedTaskDataSecurityMessageHandler : DelegatingHandler
```

```
{
    private readonly ILog _log;
    private readonly IUserSession _userSession;

    public PagedTaskDataSecurityMessageHandler(ILogManager logManager, IUserSession userSession)
    {
        _log = logManager.GetLog(typeof (PagedTaskDataSecurityMessageHandler));
        _userSession = userSession;
    }

    protected override async Task<HttpResponseMessage> SendAsync(
        HttpRequestMessage request,
        CancellationToken cancellationToken)
    {
        var response = await base.SendAsync(request, cancellationToken);

        if (CanHandleResponse(response))
        {
            ApplySecurityToResponseData((ObjectContent) response.Content);
        }

        return response;
    }

    public bool CanHandleResponse(HttpResponseMessage response)
    {
        var objectContent = response.Content as ObjectContent;
        var canHandleResponse = objectContent != null &&
                                objectContent.ObjectType == typeof (PagedDataInquiryResponse<Task>);
        return canHandleResponse;
    }

    public void ApplySecurityToResponseData(ObjectContent responseObjectContent)
    {
        var maskData = !_userSession.IsInRole(Constants.RoleNames.SeniorWorker);

        if (maskData)
        {
            _log.DebugFormat("Applying security data masking for user {0}", _userSession.Username);
        }

        ((PagedDataInquiryResponse<Task>) responseObjectContent.Value).Items.ForEach(
            x => x.SetShouldSerializeAssignees(!maskData));
    }
}
}
```

Next, write the code to configure it at run time. The handler is configured during application startup, so let's return to the WebApiApplication class and add the following to the RegisterHandlers method:

```
GlobalConfiguration.Configuration.MessageHandlers.Add(
    new PagedTaskDataSecurityMessageHandler(logManager,userSession));
```

Looking back at the PagedTaskDataSecurityMessageHandler implementation, we see that it is similar to the TaskDataSecurityMessageHandler implementation. It derives from the ASP.NET Web API's DelegatingHandler base class, and it overrides SendAsync.

One difference, though, is in CanHandleResponse, because this time the handler is checking for a different type in the response. ApplySecurityToResponseData is also different, modified to handle Task instances that are elements in a response of type PagedDataInquiryResponse<Task>.

With our new handler in place, we are now ready to replay the request we just issued. Our result is shown in Figure 7-2.

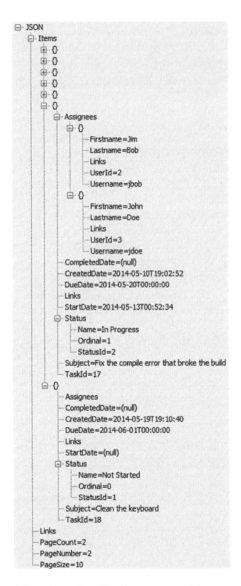

Figure 7-2. *Paged tasks response, with assignees (abbreviated)*

The data looks correct—and complete—this time! There are many more tests that could be done to demonstrate the functionality (e.g., issue a request with no query string, issue a request with an invalid query string, etc.), and we encourage you to experiment on your own. However, at this point, we will move on to adding hypermedia links to our application.

Hypermedia Links

We introduced (and stated the importance of) hypermedia links in Chapter 2, we modeled them in Chapter 3, and we hacked in a hard-coded link to the `AddTaskMaintenanceProcessor` in Chapter 5. We've even alluded to them a couple of times since then. Now it's time to give links the attention they deserve. In this section, we will revisit the functionality we just implemented to get all tasks, but this time we will enhance the response with hypermedia links.

As a refresher, these are the properties on the `Link` class that we introduced in Chapter 3:

- `Rel` Specifies the relationship between the resource and the resource identified in the link

- `Href` Specifies the linked resource's address

- `Method` Specifies the HTTP method used to access the resource

Note how this class is patterned off of the standard HTML `link` element. This is intentional. Guided by the REST principle of HATEOS (Hypermedia as the Engine of Application State), the caller, given a root or starting URI, should be able to navigate the collection of resources without prior knowledge of the possible navigation paths. What better model to use than the `link` element?

With that brief refresher on hypermedia links and their relationship to HATEOS, let's begin the implementation.

Common Link Service

We've already added some infrastructural support for hypermedia links over the course of the past few chapters. For example, in the previous section we implemented `IPageLinkContaining`. Now we need to finish building out that infrastructural support. We'll begin by implementing a couple of utility types. First, implement the `UriExtensions` class as follows:

UriExtensions Class

```
using System;

namespace WebApi2Book.Common.Extensions
{
    public static class UriExtensions
    {
        public static Uri GetBaseUri(this Uri originalUri)
        {
            var queryDelimiterIndex = originalUri.AbsoluteUri.IndexOf("?", StringComparison.Ordinal);
            return queryDelimiterIndex < 0
                ? originalUri
                : new Uri(originalUri.AbsoluteUri.Substring(0, queryDelimiterIndex));
        }
    }
}
```

```
        public static string QueryWithoutLeadingQuestionMark(this Uri uri)
        {
            const int indexToSkipQueryDelimiter = 1;
            return uri.Query.Length > 1 ? uri.Query.Substring(indexToSkipQueryDelimiter) : string.Empty;
        }
    }
}
```

UriExtensions provides a couple of convenience extensions that seem to naturally belong to the Uri class. GetBaseUri returns the portion of the request URL to the left of the query-string delimiter, and QueryWithoutLeadingQuestionMark returns the query string sans the query-string delimiter.

Our next dependency, ICommonLinkService, relies on UriExtensions. It provides functionality required by the business domain-specific link services (e.g., TaskLinkService) that we'll implement soon. Implement ICommonLinkService as follows:

ICommonLinkService Interface

```
using System.Net.Http;
using WebApi2Book.Web.Api.Models;

namespace WebApi2Book.Web.Api.LinkServices
{
    public interface ICommonLinkService
    {
        void AddPageLinks(IPageLinkContaining linkContainer,
            string currentPageQueryString,
            string previousPageQueryString,
            string nextPageQueryString);

        Link GetLink(string pathFragment, string relValue, HttpMethod httpMethod);
    }
}
```

CommonLinkService Class

```
using System;
using System.Net.Http;
using WebApi2Book.Common;
using WebApi2Book.Common.Extensions;
using WebApi2Book.Web.Api.Models;
using WebApi2Book.Web.Common.Security;

namespace WebApi2Book.Web.Api.LinkServices
{
    public class CommonLinkService : ICommonLinkService
    {
        private readonly IWebUserSession _userSession;

        public CommonLinkService(IWebUserSession userSession)
        {
            _userSession = userSession;
        }
```

```
public virtual Link GetLink(string pathFragment, string relValue, HttpMethod httpMethod)
{
    const string delimitedVersionedApiRouteBaseFormatString =
        Constants.CommonRoutingDefinitions.ApiSegmentName + "/{0}/";

    var path =
        string.Concat(
            string.Format(
                delimitedVersionedApiRouteBaseFormatString,
                _userSession.ApiVersionInUse), pathFragment);

    var uriBuilder = new UriBuilder
    {
        Scheme = _userSession.RequestUri.Scheme,
        Host = _userSession.RequestUri.Host,
        Port = _userSession.RequestUri.Port,
        Path = path
    };

    var link = new Link
    {
        Href = uriBuilder.Uri.AbsoluteUri,
        Rel = relValue,
        Method = httpMethod.Method
    };
    return link;
}

public void AddPageLinks(IPageLinkContaining linkContainer,
    string currentPageQueryString,
    string previousPageQueryString,
    string nextPageQueryString)
{
    var versionedBaseUri = _userSession.RequestUri.GetBaseUri();

    AddCurrentPageLink(linkContainer, versionedBaseUri, currentPageQueryString);

    var addPrevPageLink = ShouldAddPreviousPageLink(linkContainer.PageNumber);
    var addNextPageLink = ShouldAddNextPageLink(linkContainer.PageNumber,
        linkContainer.PageCount);

    if (addPrevPageLink || addNextPageLink)
    {
        if (addPrevPageLink)
        {
            AddPreviousPageLink(linkContainer, versionedBaseUri, previousPageQueryString);
        }
```

```
            if (addNextPageLink)
            {
                AddNextPageLink(linkContainer, versionedBaseUri, nextPageQueryString);
            }
        }
    }

    public virtual void AddCurrentPageLink(IPageLinkContaining linkContainer, Uri versionedBaseUri,
        string pageQueryString)
    {
        var currentPageUriBuilder = new UriBuilder(versionedBaseUri)
        {
            Query = pageQueryString
        };
        linkContainer.AddLink(GetCurrentPageLink(currentPageUriBuilder.Uri));
    }

    public virtual void AddPreviousPageLink(IPageLinkContaining linkContainer, Uri versionedBaseUri,
        string pageQueryString)
    {
        var uriBuilder = new UriBuilder(versionedBaseUri)
        {
            Query = pageQueryString
        };
        linkContainer.AddLink(GetPreviousPageLink(uriBuilder.Uri));
    }

    public virtual void AddNextPageLink(IPageLinkContaining linkContainer, Uri versionedBaseUri,
        string pageQueryString)
    {
        var uriBuilder = new UriBuilder(versionedBaseUri)
        {
            Query = pageQueryString
        };
        linkContainer.AddLink(GetNextPageLink(uriBuilder.Uri));
    }

    public virtual Link GetCurrentPageLink(Uri uri)
    {
        return new Link
        {
            Href = uri.AbsoluteUri,
            Rel = Constants.CommonLinkRelValues.CurrentPage,
            Method = HttpMethod.Get.Method
        };
    }
```

```csharp
        public virtual Link GetPreviousPageLink(Uri uri)
        {
            return new Link
            {
                Href = uri.AbsoluteUri,
                Rel = Constants.CommonLinkRelValues.PreviousPage,
                Method = HttpMethod.Get.Method
            };
        }

        public virtual Link GetNextPageLink(Uri uri)
        {
            return new Link
            {
                Href = uri.AbsoluteUri,
                Rel = Constants.CommonLinkRelValues.NextPage,
                Method = HttpMethod.Get.Method
            };
        }

        public bool ShouldAddPreviousPageLink(int pageNumber)
        {
            return pageNumber > 1;
        }

        public bool ShouldAddNextPageLink(int pageNumber, int pageCount)
        {
            return pageNumber < pageCount;
        }
    }
}
```

Dependency Configuration (add to NinjectConfigurator.AddBindings)

```csharp
container.Bind<ICommonLinkService>().To<CommonLinkService>().InRequestScope();
```

■ **Note**   You'll need to add a using directive for WebApi2Book.Web.Api.LinkServices to satisfy the compiler.

Let's review. GetLink computes a Uri.Path by prepending a versioned base path prefix to a specified path fragment. For example, while processing a message routed to a version 1 controller, the method would calculate a Uri.Path value of api/v1/tasks for a supplied pathFragment equal to tasks. GetLink uses the UriBuilder to construct a properly-formed URI, which is assigned to the Href property of the returned link. The Rel and Method properties are specified by the invoker.

Next, let's look at some of the helper methods that support the AddPageLinks interface method. We'll start with GetCurrentPageLink, GetPreviousPageLink, and GetNextPageLink. Each of these is a factory method, creating an appropriate Link instance based on the specified URI.

The ShouldAddPreviousPageLink and ShouldAddNextPageLink methods encapsulate simple logic to determine whether previous and/or next page links should be added to a response, respectively.

The last of the helper methods—AddCurrentPageLink, AddPreviousPageLink, and AddNextPageLink—build a proper URI from the specified base and query string. They pass this URI to the appropriate Get*PageLink method (which we just discussed) and add the resulting Link instance to the specified IPageLinkContaining instance.

These helper methods are used by the AddPageLinks interface method, which begins by invoking AddCurrentPageLink with the base URI it received from the GetBaseUri extension method. AddPageLinks then conditionally adds links to the previous and next pages using the ShouldAdd*PageLink and Add*PageLink helper methods, respectively.

Business Domain-Specific Link Services

With that infrastructure in place, we are now ready to implement some of the business domain-specific link services. Let's begin with a simple one: the one used to add links to User instances. Implement it as follows:

IUserLinkService Interface

```
using WebApi2Book.Web.Api.Models;

namespace WebApi2Book.Web.Api.LinkServices
{
    public interface IUserLinkService
    {
        void AddSelfLink(User user);
    }
}
```

UserLinkService Class

```
using System.Net.Http;
using WebApi2Book.Common;
using WebApi2Book.Web.Api.Models;

namespace WebApi2Book.Web.Api.LinkServices
{
    public class UserLinkService : IUserLinkService
    {
        private readonly ICommonLinkService _commonLinkService;

        public UserLinkService(ICommonLinkService commonLinkService)
        {
            _commonLinkService = commonLinkService;
        }

        public virtual void AddSelfLink(User user)
        {
            user.AddLink(GetSelfLink(user));
        }
```

```
        public virtual Link GetSelfLink(User user)
        {
            var pathFragment = string.Format("users/{0}", user.UserId);
            var link = _commonLinkService.GetLink(pathFragment, Constants.CommonLinkRelValues.Self,
                HttpMethod.Get);
            return link;
        }
    }
}
```

Dependency Configuration (add to NinjectConfigurator.AddBindings)

```
container.Bind<IUserLinkService>().To<UserLinkService>().InRequestScope();
```

The AddSelfLink interface method could easily implement all of its own logic, but instead it delegates most of its work to the GetSelfLink helper method. This is because GetSelfLink implements logic shared by another interface method, not shown or used here, which appears in the full task-management service implementation available in our GitHub repository for this book. GetSelfLink uses the ICommonLinkService to build a link with an Href similar to http://localhost:61589/api/v1/users/1. There's nothing more to see in this class, so we'll move on to another domain-specific link service: ITaskLinkService. Implement it as follows:

ITaskLinkService Interface

```
using WebApi2Book.Web.Api.Models;

namespace WebApi2Book.Web.Api.LinkServices
{
    public interface ITaskLinkService
    {
        Link GetAllTasksLink();
        void AddSelfLink(Task task);
        void AddLinksToChildObjects(Task task);
    }
}
```

TaskLinkService Class

```
using System.Net.Http;
using WebApi2Book.Common;
using WebApi2Book.Web.Api.Models;

namespace WebApi2Book.Web.Api.LinkServices
{
    public class TaskLinkService : ITaskLinkService
    {
        private readonly ICommonLinkService _commonLinkService;
        private readonly IUserLinkService _userLinkService;
```

```
public TaskLinkService(ICommonLinkService commonLinkService,
    IUserLinkService userLinkService)
{
    _commonLinkService = commonLinkService;
    _userLinkService = userLinkService;
}

public void AddLinksToChildObjects(Task task)
{
    task.Assignees.ForEach(x => _userLinkService.AddSelfLink(x));
}

public virtual void AddSelfLink(Task task)
{
    task.AddLink(GetSelfLink(task.TaskId.Value));
}

public virtual Link GetAllTasksLink()
{
    const string pathFragment = "tasks";
    return _commonLinkService.GetLink(pathFragment, Constants.CommonLinkRelValues.All,
        HttpMethod.Get);
}

public virtual Link GetSelfLink(long taskId)
{
    var pathFragment = string.Format("tasks/{0}", taskId);
    var link = _commonLinkService.GetLink(pathFragment, Constants.CommonLinkRelValues.Self,
        HttpMethod.Get);
    return link;
}
    }
}
```

Dependency Configuration (add to NinjectConfigurator.AddBindings)

```
container.Bind<ITaskLinkService>().To<TaskLinkService>().InRequestScope();
```

This simple class relies on the functionality provided by the ICommonLinkService and IUserLinkService implementations we just added. Here's a quick overview:

- AddLinksToChildObjects iterates the Assignees list, leaning on the IUserLinkService to add the appropriate link to each User.

- The AddSelfLink interface method could easily implement all of its own logic, but instead it delegates most of its work to the GetSelfLink helper method. This is because GetSelfLink implements logic shared by another interface method, not shown or used here, which appears in the full task-management service implementation available in GitHub.

- GetAllTasksLink uses the ICommonLinkService to build a link with an Href similar to Href=http://localhost:61589/api/v1/tasks.

- GetSelfLink uses the ICommonLinkService to build a link with an Href similar to http://localhost:61589/api/v1/tasks/17.

Now we've laid the groundwork to wire all of this into the AllTasksInquiryProcessor that we implemented in the "Paging of Results" section. Let's do that now.

Putting It Together

We're going to modify the AllTasksInquiryProcessor class so that it adds the relevant hypermedia links to the "All Tasks" inquiry we implemented in the "Paging of Results" section. Let's begin by modifying the class to accept the necessary dependencies, ICommonLinkService and ITaskLinkService (modifying it so that it appears as follows):

```
using System.Collections.Generic;
using System.Linq;
using WebApi2Book.Common.TypeMapping;
using WebApi2Book.Data;
using WebApi2Book.Data.QueryProcessors;
using WebApi2Book.Web.Api.LinkServices;
using WebApi2Book.Web.Api.Models;
using PagedTaskDataInquiryResponse =
WebApi2Book.Web.Api.Models.PagedDataInquiryResponse<WebApi2Book.Web.Api.Models.Task>;

namespace WebApi2Book.Web.Api.InquiryProcessing
{
    public class AllTasksInquiryProcessor : IAllTasksInquiryProcessor
    {
        public const string QueryStringFormat = "pagenumber={0}&pagesize={1}";

        private readonly IAutoMapper _autoMapper;
        private readonly ICommonLinkService _commonLinkService;
        private readonly IAllTasksQueryProcessor _queryProcessor;
        private readonly ITaskLinkService _taskLinkService;

        public AllTasksInquiryProcessor(IAllTasksQueryProcessor queryProcessor, IAutoMapper autoMapper,
            ITaskLinkService taskLinkService, ICommonLinkService commonLinkService)
        {
            _queryProcessor = queryProcessor;
            _autoMapper = autoMapper;
            _taskLinkService = taskLinkService;
            _commonLinkService = commonLinkService;
        }
```

```csharp
public PagedTaskDataInquiryResponse GetTasks(PagedDataRequest requestInfo)
{
    var queryResult = _queryProcessor.GetTasks(requestInfo);

    var tasks = GetTasks(queryResult.QueriedItems).ToList();

    var inquiryResponse = new PagedTaskDataInquiryResponse
    {
        Items = tasks,
        PageCount = queryResult.TotalPageCount,
        PageNumber = requestInfo.PageNumber,
        PageSize = requestInfo.PageSize
    };

    AddLinksToInquiryResponse(inquiryResponse);

    return inquiryResponse;
}

public virtual void AddLinksToInquiryResponse(PagedTaskDataInquiryResponse inquiryResponse)
{
    inquiryResponse.AddLink(_taskLinkService.GetAllTasksLink());

    _commonLinkService.AddPageLinks(inquiryResponse,
        GetCurrentPageQueryString(inquiryResponse),
        GetPreviousPageQueryString(inquiryResponse),
        GetNextPageQueryString(inquiryResponse));
}

public virtual IEnumerable<Task> GetTasks(IEnumerable<Data.Entities.Task> taskEntities)
{
    var tasks = taskEntities.Select(x => _autoMapper.Map<Task>(x)).ToList();

    tasks.ForEach(x =>
    {
        _taskLinkService.AddSelfLink(x);
        _taskLinkService.AddLinksToChildObjects(x);
    });

    return tasks;
}

public virtual string GetCurrentPageQueryString(PagedTaskDataInquiryResponse inquiryResponse)
{
    return
        string.Format(QueryStringFormat,
            inquiryResponse.PageNumber,
            inquiryResponse.PageSize);
}
```

```
public virtual string GetPreviousPageQueryString(PagedTaskDataInquiryResponse inquiryResponse)
{
    return
        string.Format(QueryStringFormat,
            inquiryResponse.PageNumber - 1,
            inquiryResponse.PageSize);
}

public virtual string GetNextPageQueryString(PagedTaskDataInquiryResponse inquiryResponse)
{
    return string.Format(QueryStringFormat,
        inquiryResponse.PageNumber + 1,
        inquiryResponse.PageSize);
}
    }
}
```

The first thing we note is that a call to the AddLinksInquiryResponse helper method has been added to GetTasks. This new method relies on the ITaskLinkService and on the Get*PageQueryString helper methods. And, as you can see, the Get*PageQueryString methods are quite simple, each encapsulating a string formatting operation that builds an appropriate query string.

Similarly, we modified the GetTasks helper method to add a self link and child links to each Task service-model object. These link-enhanced tasks are then packaged up in the GetTasks interface method and returned to the caller, which, as you remember, is the TasksController.

Now let's test our hypermedia link functionality. We'll repeat the request that we sent to the task-management service at the end of the "Paging of Results" section and compare the results. Here's the request to fetch the second page, specifying a page size of 10 (using bhogg's credentials, as usual):

Paged Tasks Request - With Links (abbreviated)

```
GET http://localhost:61589/api/v1/tasks?pageNumber=2&pageSize=10 HTTP/1.1
Content-Type: text/json
Authorization: Basic YmhvZ2c6aWdub3JlZA==
```

The response is shown in Figure 7-3.

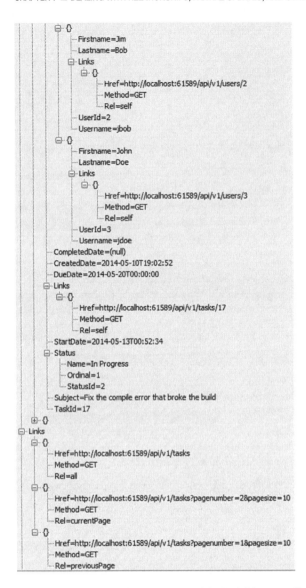

Figure 7-3. *Paged tasks response, with links (abbreviated)*

You can see that the links have now been added to the response. Links are present at the response level (i.e., the *All Tasks Inquiry* link and the page-specific inquiry links), task level, and user level. Great work!

Summary

We've reached the point in this book where we have implemented at least one example of virtually everything you need to know to build your own web API. We've implemented the following:

- API versioning

- Routing

- Each of the main HTTP verbs

- Relationships

- Partial updates

- Hypermedia links

- Paging of results

- Non-resource API operations

- Persistence

- Dependency Injection

- Tracing/Logging

- Error handling

- Input validation

- Authentication/authorization

- Auditing

- Removing sensitive data from response messages

And we did it in such a way as to leverage and highlight the great framework-level support you get from the ASP. NET Web API.

In the next chapter, we will demonstrate how ASP.NET Web API can be leveraged to support existing legacy (SOAP-based) clients. Then, in Chapter 9, we'll wrap things up with some unit testing and a Web page that consumes our task-management service.

CHAPTER 8

Supporting Diverse Clients

At this point, we've demonstrated that ASP.NET Web API is an excellent platform on which to implement REST-based services. However, what if you found yourself in a situation where you had to support existing legacy (asmx-based or SOAP-based) clients? Or clients that required messages to be in XML format? Would that automatically eliminate ASP.NET Web API as a technology choice? Fortunately, the answer is *no*.

And that leads us to the subject of this chapter—namely, how to use ASP.NET Web API to simultaneously support legacy clients and extend reach to clients requiring various message formats. Along the way, we'll throw in some ASP.NET Web API goodies, of course, just to keep it interesting for those who don't need to support SOAP-based clients or multiple message formats.

Project Requirements

Recently, we were given the job of developing a REST-based Web API for an existing system. There were a couple of interesting requirements for this project:

1. New clients must be able to consume the service using their choice of either an XML or JSON message format.

2. The new REST-based API and the legacy SOAP-based API must be implemented and deployed as a single application.

3. Existing clients must be able to benefit from the new features of the new application without affecting any existing integration points; in other words, backward compatibility with existing SOAP-based clients is required.

An architectural overview of this project is depicted in Figure 8-1 and Figure 8-2. Note that though the actual system didn't have anything to do with task management, we will use our task-management service example to illustrate and explain key concepts throughout this chapter.

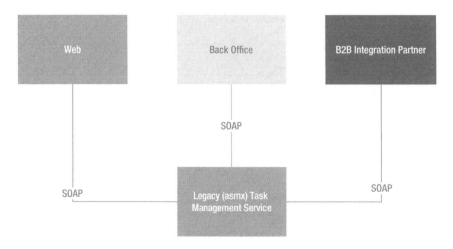

Figure 8-1. *Architectural overview, current state*

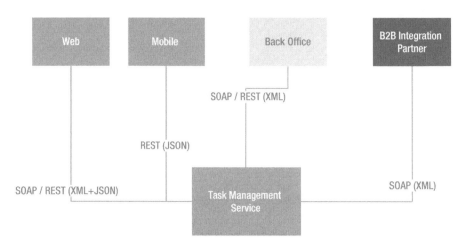

Figure 8-2. *Architectural overview, target state*

In the current state (Figure 8-1), we see the legacy service integrating with clients via the SOAP messaging protocol. The target architecture (Figure 8-2), however, shows the task-management service concurrently supporting existing clients and new clients by offering a choice of messaging protocols and formats.

We'll begin this chapter by demonstrating how to support various message formats (i.e., XML and JSON) in our REST-based API; this will satisfy requirement 1. Then we will demonstrate how to support the existing SOAP-based clients with the same application, satisfying requirements 2 and 3.

Content Negotiation

Way back in Chapter 1, we introduced the concept of content negotiation, defined by the HTTP specification as "the process of selecting the best representation for a given response when there are multiple representations available." We also made mention of it in Chapter 5. In this brief section, we will demonstrate how to leverage it to support clients that require specific message formats.

The following HTTP request headers are the primary mechanism for content negotiation with services built using ASP.NET Web API:

- Accept Used to specify which media types are acceptable for the response, such as application/json, application/xml, or a custom media type.

- Accept-Charset Used to specify which character sets are acceptable, such as UTF-8 or ISO 8859-1.

Services built using ASP.NET Web API will respond to request messages received without these headers with a default content type and character set (application/json and utf-8, respectively). For example, here is the request-response message pair that gets all tasks using bhogg's highly-privileged credentials:

Get Tasks Request - Without Accept Header (abbreviated)

```
GET http://localhost:61589/api/v1/tasks HTTP/1.1
Authorization: Basic YmhvZ2c6aWdub3J1ZA==
```

Get Tasks Response - Without Accept Header (abbreviated)

```
HTTP/1.1 200 OK
Content-Type: application/json; charset=utf-8
```

```
{"Items":[{"TaskId":1,"Subject":"Triage the important tasks","StartDate":"2014-04-24T15:20:58",
"DueDate":null,"CreatedDate":"2014-04-24T11:19:41","CompletedDate":null,"Status":{"StatusId":2...
```

Note that the service responded with the default content type and character set (as shown in the preceding example), and notice the difference when the caller specifies that it would like to receive the response in XML format (as shown in the next example):

Get Tasks Request - With Accept Header (abbreviated)

```
GET http://localhost:61589/api/v1/tasks HTTP/1.1
Authorization: Basic YmhvZ2c6aWdub3J1ZA==
Accept: application/xml
```

Get Tasks Response - With Accept Header (abbreviated)

```
HTTP/1.1 200 OK
Content-Type: application/xml; charset=utf-8
```

```
<PagedDataInquiryResponseOfTaskQgo2FNlC xmlns:i="http://www.w3.org/2001/XMLSchema-instance"
xmlns="http://schemas.datacontract.org/2004/07/WebApi2Book.Web.Api.Models"><Items><Task>
<Assignees><User><Firstname>Boss</Firstname><Lastname>Hogg</Lastname><Links>
<Link><Href>http://localhost:61589/api/v1/users/1</Href><Method>GET</Method>
<Rel>self</Rel></Link></Links><UserId>1</UserId><Username>bhogg</Username>...
```

The best part is that this content negotiation is built into ASP.NET Web API. Simply by specifying the Accept header, the caller is able to control the format that the server uses to create the response message. Pretty cool—we have satisfied requirement 1!

There are limitations to this, of course. For example, the service cannot produce a response message in a format it knows nothing of (i.e., fooBar):

Get Tasks Request - Unknown Content Type (abbreviated)

```
GET http://localhost:61589/api/v1/tasks HTTP/1.1
Authorization: Basic YmhvZ2c6aWdub3JlZA==
Accept: application/fooBar
```

Get Tasks Response - Unknown Content Type (abbreviated)

```
HTTP/1.1 200 OK
Content-Type: application/json; charset=utf-8
```

```json
{"Items":[{"TaskId":1,"Subject":"Triage the important tasks","StartDate":"2014-04-24T15:20:58",
"DueDate":null,"CreatedDate":"2014-04-24T11:19:41","CompletedDate":null,"Status":{"StatusId":2...
```

When presented with a request for an unknown content type like this, ASP.NET Web API tries to match the media type of the request body, if any. In this case, the message was a GET, with no request body; therefore, the service simply returned the response message using the default format.

For request messages with an XML request body (i.e., PUT and POST messages), one very important thing to note is that you will need to specify the XML serializer so that the body can be parsed for model binding. This can easily be accomplished by adding the following line to the WebApiConfig.Register method:

```
config.Formatters.XmlFormatter.UseXmlSerializer = true;
```

This concludes our brief introduction to content negotiation, and this is probably all you'll need to know about it for most projects. However, content negotiation, and related concerns such as serialization and formatting, can be highly customized on the server side. If you'd like to learn more about this, we encourage you to visit the official Microsoft ASP.NET Web API site and make use of the excellent resources they have available. This one is particularly apropos: http://www.asp.net/web-api/overview/formats-and-model-binding/content-negotiation.

Supporting SOAP-Based Clients

A couple of things made it relatively easy for us to satisfy the remaining requirements, 2 and 3. First, the legacy task-management service was well-architected. We were able to use virtually all of the code implementing the business logic because it was decoupled from the asmx-based host plumbing. This example underscores why throughout this book we have emphasized the importance of "thin" controllers. After all, someday some exciting new platform will replace ASP.NET Web API, and it will be a whole lot easier to reuse your core business logic if it is not all entangled with ASP.NET Web API–specific types.

Second—and this was key—was the realization that *SOAP requests are merely HTTP POST messages with an XML body*. Once we knew this, we were sure that we could support existing clients with ASP.NET Web API—and some custom parsing and formatting to replace the functionality provided by the former asmx-based host.

Now we're ready to explore the implementation. We will also demonstrate the following cool ASP.NET Web API features:

- A message handler that takes the place of a controller

- Route-specific message handlers

- Mixing convention-based routing with attribute-based routing

- A custom formatter

Let's begin!

> # A WORD ABOUT THE IMPLEMENTATION
>
> Because this particular topic may tend to appeal to a smaller audience than the rest of the book, our explanation will be abridged. Instead of our usual exhaustive code walkthrough, including explanations of every dependency, we will highlight only the major components (and, of course, the ASP.NET Web API features).
>
> The complete implementation, including demo instructions, can be found on the book's GitHub site: https://github.com/jamiekurtz/WebAPI2Book.

Where Is the Controller?

First off, we decided to use a message handler, rather than a controller, to orchestrate the processing of request messages. The main reasons for this were

- We needed full control of the message parsing and formatting, both inbound and outbound.

- We had no need for controller selection, action selection, or model binding, and we therefore didn't want to incur the overhead of these functions.

Regarding that second point, remember that SOAP clients aren't concerned with REST-style routes; they are merely pointing to a service file (e.g., TaskService.asmx) and calling a method on that service by issuing a POST. As such, the capabilities of ASP.NET Web API routes and controllers don't need to be leveraged when emulating a SOAP-based endpoint.

Keeping with our "thin" controller approach, we implemented the "thin" handler, and the supporting processor, as follows:

Message Handler

```
using System.Net;
using System.Net.Http;
using System.Threading;
using System.Threading.Tasks;
using System.Xml.Linq;
using WebApi2Book.Web.Common;

namespace WebApi2Book.Web.Api.LegacyProcessing
{
    public class LegacyMessageHandler : DelegatingHandler
    {
        public virtual ILegacyMessageProcessor LegacyMessageProcessor
        {
            get { return WebContainerManager.Get<ILegacyMessageProcessor>(); }
        }

        protected override Task<HttpResponseMessage> SendAsync(HttpRequestMessage request,
            CancellationToken cancellationToken)
        {
            var requestContentAsString = request.Content.ReadAsStringAsync().Result;
            var requestContentAsDocument = XDocument.Parse(requestContentAsString);

            var legacyResponse = LegacyMessageProcessor.ProcessLegacyMessage(
                requestContentAsDocument);
```

```csharp
            var responseMsg = request.CreateResponse(HttpStatusCode.OK, legacyResponse);

            return Task.FromResult(responseMsg);
        }
    }
}
```

Message Processor

```csharp
using System;
using System.Collections.Generic;
using System.Xml.Linq;
using WebApi2Book.Web.Api.LegacyProcessing.ProcessingStrategies;

namespace WebApi2Book.Web.Api.LegacyProcessing
{
    public class LegacyMessageProcessor : ILegacyMessageProcessor
    {
        private readonly ILegacyMessageParser _legacyMessageParser;
        private readonly IEnumerable<ILegacyMessageProcessingStrategy>
            _legacyMessageProcessingStrategies;

        public LegacyMessageProcessor(ILegacyMessageParser legacyMessageParser,
            IEnumerable<ILegacyMessageProcessingStrategy> legacyMessageProcessingStrategies)
        {
            _legacyMessageParser = legacyMessageParser;
            _legacyMessageProcessingStrategies = legacyMessageProcessingStrategies;
        }

        public virtual LegacyResponse ProcessLegacyMessage(XDocument request)
        {
            var operationElement = _legacyMessageParser.GetOperationElement(request);
            var opName = operationElement.Name.LocalName;

            foreach (var legacyMessageProcessingStrategy in _legacyMessageProcessingStrategies)
            {
                if (legacyMessageProcessingStrategy.CanProcess(opName))
                {
                    var legacyResponse = new LegacyResponse
                    {
                        Request = request,
                        ProcessingResult = legacyMessageProcessingStrategy.Execute(operationElement)
                    };
                    return legacyResponse;
                }
            }

            throw new NotSupportedException(opName);
        }
    }
}
```

This implementation provides a nice overview of the processing. The message contents are read by the message handler and then parsed into an object that can be processed by the message processor. The result from the message processor is then packaged up in the response and returned as a generic Task as required by the SendAsync method signature.

The message processor is straightforward as well. It simply parses the operation element from the SOAP request message body and, based on the operation name, finds the appropriate dependency to which it can delegate the rest of the work.

As an example, consider the following request:

Get Tasks Request - SOAP (abbreviated)

```
POST http://localhost:61589/TeamTaskService.asmx HTTP/1.1
Content-Type: text/xml; charset=utf-8
SOAPAction: "http://tempuri.org/GetTasks"

<s:Envelope xmlns:s="http://schemas.xmlsoap.org/soap/envelope/"><s:Body>
<GetTasks xmlns="http://tempuri.org/" xmlns:a=
"http://schemas.datacontract.org/2004/07/WebApi2Book.Windows.Legacy.Client.TaskServiceReference"
xmlns:i="http://www.w3.org/2001/XMLSchema-instance"/></s:Body></s:Envelope>
```

The following ILegacyMessageProcessingStrategy implementation would be used to do the work in this case because it supports the GetTasks operation (note the CanProcess method):

GetTasksMessageProcessingStrategy Class (abbreviated)

```
namespace WebApi2Book.Web.Api.LegacyProcessing.ProcessingStrategies
{
    public class GetTasksMessageProcessingStrategy : ILegacyMessageProcessingStrategy
    {
        private readonly IAllTasksInquiryProcessor _inquiryProcessor;

        public GetTasksMessageProcessingStrategy(IAllTasksInquiryProcessor inquiryProcessor)
        {
            _inquiryProcessor = inquiryProcessor;
        }

        public bool CanProcess(string operationName)
        {
            return operationName == "GetTasks";
        }
...
```

You can view the rest of the related code in the book's GitHub.com repository.

Let's move on to explaining how we configured routing for this message handler.

Configuring the Route

As we discussed in Chapter 5, attribute-based routing is a powerful feature to have at your disposal. However, attribute-based routing is designed for controllers and controller actions, not for message handlers. Fortunately, convention-based routing is still available, it supports routing directly to message handlers, and it can be used in the same application as attribute-based routing. Therefore, we modified the WebApiConfig class to appear as follows:

```
using System.Web.Http;
using System.Web.Http.Dispatcher;
using System.Web.Http.ExceptionHandling;
using System.Web.Http.Routing;
using System.Web.Http.Tracing;
using WebApi2Book.Common.Logging;
using WebApi2Book.Web.Api.LegacyProcessing;
using WebApi2Book.Web.Common;
using WebApi2Book.Web.Common.ErrorHandling;
using WebApi2Book.Web.Common.Routing;

namespace WebApi2Book.Web.Api
{
    public static class WebApiConfig
    {
        public static void Register(HttpConfiguration config)
        {
            config.Formatters.XmlFormatter.UseXmlSerializer = true;

            ConfigureRouting(config);

            config.Services.Replace(typeof(ITraceWriter),
                new SimpleTraceWriter(WebContainerManager.Get<ILogManager>()));

            config.Services.Add(typeof (IExceptionLogger),
                new SimpleExceptionLogger(WebContainerManager.Get<ILogManager>()));

            config.Services.Replace(typeof(IExceptionHandler), new GlobalExceptionHandler());
        }

        private static void ConfigureRouting(HttpConfiguration config)
        {
            config.Routes.MapHttpRoute(
                name: "legacyRoute",
                routeTemplate: "TeamTaskService.asmx",
                defaults: null,
                constraints: null,
                handler: new LegacyAuthenticationMessageHandler(WebContainerManager
                    .Get<ILogManager>())
                {
                    InnerHandler = new LegacyMessageHandler
                        { InnerHandler = new HttpControllerDispatcher(config) }
                });
```

```
        var constraintsResolver = new DefaultInlineConstraintResolver();
        constraintsResolver.ConstraintMap.Add("apiVersionConstraint",
            typeof(ApiVersionConstraint));
        config.MapHttpAttributeRoutes(constraintsResolver);

        config.Services.Replace(typeof(IHttpControllerSelector),
            new NamespaceHttpControllerSelector(config));
    }
  }
}
```

Besides the addition of the new "legacyRoute" route, you may have noticed that we also factored the routing code out into a separate method, ConfigureRouting. This was because the Register method was getting too complicated. As for the new route, the template was developed by examining the URLs of messages to the legacy task-management service (using Fiddler) to ensure that existing clients wouldn't break when they pointed their proxies to the new service.

Now let's turn our attention to the handler parameter. Here we have a route-specific handler, LegacyAuthenticationMessageHandler, used to perform custom legacy authentication. The LegacyAuthenticationMessageHandler implementation isn't particularly interesting (it's similar to the BasicAuthenticationMessageHandler discussed in Chapter 6), so we won't discuss it. However, the reason we configured LegacyAuthenticationMessageHandler here as a route-specific handler instead of a global handler (like BasicAuthenticationMessageHandler, for example) is so that the handler would not burden other routes with unnecessary overhead; the handler is relevant only for this particular route.

Another reason is that we knew this would be a great way to demonstrate nested handlers. So, nested inside of the LegacyAuthenticationMessageHandler is our LegacyMessageHandler, which at run time is the next handler in the processing chain to receive the request message. Note how its inner handler is an HttpControllerDispatcher instance. Though nesting can go many levels deep, ultimately the nesting has to end, and it ends this way so that ASP.NET Web API is able to complete the processing pipeline diagrammed in Figure 5-1 of Chapter 5.

Adding a Custom Formatter

As we noted earlier, the LegacyMessageHandler returns a LegacyResponse object as part of the HttpResponseMessage. ASP.NET Web API will then serialize that object into the response message that the caller receives. Normally, this is all that is required. However, in the case of SOAP, the response message needs to be tweaked a bit so that it can consumed by the callers—who are expecting a full-blown SOAP response. We added the following custom formatter to do this tweaking:

```
using System;
using System.IO;
using System.Net;
using System.Net.Http;
using System.Net.Http.Formatting;
using System.Net.Http.Headers;
using System.Text;
using System.Threading.Tasks;
using System.Xml;
using System.Xml.Linq;
using WebApi2Book.Common;
using WebApi2Book.Common.Extensions;
```

```csharp
namespace WebApi2Book.Web.Api.LegacyProcessing
{
    public class LegacyMessageTypeFormatter : MediaTypeFormatter, ILegacyMessageTypeFormatter
    {
        private readonly ILegacyMessageParser _legacyMessageParser;

        public LegacyMessageTypeFormatter(ILegacyMessageParser legacyMessageParser)
        {
            _legacyMessageParser = legacyMessageParser;

            SupportedMediaTypes.Add(new MediaTypeHeaderValue(Constants.MediaTypeNames.TextXml));
        }

        public override bool CanReadType(Type type)
        {
            return false;
        }

        public override bool CanWriteType(Type type)
        {
            return type == typeof (LegacyResponse);
        }

        public override Task WriteToStreamAsync(Type type, object value, Stream writeStream,
            HttpContent content, TransportContext transportContext)
        {
            return Task.Factory.StartNew(() => WriteResponseToStream(
                (LegacyResponse) value, writeStream));
        }

        public void WriteResponseToStream(LegacyResponse legacyResponse, Stream writeStream)
        {
            var request = legacyResponse.Request;

            var body = request.GetSoapBody();
            var operationElement = _legacyMessageParser.GetOperationElement(body);
            var operationElementName = operationElement.Name;
            var namespaceName = operationElementName.NamespaceName;
            var operationName = operationElementName.LocalName;

            var operationResultInnerElement = new XElement(
                string.Concat("{", namespaceName, "}", operationName, "Result"));

            var processResult = legacyResponse.ProcessingResult;
            if (processResult != null)
            {
                operationResultInnerElement.Add(processResult);
            }

            var operationResultOuterElement = new XElement(
                string.Concat("{", namespaceName, "}", operationName, "Response"));
            operationResultOuterElement.Add(operationResultInnerElement);
```

```
            operationElement.ReplaceWith(operationResultOuterElement);

            using (var outWriter = new XmlTextWriter(writeStream, Encoding.UTF8))
            {
                request.WriteTo(outWriter);
                outWriter.Flush();
            }
        }
    }
}
```

Rather than going into all of the details of how the SOAP message body is being constructed, we will instead point out the following highlights:

- The formatter derives from the ASP.NET Web API's MediaTypeFormatter class. If you need to handle serializing and deserializing strongly-typed objects, you'll want to derive from this class.

- The supported media types should be specified in the constructor. SOAP is XML, so in this case we only specify XML as a supported media type.

- The CanReadType and CanWriteType methods are interrogated by ASP.NET Web API when it needs to deserialize or serialize data in a request message or response message, respectively. This formatter is used only to write LegacyResponse objects, so we implemented the methods to reflect this.

Finally, we needed to configure the formatter to make ASP.NET Web API aware of it. We configured it by adding the ConfigureFormatters method to the WebApiApplication class and invoking it from the Application_Start method, as follows:

```
namespace WebApi2Book.Web.Api
{
    public class WebApiApplication : HttpApplication
    {
        protected void Application_Start()
        {
            GlobalConfiguration.Configure(WebApiConfig.Register);

            ConfigureFormatters();

            RegisterHandlers();

            new AutoMapperConfigurator().Configure(
                WebContainerManager.GetAll<IAutoMapperTypeConfigurator>());
        }

        private void ConfigureFormatters()
        {
            var legacyFormatter = (MediaTypeFormatter)WebContainerManager
                .Get<ILegacyMessageTypeFormatter>();
            GlobalConfiguration.Configuration.Formatters.Insert(0, legacyFormatter);
        }
...
```

Note that we inserted it as the first formatter in the list. This was to ensure that our specialized formatter was picked first at run time by ASP.NET Web API, instead of some other, general-purpose XML formatter (e.g., the default XML formatter).

This concludes our brief tour of how to support SOAP-based clients, so now it's demo time! You saw the request earlier in this section. Here's the corresponding response:

Get Tasks Response - SOAP (abbreviated)

```
HTTP/1.1 200 OK
Content-Type: text/xml

<?xml version="1.0" encoding="utf-8"?>
<s:Envelope xmlns:s="http://schemas.xmlsoap.org/soap/envelope/"><s:Body>
<GetTasksResponse xmlns="http://tempuri.org/"><GetTasksResult><Task><TaskId>1</TaskId>
<Subject>Triage the important tasks</Subject><StartDate>2014-04-24T15:20:58</StartDate>
<DueDate d6p1:nil="true" xmlns:d6p1="http://www.w3.org/2001/XMLSchema-instance" />
<CreatedDate>2014-04-24T11:19:41</CreatedDate>
<CompletedDate d6p1:nil="true" xmlns:d6p1="http://www.w3.org/2001/XMLSchema-instance" />
<Status><StatusId>2</StatusId><Name>In Progress</Name><Ordinal>1</Ordinal></Status>
<Links><Link><Rel>self</Rel><Href>http://localhost:61589/api//tasks/1</Href>
<Method>GET</Method></Link></Links></Task>...
```

Notice how different it is from the "Get Tasks Response - With Accept Header" example from the "Content Negotiation" section. This custom-formatted response is encapsulated inside of a SOAP body, which is enclosed inside of a SOAP envelope and ready to be consumed by the existing legacy SOAP clients—all without requiring any modification to the client code. Requirements 2 and 3 are hereby satisfied.

Summary

In this chapter, we explored how to use ASP.NET Web API to simulteneously support legacy SOAP clients and extend reach to clients requiring various message formats. Over the course of our journey, we were also introduced to the following important ASP.NET Web API features that aren't necessarily tied to supporting legacy clients:

- Content negotiation

- A message handler that takes the place of a controller

- Route-specific message handlers

- Mixing convention-based routing with attribute-based routing

- A custom formatter

Though we broke from our usual exhaustive explanation of the implementation and instead provided more of an overview, all of the source code is available on our project web site for those interested in getting into the details of manipulating SOAP messages.

In the next chapter, we'll tie up some loose ends, so to speak, by showing you how to consume the task-management service using a Single Page Application (SPA), including some attention paid to a couple of additional security concerns. We'll also demonstrate how to test the functionality we've developed. Don't worry, ASP.NET Web API, and our loosely-couple architecture, will actually help make testing enjoyable!

CHAPTER 9

■ ■ ■

Completing the Picture

In his highly-acclaimed book, *Working Effectively with Legacy Code* (Prentice Hall, 2004), Michael Feathers states:

> *Code without tests is bad code. It doesn't matter how well written it is; it doesn't matter how pretty or object-oriented or well-encapsulated it is. With tests, we can change the behavior of our code quickly and verifiably. Without them, we really don't know if our code is getting better or worse.*

He demonstrates how what he calls the "Cover [with tests] and Modify" approach is more efficient than the "Edit and Pray [because there are no automated tests]" approach. And although most of us know this, either through our formal education or through the "school of hard knocks," oftentimes we find ourselves writing what Mr. Feathers calls "bad code." The reasons vary, but typically it's because writing testable code can be difficult, especially when developing on top of certain frameworks.

The good news, in this regard, is that ASP.NET Web API was developed with testability in mind. In this chapter, we will demonstrate how to achieve high levels of code coverage relatively easily, and how to safely refactor code.

Finally, based on feedback from the previous edition of the book, we will demonstrate how to consume the task-management service using a simple ASP.NET MVC–based Single Page Application (SPA).

We're in the homestretch now, so let's finish strong!

■ **Note** As in previous chapters, unless otherwise noted, we implement one public type per file. The file name should match the type name, and the file location should match the namespace name. For example, the `WebApi2Book.Web.Common.Routing.ApiVersionConstraint` class is in a file named "ApiVersionConstraint.cs," which is located in a project folder named "Routing" in the `WebApi2Book.Web.Common` project.

Testing the API

Our usual approach to automated testing employs a mix of automated integration tests and unit tests, with a bias toward unit tests. This is because, even though integration tests are needed to ensure everything works together, unit tests typically provide much less friction when trying to achieve high levels of code coverage (e.g., unit tests don't require access to a database).

In this section, we will test the *Get Tasks* operation. We have chosen *Get Tasks* because it represents a superset of most of the other operations (i.e., it involves paging, database access, type mapping, hypermedia links, etc.). We'll begin by putting unit tests in place, and then we'll go end to end with an integration test. A familiarity with NUnit and Moq would certainly be helpful at this point; however, you will still be able to benefit by following along with the test implementation, regardless of your experience with these frameworks.

Unit Testing

The first thing we need to do is add some dependencies to the WebApi2Book.Web.Api.Tests project. With the solution open, run the following commands in the Package Manager console to install the testing and mocking frameworks, respectively, that we introduced in Chapter 3:

```
install-package NUnit WebApi2Book.Web.Api.Tests
install-package Moq WebApi2Book.Web.Api.Tests
```

Next, run the following commands, *in this order*, in the Package Manager console to install some ASP.NET Web API framework dependencies:

```
install-package Microsoft.AspNet.WebApi.WebHost WebApi2Book.Web.Api.Tests
install-package Microsoft.Net.Http WebApi2Book.Web.Api.Tests
```

Now that the external dependencies have been added, add the following project references to the WebApi2Book.Web.Api.Tests project:

```
WebApi2Book.Data
WebApi2Book.Web.Api.Models
WebApi2Book.Web.Api
```

Testing the Controller

We are now ready to write test some code. Implement the TasksControllerTest class as follows, after creating the Controllers folder and then the V1 folder within it:

```csharp
using System;
using System.Net.Http;
using System.Web.Http;
using Moq;
using NUnit.Framework;
using WebApi2Book.Data;
using WebApi2Book.Web.Api.Controllers.V1;
using WebApi2Book.Web.Api.InquiryProcessing;
using WebApi2Book.Web.Api.MaintenanceProcessing;
using WebApi2Book.Web.Api.Models;

namespace WebApi2Book.Web.Api.Tests.Controllers.V1
{
    [TestFixture]
    public class TasksControllerTest
    {
        [SetUp]
        public void SetUp()
        {
            _pagedDataRequestFactoryMock = new Mock<IPagedDataRequestFactory>();
            _allTasksInquiryProcessorMock = new Mock<IAllTasksInquiryProcessor>();
            _taskByIdInquiryProcessorMock = new Mock<ITaskByIdInquiryProcessor>();
            _addTaskMaintenanceProcessorMock = new Mock<IAddTaskMaintenanceProcessor>();
            _updateTaskMaintenanceProcessorMock = new Mock<IUpdateTaskMaintenanceProcessor>();
```

```
        _controller = new TasksController(
            _addTaskMaintenanceProcessorMock.Object,
            _taskByIdInquiryProcessorMock.Object,
            _updateTaskMaintenanceProcessorMock.Object,
            _pagedDataRequestFactoryMock.Object,
            _allTasksInquiryProcessorMock.Object);
    }

    private Mock<IPagedDataRequestFactory> _pagedDataRequestFactoryMock;
    private Mock<IAllTasksInquiryProcessor> _allTasksInquiryProcessorMock;
    private Mock<ITaskByIdInquiryProcessor> _taskByIdInquiryProcessorMock;
    private Mock<IAddTaskMaintenanceProcessor> _addTaskMaintenanceProcessorMock;
    private Mock<IUpdateTaskMaintenanceProcessor> _updateTaskMaintenanceProcessorMock;

    private TasksController _controller;

    public HttpRequestMessage CreateRequestMessage(HttpMethod method = null, string uriString = null)
    {
        method = method ?? HttpMethod.Get;
        var uri = string.IsNullOrWhiteSpace(uriString)
            ? new Uri("http://localhost:12345/api/whatever")
            : new Uri(uriString);
        var requestMessage = new HttpRequestMessage(method, uri);
        requestMessage.SetConfiguration(new HttpConfiguration());
        return requestMessage;
    }

    [Test]
    public void GetTasks_returns_correct_response()
    {
        var requestMessage = CreateRequestMessage();
        var request = new PagedDataRequest(1, 25);
        var response = new PagedDataInquiryResponse<Task>();

        _pagedDataRequestFactoryMock.Setup(x =>
            x.Create(requestMessage.RequestUri)).Returns(request);
        _allTasksInquiryProcessorMock.Setup(x => x.GetTasks(request)).Returns(response);

        var actualResponse = _controller.GetTasks(requestMessage);

        Assert.AreSame(response, actualResponse);
    }
    }
}
```

Paradoxically, it seems that this required a lot of code, yet the test itself required very little code. Let's first talk about the test itself.

It required very little code because the GetTasks controller method is quite simple. We extolled the virtues of "thin" controller methods and a loosely-coupled architecture in the previous chapter, and now we are experiencing one of the benefits: namely, it makes unit testing easy to do. In the GetTasks_returns_correct_response test method, all we are doing is setting up the mocked dependencies, invoking the target method, and comparing the result with the expected value. Go ahead and build and run the test; the test should pass.

Now let's address the problem of so much apparent "noise" code in this test class. In particular, we're mocking a bunch of dependencies to satisfy the `TasksController` constructor, yet we're using only one of them. Well, for one thing, if we were to test all of the controller methods we *would* be using all of the dependencies; so, in that sense, they aren't gratuitous. However, from a design perspective, this arrangement is suboptimal; we are breaking the Open/Closed and Single Responsibility principles. For example, if we were to implement the `DeleteTask` action method, we would need to modify the `TasksController` constructor to accept a parameter of type `IDeleteTaskQueryProcessor`. (Note, this method is implemented in the example code on the book's GitHub site.) We would also need to modify the unit test class to pass an `IDeleteTaskQueryProcessor` instance to the updated constructor. How do we improve this design?

The good news here is that we've already made the first step toward improving, or refactoring, the code: we've *covered* the implementation with a test that passes. Now that the implementation is *covered*, it can be safely *modified*.

For the next step, let's fold all of these dependencies into a single dependency. Implement it as follows:

ITasksControllerDependencyBlock Interface

```
using WebApi2Book.Web.Api.InquiryProcessing;
using WebApi2Book.Web.Api.MaintenanceProcessing;

namespace WebApi2Book.Web.Api.Controllers.V1
{
    public interface ITasksControllerDependencyBlock
    {
        IAddTaskMaintenanceProcessor AddTaskMaintenanceProcessor { get; }
        ITaskByIdInquiryProcessor TaskByIdInquiryProcessor { get; }
        IUpdateTaskMaintenanceProcessor UpdateTaskMaintenanceProcessor { get; }
        IPagedDataRequestFactory PagedDataRequestFactory { get; }
        IAllTasksInquiryProcessor AllTasksInquiryProcessor { get; }
    }
}
```

TasksControllerDependencyBlock Class

```
using WebApi2Book.Web.Api.InquiryProcessing;
using WebApi2Book.Web.Api.MaintenanceProcessing;

namespace WebApi2Book.Web.Api.Controllers.V1
{
    public class TasksControllerDependencyBlock : ITasksControllerDependencyBlock
    {
        public IAddTaskMaintenanceProcessor AddTaskMaintenanceProcessor { get; private set; }
        public ITaskByIdInquiryProcessor TaskByIdInquiryProcessor { get; private set; }
        public IUpdateTaskMaintenanceProcessor UpdateTaskMaintenanceProcessor { get; private set; }
        public IPagedDataRequestFactory PagedDataRequestFactory { get; private set; }
        public IAllTasksInquiryProcessor AllTasksInquiryProcessor { get; private set; }

        public TasksControllerDependencyBlock(
            IAddTaskMaintenanceProcessor addTaskMaintenanceProcessor,
            ITaskByIdInquiryProcessor taskByIdInquiryProcessor,
            IUpdateTaskMaintenanceProcessor updateTaskMaintenanceProcessor,
            IPagedDataRequestFactory pagedDataRequestFactory,
            IAllTasksInquiryProcessor allTasksInquiryProcessor)
        {
```

```
            AddTaskMaintenanceProcessor = addTaskMaintenanceProcessor;
            TaskByIdInquiryProcessor = taskByIdInquiryProcessor;
            UpdateTaskMaintenanceProcessor = updateTaskMaintenanceProcessor;
            PagedDataRequestFactory = pagedDataRequestFactory;
            AllTasksInquiryProcessor = allTasksInquiryProcessor;
        }
    }
}
```

Dependency Configuration (add to NinjectConfigurator.AddBindings)

```
container.Bind<ITasksControllerDependencyBlock>().To<TasksControllerDependencyBlock>().
    InRequestScope();
```

▨ **Note**   You'll need to add a `using` directive for `WebApi2Book.Web.Api.Controllers.V1` to satisfy the compiler.

Now we'll update the `TasksController` implementation to make use of this new `ITasksControllerDependencyBlock`:

```
using System.Net.Http;
using System.Web.Http;
using WebApi2Book.Common;
using WebApi2Book.Web.Api.InquiryProcessing;
using WebApi2Book.Web.Api.MaintenanceProcessing;
using WebApi2Book.Web.Api.Models;
using WebApi2Book.Web.Common;
using WebApi2Book.Web.Common.Routing;
using WebApi2Book.Web.Common.Validation;

namespace WebApi2Book.Web.Api.Controllers.V1
{
    [ApiVersion1RoutePrefix("tasks")]
    [UnitOfWorkActionFilter]
    [Authorize(Roles = Constants.RoleNames.JuniorWorker)]
    public class TasksController : ApiController
    {
        private readonly IAddTaskMaintenanceProcessor _addTaskMaintenanceProcessor;
        private readonly IAllTasksInquiryProcessor _allTasksInquiryProcessor;
        private readonly IPagedDataRequestFactory _pagedDataRequestFactory;
        private readonly ITaskByIdInquiryProcessor _taskByIdInquiryProcessor;
        private readonly IUpdateTaskMaintenanceProcessor _updateTaskMaintenanceProcessor;

        public TasksController(ITasksControllerDependencyBlock tasksControllerDependencyBlock)
        {
            _addTaskMaintenanceProcessor =
                tasksControllerDependencyBlock.AddTaskMaintenanceProcessor;
            _allTasksInquiryProcessor = tasksControllerDependencyBlock.AllTasksInquiryProcessor;
            _pagedDataRequestFactory = tasksControllerDependencyBlock.PagedDataRequestFactory;
            _taskByIdInquiryProcessor = tasksControllerDependencyBlock.TaskByIdInquiryProcessor;
            _updateTaskMaintenanceProcessor =
                tasksControllerDependencyBlock.UpdateTaskMaintenanceProcessor;
        }
```

```
    [Route("", Name = "GetTasksRoute")]
    public PagedDataInquiryResponse<Task> GetTasks(HttpRequestMessage requestMessage)
    {
        var request = _pagedDataRequestFactory.Create(requestMessage.RequestUri);

        var tasks = _allTasksInquiryProcessor.GetTasks(request);
        return tasks;
    }
etc....
```

Note how the ITasksControllerDependencyBlock is now the only dependency required by the TasksController's constructor. Its single responsibility is to encapsulate the other dependencies, so new methods can be added to the TasksController without any modification to its constructor's public signature (or to the TasksControllerTest SetUp method, which is coupled to the TasksController constructor signature). The TasksControllerDependencyBlock constructor will necessarily change, but that's okay because managing dependencies is its only responsibility.

Before we become exhausted from patting ourselves on the back, however, an attempt to build the solution will abruptly remind us that we still need to update the TasksControllerTest. Let's attend to that right now by first updating it so that it appears as follows, and then adding the test utility class required by this updated implementation:

```
using NUnit.Framework;
using WebApi2Book.Data;
using WebApi2Book.Web.Api.Controllers.V1;
using WebApi2Book.Web.Api.Models;

namespace WebApi2Book.Web.Api.Tests.Controllers.V1
{
    [TestFixture]
    public class TasksControllerTest
    {
        [SetUp]
        public void SetUp()
        {
            _mockBlock = new TasksControllerDependencyBlockMock();

            _controller = new TasksController(_mockBlock.Object);
        }

        private TasksControllerDependencyBlockMock _mockBlock;
        private TasksController _controller;

        [Test]
        public void GetTasks_returns_correct_response()
        {
            var requestMessage = HttpRequestMessageFactory.CreateRequestMessage();
            var request = new PagedDataRequest(1, 25);
            var response = new PagedDataInquiryResponse<Task>();
```

```
            _mockBlock.PagedDataRequestFactoryMock.Setup(
                x => x.Create(requestMessage.RequestUri)).Returns(request);
            _mockBlock.AllTasksInquiryProcessorMock.Setup(x => x.GetTasks(request)).Returns(response);

            var actualResponse = _controller.GetTasks(requestMessage);

            Assert.AreSame(response, actualResponse);
        }
    }
}
```

Note how we've replaced all of the various mocked TasksController dependencies with a single dependency (i.e., TasksControllerDependencyBlockMock), significantly cutting down on the "noise" in the test class. We took things a step further and factored the CreateRequestMessage method out into a separate test utility class, because we anticipate that other test classes will require the functionality provided by the method and we don't want to, in any way, encourage a "copy and paste" coding style. Here's that test utility class (implement it as follows):

```
using System;
using System.Net.Http;
using System.Web.Http;

namespace WebApi2Book.Web.Api.Tests
{
    public static class HttpRequestMessageFactory
    {
        public static HttpRequestMessage CreateRequestMessage(
            HttpMethod method = null, string uriString = null)
        {
            method = method ?? HttpMethod.Get;
            var uri = string.IsNullOrWhiteSpace(uriString)
                ? new Uri("http://localhost:12345/api/whatever")
                : new Uri(uriString);
            var requestMessage = new HttpRequestMessage(method, uri);
            requestMessage.SetConfiguration(new HttpConfiguration());
            return requestMessage;
        }
    }
}
```

You've probably noticed that we have one more class to add before we can build and re-run the test, and that's the new TasksControllerDependencyBlockMock class. Let's add it as follows:

```
using Moq;
using WebApi2Book.Web.Api.Controllers.V1;
using WebApi2Book.Web.Api.InquiryProcessing;
using WebApi2Book.Web.Api.MaintenanceProcessing;
```

227

```csharp
namespace WebApi2Book.Web.Api.Tests.Controllers.V1
{
    public class TasksControllerDependencyBlockMock : Mock<ITasksControllerDependencyBlock>
    {
        private Mock<IAddTaskMaintenanceProcessor> _addTaskMaintenanceProcessorMock;
        private Mock<ITaskByIdInquiryProcessor> _taskByIdInquiryProcessorMock;
        private Mock<IUpdateTaskMaintenanceProcessor> _updateTaskMaintenanceProcessorMock;
        private Mock<IPagedDataRequestFactory> _pagedDataRequestFactoryMock;
        private Mock<IAllTasksInquiryProcessor> _allTasksInquiryProcessorMock;

        public TasksControllerDependencyBlockMock()
        {
            Setup(x => x.AddTaskMaintenanceProcessor)
                .Returns(AddTaskMaintenanceProcessorMock.Object);
            Setup(x => x.TaskByIdInquiryProcessor).Returns(TaskByIdInquiryProcessorMock.Object);
            Setup(x => x.UpdateTaskMaintenanceProcessor)
                .Returns(UpdateTaskMaintenanceProcessorMock.Object);
            Setup(x => x.PagedDataRequestFactory).Returns(PagedDataRequestFactoryMock.Object);
            Setup(x => x.AllTasksInquiryProcessor).Returns(AllTasksInquiryProcessorMock.Object);
        }

        public Mock<IAddTaskMaintenanceProcessor> AddTaskMaintenanceProcessorMock
        {
            get { return _addTaskMaintenanceProcessorMock ??
                        (_addTaskMaintenanceProcessorMock = new Mock<IAddTaskMaintenanceProcessor>());
            }
            set { _addTaskMaintenanceProcessorMock = value; }
        }

        public Mock<ITaskByIdInquiryProcessor> TaskByIdInquiryProcessorMock
        {
            get { return _taskByIdInquiryProcessorMock ??
                        (_taskByIdInquiryProcessorMock = new Mock<ITaskByIdInquiryProcessor>()); }
            set { _taskByIdInquiryProcessorMock = value; }
        }

        public Mock<IUpdateTaskMaintenanceProcessor> UpdateTaskMaintenanceProcessorMock
        {
            get { return _updateTaskMaintenanceProcessorMock ??
                        (_updateTaskMaintenanceProcessorMock =
                            new Mock<IUpdateTaskMaintenanceProcessor>()); }
            set { _updateTaskMaintenanceProcessorMock = value; }
        }

        public Mock<IPagedDataRequestFactory> PagedDataRequestFactoryMock
        {
            get { return _pagedDataRequestFactoryMock ??
                        (_pagedDataRequestFactoryMock = new Mock<IPagedDataRequestFactory>()); }
            set { _pagedDataRequestFactoryMock = value; }
        }
```

```
        public Mock<IAllTasksInquiryProcessor> AllTasksInquiryProcessorMock
        {
            get { return _allTasksInquiryProcessorMock ??
                            (_allTasksInquiryProcessorMock = new Mock<IAllTasksInquiryProcessor>()); }
            set { _allTasksInquiryProcessorMock = value; }
        }
    }
}
```

This simple class is simply a mock of mocks, encapsulating all of the mocked dependencies required by the TasksController. And now, with that in place, we are ready to build and re-run the GetTasks_returns_correct_response test. It should pass. Congratulations, you have tested and safely refactored a controller action method. Go ahead and celebrate this little victory, but make it quick because now we've got to test the dependencies that were used in the GetTasks implementation.

Testing the Dependencies

The first thing we need to do is add some more dependencies to the WebApi2Book.Web.Api.Tests project. With the solution open, run the following commands in the Package Manager console to install the logging framework that we introduced in Chapter 3:

```
install-package log4net WebApi2Book.Web.Api.Tests
```

Next, reference System.Web and the WebApi2Book.Common project from the WebApi2Book.Web.Api.Tests project. With that complete, we are now ready to test the first dependency that we used in the GetTasks method—namely, PagedDataRequestFactory. Therefore, let's add a new test, PagedDataRequestFactoryTest, as follows:

```
using System;
using System.Net;
using System.Net.Http;
using System.Web;
using log4net;
using Moq;
using NUnit.Framework;
using WebApi2Book.Common.Logging;
using WebApi2Book.Web.Api.InquiryProcessing;

namespace WebApi2Book.Web.Api.Tests.InquiryProcessing
{
    [TestFixture]
    public class PagedDataRequestFactoryTest
    {
        [SetUp]
        public void SetUp()
        {
            _logMock = new Mock<ILog>();
            _logManagerMock = new Mock<ILogManager>();

            _logManagerMock.Setup(x => x.GetLog(It.IsAny<Type>())).Returns(_logMock.Object);

            _requestFactory = new PagedDataRequestFactory(_logManagerMock.Object);
        }
```

```
        private const int DefaultPageNumber = 1;
        private const int MaxPageSize = 50;
        private const int DefaultPageSize = 25;

        private Mock<ILog> _logMock;
        private Mock<ILogManager> _logManagerMock;

        private PagedDataRequestFactory _requestFactory;

        [Test]
        public void Create_throws_HttpException_when_given_invalid_query_string()
        {
            var requestMessage = HttpRequestMessageFactory.CreateRequestMessage(HttpMethod.Get,
                "http://www.foo.com/bar?pageNumber=2&pageSize=10&pageNumber=50");

            try
            {
                _requestFactory.Create(requestMessage.RequestUri);
                Assert.Fail();
            }
            catch (HttpException e)
            {
                Assert.AreEqual((int) HttpStatusCode.BadRequest, e.GetHttpCode());
            }
        }

        [Test]
        public void Create_uses_corrected_supplied_pageNumber()
        {
            const int pageNumber = 0;

            var requestMessage = HttpRequestMessageFactory.CreateRequestMessage(HttpMethod.Get,
                string.Format("http://www.foo.com/bar?pageNumber={0}", pageNumber));

            var inquiryRequestData = _requestFactory.Create(requestMessage.RequestUri);

            Assert.AreEqual(DefaultPageNumber, inquiryRequestData.PageNumber);
        }

        [Test]
        public void Create_uses_corrected_supplied_pageSize()
        {
            const int pageSize = 2000;

            var requestMessage = HttpRequestMessageFactory.CreateRequestMessage(HttpMethod.Get,
                string.Format("http://www.foo.com/bar?pageSize={0}", pageSize));

            var inquiryRequestData = _requestFactory.Create(requestMessage.RequestUri);

            Assert.AreEqual(MaxPageSize, inquiryRequestData.PageSize);
        }
```

```
[Test]
public void Create_uses_default_pageNumber()
{
    var requestMessage = HttpRequestMessageFactory.CreateRequestMessage();
    var inquiryRequestData = _requestFactory.Create(requestMessage.RequestUri);

    Assert.AreEqual(DefaultPageNumber, inquiryRequestData.PageNumber);
}

[Test]
public void Create_uses_default_pageSize()
{
    var requestMessage = HttpRequestMessageFactory.CreateRequestMessage();
    var inquiryRequestData = _requestFactory.Create(requestMessage.RequestUri);

    Assert.AreEqual(DefaultPageSize, inquiryRequestData.PageSize);
}

[Test]
public void Create_uses_supplied_pageNumber()
{
    const int pageNumber = 1;

    var requestMessage = HttpRequestMessageFactory.CreateRequestMessage(HttpMethod.Get,
        string.Format(
            "http://www.foo.com/bar?pageNumber={0}", pageNumber));

    var inquiryRequestData = _requestFactory.Create(requestMessage.RequestUri);

    Assert.AreEqual(pageNumber, inquiryRequestData.PageNumber);
}

[Test]
public void Create_uses_supplied_pageSize()
{
    const int pageSize = 20;

    var requestMessage = HttpRequestMessageFactory.CreateRequestMessage(HttpMethod.Get,
        string.Format(
            "http://www.foo.com/bar?pageSize={0}", pageSize));

    var inquiryRequestData = _requestFactory.Create(requestMessage.RequestUri);

    Assert.AreEqual(pageSize, inquiryRequestData.PageSize);
}
    }
}
```

If this test class does not appear to be very noteworthy (aside from the fact that it is self-documenting), consider this: with it, we have achieved virtually 100 percent code coverage of the PagedDataRequestFactory class. The CreateRequestMessage utility that we introduced in the previous section helped make this relatively easy to accomplish. And, with the TasksController and PagedDataRequestFactory tests now out of the way, we are finished dealing with classes that have any dependency on the ASP.NET Web API. It's all just plain old C# from here on out, which is ideal from a code-reuse perspective.

The final class that we're going to unit test in this section is AllTasksInquiryProcessor. The last time we saw this class' implementation was all the way back in Chapter 7, so we'll show it again as a bit of a memory refresher:

```
using System.Collections.Generic;
using System.Linq;
using WebApi2Book.Common.TypeMapping;
using WebApi2Book.Data;
using WebApi2Book.Web.Api.LinkServices;
using WebApi2Book.Web.Api.Models;
using PagedTaskDataInquiryResponse =
    WebApi2Book.Web.Api.Models.PagedDataInquiryResponse<WebApi2Book.Web.Api.Models.Task>;

namespace WebApi2Book.Web.Api.InquiryProcessing
{
    public class AllTasksInquiryProcessor : IAllTasksInquiryProcessor
    {
        public const string QueryStringFormat = "pagenumber={0}&pagesize={1}";

        private readonly IAutoMapper _autoMapper;
        private readonly ICommonLinkService _commonLinkService;
        private readonly IAllTasksQueryProcessor _queryProcessor;
        private readonly ITaskLinkService _taskLinkService;

        public AllTasksInquiryProcessor(IAllTasksQueryProcessor queryProcessor, IAutoMapper autoMapper,
            ITaskLinkService taskLinkService, ICommonLinkService commonLinkService)
        {
            _queryProcessor = queryProcessor;
            _autoMapper = autoMapper;
            _taskLinkService = taskLinkService;
            _commonLinkService = commonLinkService;
        }

        public PagedTaskDataInquiryResponse GetTasks(PagedDataRequest requestInfo)
        {
            var queryResult = _queryProcessor.GetTasks(requestInfo);

            var tasks = GetTasks(queryResult.QueriedItems).ToList();

            var inquiryResponse = new PagedTaskDataInquiryResponse
            {
                Items = tasks,
                PageCount = queryResult.TotalPageCount,
                PageNumber = requestInfo.PageNumber,
                PageSize = requestInfo.PageSize
            };
```

```csharp
        AddLinksToInquiryResponse(inquiryResponse);

        return inquiryResponse;
    }

    public virtual void AddLinksToInquiryResponse(PagedTaskDataInquiryResponse inquiryResponse)
    {
        inquiryResponse.AddLink(_taskLinkService.GetAllTasksLink());

        _commonLinkService.AddPageLinks(inquiryResponse,
            GetCurrentPageQueryString(inquiryResponse),
            GetPreviousPageQueryString(inquiryResponse),
            GetNextPageQueryString(inquiryResponse));
    }

    public virtual IEnumerable<Task> GetTasks(IEnumerable<Data.Entities.Task> taskEntities)
    {
        var tasks = taskEntities.Select(x => _autoMapper.Map<Task>(x)).ToList();

        tasks.ForEach(x =>
        {
            _taskLinkService.AddSelfLink(x);
            _taskLinkService.AddLinksToChildObjects(x);
        });

        return tasks;
    }

    public virtual string GetCurrentPageQueryString(PagedTaskDataInquiryResponse
    inquiryResponse)
    {
        return
            string.Format(QueryStringFormat,
                inquiryResponse.PageNumber,
                inquiryResponse.PageSize);
    }

    public virtual string GetPreviousPageQueryString(PagedTaskDataInquiryResponse
    inquiryResponse)
    {
        return
            string.Format(QueryStringFormat,
                inquiryResponse.PageNumber - 1,
                inquiryResponse.PageSize);
    }
```

```
        public virtual string GetNextPageQueryString(PagedTaskDataInquiryResponse inquiryResponse)
        {
            return string.Format(QueryStringFormat,
                inquiryResponse.PageNumber + 1,
                inquiryResponse.PageSize);
        }
    }
}
```

Now let's implement the test for this class as follows:

```
using System;
using System.Collections.Generic;
using System.Linq;
using Moq;
using NUnit.Framework;
using WebApi2Book.Common.TypeMapping;
using WebApi2Book.Data;
using WebApi2Book.Data.QueryProcessors;
using WebApi2Book.Web.Api.InquiryProcessing;
using WebApi2Book.Web.Api.LinkServices;
using WebApi2Book.Web.Api.Models;
using PagedTaskDataInquiryResponse =
    WebApi2Book.Web.Api.Models.PagedDataInquiryResponse<WebApi2Book.Web.Api.Models.Task>;
using Task = WebApi2Book.Data.Entities.Task;

namespace WebApi2Book.Web.Api.Tests.InquiryProcessing
{
    [TestFixture]
    public class AllTasksInquiryProcessorTest
    {
        [SetUp]
        public void SetUp()
        {
            _autoMapperMock = new Mock<IAutoMapper>();
            _commonLinkServiceMock = new Mock<ICommonLinkService>();
            _allTasksQueryProcessorMock = new Mock<IAllTasksQueryProcessor>();
            _taskLinkServiceMock = new Mock<ITaskLinkService>();

            _inquiryProcessor = new AllTasksInquiryProcessorTestDouble(
                _allTasksQueryProcessorMock.Object, _autoMapperMock.Object, _taskLinkServiceMock.Object,
                _commonLinkServiceMock.Object);
        }

        private const string QueryStringFormat = "pagenumber={0}&pagesize={1}";

        private Mock<IAutoMapper> _autoMapperMock;
        private Mock<ICommonLinkService> _commonLinkServiceMock;
        private Mock<IAllTasksQueryProcessor> _allTasksQueryProcessorMock;
        private Mock<ITaskLinkService> _taskLinkServiceMock;
```

```csharp
private AllTasksInquiryProcessorTestDouble _inquiryProcessor;

private const int PageNumber = 1;
private const int PageSize = 20;

private class AllTasksInquiryProcessorTestDouble : AllTasksInquiryProcessor
{
    public AllTasksInquiryProcessorTestDouble(IAllTasksQueryProcessor queryProcessor,
        IAutoMapper autoMapper, ITaskLinkService taskLinkService,
        ICommonLinkService commonLinkService)
        : base(queryProcessor, autoMapper, taskLinkService, commonLinkService)
    {
    }

    public Func<IEnumerable<Task>, IEnumerable<Models.Task>>GetTasksTestDouble { get; set; }

    public Action<PagedTaskDataInquiryResponse>
        AddLinksToInquiryResponseTestDouble { get; set; }

    public Func<PagedTaskDataInquiryResponse, string> GetCurrentPageQueryStringTestDouble {
    get; set; }

    public Func<PagedTaskDataInquiryResponse, string> GetNextPageQueryStringTestDouble {
    get; set; }

    public Func<PagedTaskDataInquiryResponse, string> GetPreviousPageQueryStringTestDouble {
    get; set; }

    public override IEnumerable<Models.Task> GetTasks(IEnumerable<Task> taskEntities)
    {
        return GetTasksTestDouble == null ? base.GetTasks(taskEntities) :
                GetTasksTestDouble(taskEntities);
    }

    public override void AddLinksToInquiryResponse(
        PagedTaskDataInquiryResponse inquiryResponse)
    {
        if (AddLinksToInquiryResponseTestDouble == null)
        {
            base.AddLinksToInquiryResponse(inquiryResponse);
        }
        else
        {
            AddLinksToInquiryResponseTestDouble(inquiryResponse);
        }
    }
}
```

```csharp
    public override string GetCurrentPageQueryString(
        PagedTaskDataInquiryResponse inquiryResponse)
    {
        return GetCurrentPageQueryStringTestDouble == null
            ? base.GetCurrentPageQueryString(inquiryResponse)
            : GetCurrentPageQueryStringTestDouble(inquiryResponse);
    }

    public override string GetNextPageQueryString(PagedTaskDataInquiryResponse
    inquiryResponse)
    {
        return GetNextPageQueryStringTestDouble == null
            ? base.GetNextPageQueryString(inquiryResponse)
            : GetNextPageQueryStringTestDouble(inquiryResponse);
    }

    public override string GetPreviousPageQueryString(
        PagedTaskDataInquiryResponse inquiryResponse)
    {
        return GetPreviousPageQueryStringTestDouble == null
            ? base.GetPreviousPageQueryString(inquiryResponse)
            : GetPreviousPageQueryStringTestDouble(inquiryResponse);
    }
}

[Test]
public void AddLinksToInquiryResponse_adds_AllTasks_link()
{
    var link = new Link();
    var inquiryResponse = new PagedTaskDataInquiryResponse();

    _taskLinkServiceMock.Setup(x => x.GetAllTasksLink()).Returns(link);

    _inquiryProcessor.AddLinksToInquiryResponse(inquiryResponse);

    Assert.AreSame(link, inquiryResponse.Links.Single());
}

[Test]
public void AddLinksToInquiryResponse_adds_page_links()
{
    var inquiryResponse = new PagedTaskDataInquiryResponse();
    const string currentPageQueryString = "current";
    const string previousPageQueryString = "previous";
    const string nextPageQueryString = "next";

    _inquiryProcessor.GetCurrentPageQueryStringTestDouble = response => currentPageQueryString;
    _inquiryProcessor.GetPreviousPageQueryStringTestDouble =
        response => previousPageQueryString;
    _inquiryProcessor.GetNextPageQueryStringTestDouble = response => nextPageQueryString;
```

```csharp
    _inquiryProcessor.AddLinksToInquiryResponse(inquiryResponse);

    _commonLinkServiceMock.Verify(
        x =>
            x.AddPageLinks(inquiryResponse, currentPageQueryString,
                previousPageQueryString, nextPageQueryString));
}

[Test]
public void GetCurrentPageQueryString_returns_correct_value()
{
    var expectedResult = string.Format(QueryStringFormat, PageNumber, PageSize);
    var inquiryResponse = new PagedTaskDataInquiryResponse {PageNumber = PageNumber,
        PageSize = PageSize};
    var actualResult = _inquiryProcessor.GetCurrentPageQueryString(inquiryResponse);
    Assert.AreEqual(expectedResult, actualResult);
}

[Test]
public void GetNextPageQueryString_returns_correct_value()
{
    var expectedResult = string.Format(QueryStringFormat, PageNumber + 1, PageSize);
    var inquiryResponse = new PagedTaskDataInquiryResponse {PageNumber = PageNumber,
        PageSize = PageSize};
    var actualResult = _inquiryProcessor.GetNextPageQueryString(inquiryResponse);
    Assert.AreEqual(expectedResult, actualResult);
}

[Test]
public void GetPreviousPageQueryString_returns_correct_value()
{
    var expectedResult = string.Format(QueryStringFormat, PageNumber - 1, PageSize);
    var inquiryResponse = new PagedTaskDataInquiryResponse {PageNumber = PageNumber,
        PageSize = PageSize};
    var actualResult = _inquiryProcessor.GetPreviousPageQueryString(inquiryResponse);
    Assert.AreEqual(expectedResult, actualResult);
}

[Test]
public void GetTasks_adds_child_links()
{
    var taskEntity1 = new Task {TaskId = 300};
    var taskEntity2 = new Task {TaskId = 600};
    var task1 = new Models.Task {TaskId = taskEntity1.TaskId};
    var task2 = new Models.Task {TaskId = taskEntity2.TaskId};

    var taskEntities = new List<Task> {taskEntity1, taskEntity2};
    var tasks = new List<Models.Task> {task1, task2};
```

```
    for (var i = 0; i < taskEntities.Count; ++i)
    {
        var index = i;
        _autoMapperMock.Setup(x => x.Map<Models.Task>(taskEntities[index])).
        Returns(tasks[index]);

        _taskLinkServiceMock.Setup(x => x.AddLinksToChildObjects(tasks[index])).
        Verifiable();
    }

    _inquiryProcessor.GetTasks(taskEntities);

    _taskLinkServiceMock.VerifyAll();
}

[Test]
public void GetTasks_adds_links()
{
    var requestInfo = new PagedDataRequest(PageNumber, PageSize);
    var taskEntity = new Task {TaskId = 300};
    var queriedItems = new[] {taskEntity};
    var queryResult = new QueryResult<Task>(queriedItems, queriedItems.Count(), PageSize);

    var task = new Models.Task {TaskId = taskEntity.TaskId};
    var tasks = new[] {task};

    _allTasksQueryProcessorMock.Setup(x => x.GetTasks(requestInfo)).Returns(queryResult);
    _inquiryProcessor.GetTasksTestDouble = items => items == queriedItems ? tasks : null;

    var linksWereAdded = false;
    _inquiryProcessor.AddLinksToInquiryResponseTestDouble =
        response => linksWereAdded = tasks.SequenceEqual(response.Items)
                                    &&
                                    response.PageCount ==
                                    queryResult.TotalPageCount
                                    && response.PageNumber == PageNumber
                                    && response.PageSize == PageSize;

    _inquiryProcessor.GetTasks(requestInfo);

    Assert.IsTrue(linksWereAdded);
}

[Test]
public void GetTasks_adds_self_link_to_tasks()
{
    var taskEntity1 = new Task {TaskId = 300};
    var taskEntity2 = new Task {TaskId = 600};
    var task1 = new Models.Task {TaskId = taskEntity1.TaskId};
    var task2 = new Models.Task {TaskId = taskEntity2.TaskId};
```

```
    var taskEntities = new List<Task> {taskEntity1, taskEntity2};
    var tasks = new List<Models.Task> {task1, task2};

    for (var i = 0; i < taskEntities.Count; ++i)
    {
        var index = i;
        _autoMapperMock.Setup(x => x.Map<Models.Task>(taskEntities[index])).
        Returns(tasks[index]);

        _taskLinkServiceMock.Setup(x => x.AddSelfLink(tasks[index])).Verifiable();
    }

    _inquiryProcessor.GetTasks(taskEntities);

    _taskLinkServiceMock.VerifyAll();
}

[Test]
public void GetTasks_maps_entities_to_web_models()
{
    var taskEntity1 = new Task {TaskId = 300};
    var taskEntity2 = new Task {TaskId = 600};
    var task1 = new Models.Task {TaskId = taskEntity1.TaskId};
    var task2 = new Models.Task {TaskId = taskEntity2.TaskId};

    var taskEntities = new List<Task> {taskEntity1, taskEntity2};
    var tasks = new List<Models.Task> {task1, task2};

    for (var i = 0; i < taskEntities.Count; ++i)
    {
        var index = i;
        _autoMapperMock.Setup(x => x.Map<Models.Task>(taskEntities[index])).
        Returns(tasks[index]);
    }

    var actualResult = _inquiryProcessor.GetTasks(taskEntities);

    Assert.IsTrue(tasks.SequenceEqual(actualResult));
}

[Test]
public void GetTasks_returns_correct_result()
{
    var requestInfo = new PagedDataRequest(PageNumber, PageSize);
    var taskEntity = new Task {TaskId = 300};
    var queriedItems = new[] {taskEntity};
    var queryResult = new QueryResult<Task>(queriedItems, queriedItems.Count(), PageSize);

    var task = new Models.Task {TaskId = taskEntity.TaskId};
    var tasks = new[] {task};
```

```
            _allTasksQueryProcessorMock.Setup(x => x.GetTasks(requestInfo)).Returns(queryResult);
            _inquiryProcessor.GetTasksTestDouble = items => items == queriedItems ? tasks : null;

            var actualResult = _inquiryProcessor.GetTasks(requestInfo);

            Assert.IsTrue(tasks.SequenceEqual(actualResult.Items), "Incorrect Items in result");
            Assert.AreEqual(queryResult.TotalPageCount, actualResult.PageCount,
                "Incorrect PageCount in result");
            Assert.AreEqual(PageNumber, actualResult.PageNumber, "Incorrect PageNumber in result");
            Assert.AreEqual(PageSize, actualResult.PageSize, "Incorrect PageSize in result");
        }
    }
}
```

There are several notable items in this test class, but first let's mention some things about the AllTasksInquiryProcessor class itself. For one, all of the helper (i.e., noninterface) methods on the AllTasksInquiryProcessor class are virtual. This allows us to stub those out when unit testing.

Secondly, notice that although AllTasksInquiryProcessor requires several dependencies, we do not aggregate the dependencies in a "block" as we did with the TasksController. This is because, unlike we did with the TasksController, we don't expect the AllTasksInquiryProcessor to take on additional responsibilities. This decision should be revisited if the underlying assumption were someday proven to be incorrect.

As for the AllTasksInquiryProcessorTest class, here are some of the more noteworthy elements:

- The class contains a private class, AllTasksInquiryProcessorTestDouble, which derives from AllTasksInquiryProcessor. The AllTasksInquiryProcessorTest test methods use an instance of this private class, stubbing out functionality to allow individual test methods to isolate a single method under test.

- The class employs a mix of state verification and behavior verification, as appropriate, in order to provide high levels of code coverage. For example, AddLinksToInquiryResponse_adds_AllTasks_link employs state verification; the response is examined. On the other hand, AddLinksToInquiryResponse_adds_page_links employs behavior verification; the ICommonLinkService mock is interrogated to verify that the AddPageLinks method was invoked.

■ **Note** Martin Fowler provides a good explanation of these approaches to testing in the following article: http://martinfowler.com/articles/mocksArentStubs.html#ClassicalAndMockistTesting.

- The class defines a QueryStringFormat field, rather than relying on the AllTasksInquiryProcessor's public QueryStringFormat field. This is so that tests will break if the AllTasksInquiryProcessor's field were to ever change. Yes, this is actually desirable! If the functionality changes, the corresponding test(s) should break.

In a production situation, you would also need to test all of the other dependencies, including the ones we didn't cover here (i.e., PrimitiveTypeParser, TaskLinkService, the various extension methods, etc.). However, for the sake of keeping our readers engaged (you are still with us, right?), we will now move on to the integration tests. At this point, we trust that we've provided the basic foundation, and some helpful techniques, necessary for you to apply unit test coverage to an ASP.NET Web API–based application.

Integration Testing

The first thing we need to do is add some dependencies to the WebApi2Book.Web.Api.IntegrationTests project. With the solution open, run the following commands in the Package Manager console to install the testing and mocking frameworks, respectively, that we introduced in Chapter 3:

```
install-package NUnit WebApi2Book.Web.Api.IntegrationTests
install-package Moq WebApi2Book.Web.Api.IntegrationTests
```

Next, run the following commands, *in this order*, in the Package Manager console to install some ASP.NET Web API framework dependencies:

```
install-package Microsoft.AspNet.WebApi.WebHost WebApi2Book.Web.Api.IntegrationTests
install-package Microsoft.Net.Http WebApi2Book.Web.Api.IntegrationTests
```

Now that the external dependencies have been added, add the following project references to the WebApi2Book.Web.Api.IntegrationTests project:

```
WebApi2Book.Common
WebApi2Book.Web.Api
WebApi2Book.Web.Api.Models
```

Let's start off by adding a utility class to help the tests consume the task-management service (implement it as follows):

```
using System;
using System.Net;
using System.Text;
using WebApi2Book.Common;

namespace WebApi2Book.Web.Api.IntegrationTests
{
    public class WebClientHelper
    {
        public WebClient CreateWebClient(string username = "bhogg",
            string contentType = Constants.MediaTypeNames.TextJson)
        {
            var webClient = new WebClient();

            var creds = username + ":" + "ignored";
            var bcreds = Encoding.ASCII.GetBytes(creds);
            var base64Creds = Convert.ToBase64String(bcreds);
            webClient.Headers.Add("Authorization", "Basic " + base64Creds);
            webClient.Headers.Add("Content-Type", contentType);
            return webClient;
        }
    }
}
```

By default, the helper method uses the highly-privileged "bhogg" credentials for happy-path scenarios. The user name and content type may be specified on a per-test basis, as needed.

Now let's add the integration test (implement it as follows):

```
using Newtonsoft.Json.Linq;
using NUnit.Framework;
using WebApi2Book.Web.Api.Models;

namespace WebApi2Book.Web.Api.IntegrationTests
{
    [TestFixture]
    public class TasksControllerTest
    {
        [SetUp]
        public void Setup()
        {
            _webClientHelper = new WebClientHelper();
        }

        private const string UriRoot = "http://localhost:61589/api/v1/";

        private WebClientHelper _webClientHelper;

        [Test]
        public void GetTasks()
        {
            var client = _webClientHelper.CreateWebClient();

            try
            {
                const string address = UriRoot + "tasks";

                var responseString = client.DownloadString(address);

                var jsonResponse = JObject.Parse(responseString);
                Assert.IsNotNull(jsonResponse.ToObject<PagedDataInquiryResponse<Task>>());
            }
            finally
            {
                client.Dispose();
            }
        }
    }
}
```

This simple test creates a WebClient object using our new WebClientHelper. We went ahead and accepted the defaults for this happy-path scenario. The test simply verifies that the response is structurally valid. Other possible scenarios include passing in a bogus or restricted user name to test security or specifying a different content type to test content negotiation.

Now let's execute the test to make sure everything works properly. With the WebApi2Book.Web.Api application running, go ahead and run the test. It should pass. Excellent work, you've successfully implemented end-to-end integration testing!

Of course, as we alluded to a moment ago, other integration tests probably should be written for a production situation. However, at this point we trust that we've provided the basic foundation and some helpful techniques necessary for you to apply integration test coverage to an ASP.NET Web API–based application.

Now, by popular demand, let's wrap things up by consuming our task-management service with a simple Single Page Application.

Going Live!

In this section, we will examine a JavaScript-based consumer of our task-management service. You may have noticed a project in the WebApi2Book solution on GitHub called WebApi2BookSPA. This project is a very simple Single Page Application (SPA) built with the following technologies:

- ASP.NET MVC Framework

- Twitter Bootstrap

- KnockoutJS

- jQuery

- jQuery.Cookie

- Microsoft's JSON Web Token NuGet package

We've already covered both Basic and JWT-based authentication back in Chapter 6, so at this point we merely want to demonstrate the mechanics of how to make a jQuery AJAX call into our task-management service with a valid JWT. To keep things simple, the login page (Figure 9-1) will accept only a user name and role—no password required. Rather than complicating matters with authentication, or relying on a real token issuer, our simple SPA will generate its own JWT based on the given user name and role.

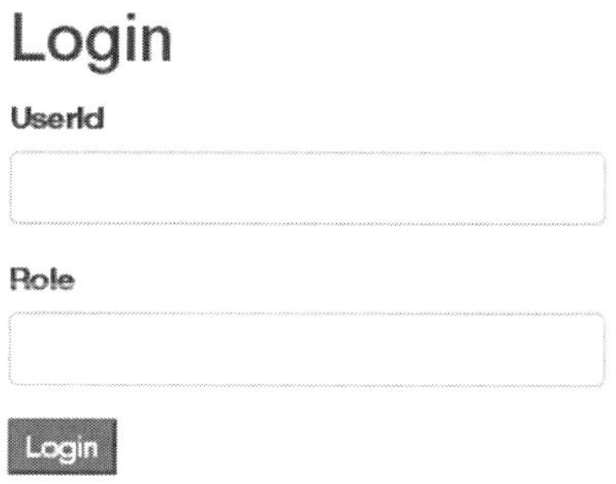

Login

UserId

Role

Login

Figure 9-1. *Single Page Application's login page*

Because this book's focus is the ASP.NET Web API, we're not going to walk through building the Single Page Application step-by-step. There are plenty of really good web-development resources out there to help you create SPAs in ASP.NET. But, if you're curious, you can find the complete code for the examples shown next in the book's GitHub repository. Throughout the rest of this chapter, we'll be pointing out the important parts from that code. So let's get started!

Logging In

Per the standard ASP.NET MVC pattern, we need to start with a model that will be used to submit our login form's data:

```
namespace WebApi2BookSPA.Models
{
    public class LoginModel
    {
        public string UserId { get; set; }
        public string Role { get; set; }
    }
}
```

And we need a view:

```
@model WebApi2BookSPA.Models.LoginModel

Login</h2>

@using (@Html.BeginForm("Login", "Login", FormMethod.Post, new {role = "form"}))
{
    <div class="form-group">
        @Html.LabelFor(m => m.UserId)
        @Html.TextBoxFor(m => m.UserId, new { @class = "form-control" })
    </div>

    <div class="form-group">
        @Html.LabelFor(m => m.Role)
        @Html.TextBoxFor(m => m.Role, new {@class = "form-control"})
    </div>

    <button type="submit" class="btn-primary">Login</button>
}
```

In case you haven't ever used Twitter Bootstrap, the various CSS classes specified in the view are included in Bootstrap, and they make it extremely easy to create good-looking web pages. Figure 9-1 is the resulting page.

And here's the controller with all that is needed to show our login page:

```
using System.Web.Mvc;

namespace WebApi2BookSPA.Controllers
{
    public class LoginController : Controller
    {
        public ActionResult Index()
        {
            return View("LoginView");
        }
    }
}
```

Nothing terribly exciting yet, of course. So now let's examine the controller action that accepts the login form's POST request and creates the JWT. Note that the key, issuer, and audience values for the created JWT must match that of the task-management service's JWT authentication handler. Normally, if you're using a real token issuer, the symmetric signing key is agreed upon and shared between parties, as is the issuer value. In our case, since we built the task-management service and configured the JwtAuthForWebApi package via web.config, we're simply going to copy the key, audience, and issuer into the LoginController.

The resulting code is actually very simple and similar to the CreateJwt console app we created back in Chapter 6. Here's the LoginController now with the required JWT-creation code:

```csharp
using System;
using System.IdentityModel.Tokens;
using System.Security.Claims;
using System.Web;
using System.Web.Mvc;
using WebApi2BookSPA.Models;

namespace WebApi2BookSPA.Controllers
{
    public class LoginController : Controller
    {
        public const string SymmetricKey = "cXdlcnR5dWlvcGFzZGZnaGprbHp4Y3Zibm0xMjMONTY=";
        public const string Issuer = "corp";
        public const string Audience = "http://www.example.com";

        public ActionResult Index()
        {
            return View("LoginView");
        }

        [HttpPost]
        public ActionResult Login(LoginModel model)
        {
            SetAuthCookie(model.UserId, model.Role);
            return RedirectToAction("Index", "Tasks");
        }

        private void SetAuthCookie(string userId, string role)
        {
            var token = CreateJwt(userId, role);
            var cookie = new HttpCookie("UserToken", token) {HttpOnly = false};
            Response.SetCookie(cookie);
        }

        private string CreateJwt(string userId, string role)
        {
            var key = Convert.FromBase64String(SymmetricKey);
            var credentials = new SigningCredentials(
                new InMemorySymmetricSecurityKey(key),
                "http://www.w3.org/2001/04/xmldsig-more#hmac-sha256",
                "http://www.w3.org/2001/04/xmlenc#sha256");

            var expiration = DateTime.UtcNow.AddMinutes(20).ToLongTimeString();
```

```
            var tokenDescriptor = new SecurityTokenDescriptor
            {
                Subject = new ClaimsIdentity(new[]
                {
                    new Claim(ClaimTypes.Name, userId),
                    new Claim(ClaimTypes.Role, role),
                    new Claim("exp", expiration)
                }),
                TokenIssuerName = Issuer,
                AppliesToAddress = Audience,
                SigningCredentials = credentials
            };

            var tokenHandler = new JwtSecurityTokenHandler();
            var token = tokenHandler.CreateToken(tokenDescriptor);
            var tokenString = tokenHandler.WriteToken(token);

            return tokenString;
        }
    }
}
```

Note the three constants that are copies of the corresponding values used in Chapter 6. All three must match; if not, the JWT validation will fail when we make the AJAX request to the service. The audience is typically the intended target (i.e., the resource server to which the user is needing access). And the issuer identifies (via any string value) the issuer of the token. This helps establish the trust relationship between the resource server (our task-management service) and the issuer of the JWT, because the service doesn't want to accept tokens from just any issuer.

Looking at the controller code, you'll see the first thing that happens when the LogIn action is invoked is we create the JWT using the supplied user name and role. Even though the act of creating a JWT would typically be handled by a token issuer of some kind, the resulting JWT is the exact same. As discussed previously, it is just a signed collection of claims.

Once the JWT is created—using the predetermined key, audience, and issuer—we create an HttpCookie in which to store the JWT for the client. In this way, the token will be readily available for use by the Tasks Viewer page's jQuery AJAX call to the task-management service.

Then, finally, we redirect the browser to the Tasks view. This next block of code shows the TasksView view:

```
Tasks Viewer</h2>
<p> </p>

<p>
    <button class="btn btn-primary"
            data-bind="click: refreshTasks">Refresh task list</button>
</p>

<p>
    <pre data-bind="text: statusMessage"
        style="width: 1000px; height: 400px; overflow-x: scroll"></pre>
</p>

<script>
    $(function () {
        var viewModel = new indexViewModel();
        ko.applyBindings(viewModel);
    });
</script>
```

In this view, we are leveraging Bootstrap to create a reasonable layout that includes a button and a big <pre> text area. We're not going to show the tasks in a grid or tree view at this point. The goal here is just to show the API-level integration with the task-management service.

The last block in that view is some JavaScript that loads our view model and then uses KnockoutJS to bind to the view. Looking at the preceding code, there are two bindings into our view model: the button click to fetch the tasks, and the text to be presented in the <pre> element.

Now let's examine the indexViewModel code:

```javascript
var taskManagementUrl = "http://localhost:61589/api/v1";

var indexViewModel = function() {

    var self = this;

    self.statusMessage = ko.observable("(Click Refresh button to load tasks)");

    self.refreshTasks = function() {
        var token = $.cookie('UserToken');

        $.ajax({
            type: 'GET',
            url: taskManagementUrl + '/tasks',
            headers: {
                Authorization : "Bearer " + token
            },
            contentType: 'application/json;charset=utf8',
            success: self.onRefreshSuccess,
            error: self.onRefreshError
        });
    };

    self.onRefreshSuccess = function(data, status) {
        self.statusMessage(JSON.stringify(data, null, 4));
    };

    self.onRefreshError = function(error) {
        self.statusMessage(error.responseText);
    };
};
```

The indexViewModel class includes a single property for displaying the returned JSON string and a function to respond to the Refresh button click. The main point here is that we're pulling the JWT from the browser's cookie collection (using the jQuery.cookie library), and then adding it to the AJAX request as a Bearer token in the Authorization header. It could hardly be simpler!

Before we move on, just a quick note: with earlier versions of jQuery, you may need to use the beforeSend event—instead of the newer headers property—to set the Authorization header.

Support for CORS

If you were to run this web site now, logging in and clicking the Refresh button to fetch some tasks from the task-management service, the call would fail. As many web developers have experienced, the browser will prevent AJAX calls being made to origins (i.e., servers) that are not the same as from where the current page was loaded. There are several security vulnerabilities associated with making cross-origin requests like this, so most (if not all) modern browsers prevent such calls from being made.

It is for this reason that a standard known as Cross-Origin Resource Sharing (CORS) was developed. CORS is meant to allow for the types of cross-origin AJAX calls we're trying to make here. It specifies that before making the desired HTTP request, the browser must first submit an OPTIONS request that essentially asks permission from the server to make the cross-origin request. Cracking open the developer tools in Chrome or Firefox while hitting the Refresh button referenced earlier, you will see two new CORS-related header values added to the OPTIONS request (as shown in Figure 9-2):

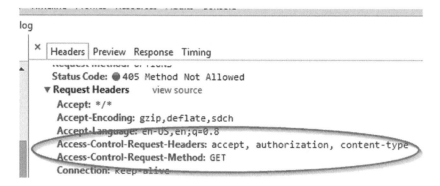

Figure 9-2. *CORS-related header values*

```
Access-Control-Request-Headers: accept, authorization, content-type
Access-Control-Request-Method: GET
```

These two header values let the server know that the browser intends to make a cross-origin request that includes, among other things, an authorization header. It's the server's responsibility, under the CORS standard, to respond with the origin(s), headers, and methods the server is willing to accept. The browser is then correspondingly responsible to respect these response headers, and not send the actual GET or POST request if the response headers don't indicate the server would allow it.

So let's enable CORS support on our task-management service. With the WebApi2Book solution open, add a couple of new NuGet packages with the following commands:

```
Install-Package Microsoft.AspNet.WebApi.Cors -Pre WebApi2Book.Web.Api
```

```
Install-Package Microsoft.AspNet.WebApi.WebHost -Pre WebApi2Book.Web.Common
```

```
Install-Package Microsoft.AspNet.WebApi.WebHost -Pre WebApi2Book.Web.Api
```

At the time of this writing, CORS support in ASP.NET Web API required the use of an alpha release of both the `Microsoft.AspNet.WebApi.WebHost` and `Microsoft.AspNet.WebApi.Cors` packages. Once those packages have been installed, add the following line of code to the `WebApiConfig` class's `Register` method:

```
config.EnableCors();
```

Then, on the TasksController class, add the following attribute:

```
[EnableCors("http://localhost:52976", "*", "*")]
```

The EnableCors attribute (along with the config.EnableCors() call) is all that is needed to add CORS support to your ASP.NET Web API service. Once configured as such, your service will appropriately respond to the browser's OPTIONS request discussed earlier.

Now recompile the solution, start up both the WebApi2Book.Web.Api and WebApi2BookSPA projects, and browse to the http://localhost:52976/login. This time, make sure you enter **JuniorWorker** for the role (as shown in Figure 9-3). If you recall from previous chapters, this role is required when fetching tasks from the task-management service.

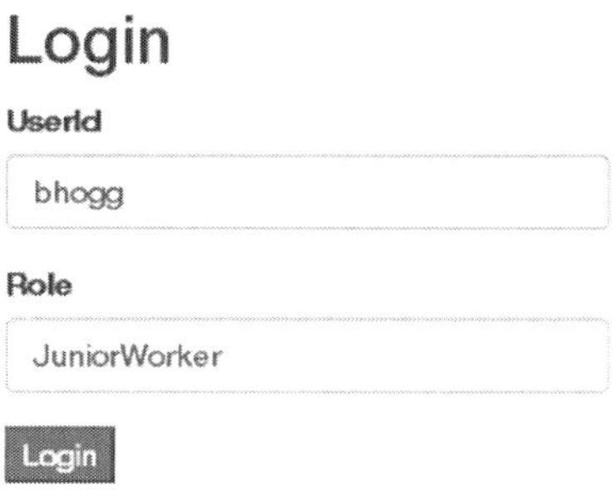

Login

UserId

bhogg

Role

JuniorWorker

Login

Figure 9-3. *Specifying the JuniorWorker role*

Once you are logged in, click the Refresh button again. This time, you should see the headers shown in Figure 9-4 included in the server's response for the OPTIONS request:

```
Access-Control-Allow-Headers: authorization,content-type
Access-Control-Allow-Origin: http://localhost:52976
```

```
× | Headers | Preview  Response  Timing
     Origin: http://localhost:52976
     Referer: http://localhost:52976/Tasks
     User-Agent: Mozilla/5.0 (Windows NT 6.2; WOW64) AppleWebKit/537.36
  ▼ Response Headers        view source
     Access-Control-Allow-Headers: authorization,content-type
     Access-Control-Allow-Origin: http://localhost:52976
     Cache-Control: no-cache
     Content-Length: 0
     Date: Mon, 09 Jun 2014 17:15:43 GMT
```

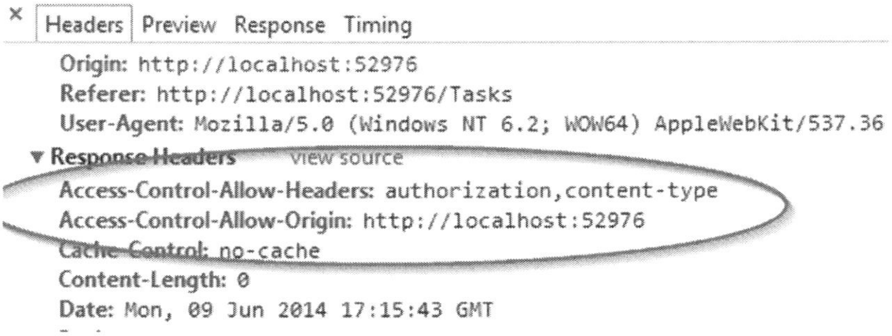

Figure 9-4. *CORS-related header values (success)*

This lets the browser know that it can go ahead and make the desired GET request from the `http://localhost:52976` origin, and it can include the Authorization header. The next request seen in the developer tools Network tab is the GET request, and it will include the JWT in the Authorization header. Finally, you should see the currently configured tasks displayed in the SPA's pre element box.

Try this now: change the `EnableCors` attribute to specify a different origin (e.g., `http://www.ourCorsExample.com`). Recompile and rerun the two projects, and try the Refresh button again. This time, the call will fail, and you will see a message similar to the following in the Developer Tools Console tab:

```
XMLHttpRequest cannot load http://localhost:61589/api/V1/tasks. No 'Access-Control-Allow-Origin'
header is present on the requested resource. Origin 'http://localhost:52976' is therefore not
allowed access.
```

This is exactly what we'd expect: our request is coming from `http://localhost:52976`, yet the task-management service now isn't going to allow a request from any origin that isn't `http://www.ourCorsExample.com`. Interestingly, per the CORS standard, it is the browser that is throwing this exception, not the server. Again, the browser is responsible for respecting the CORS-related attributes, so it is throwing the exception to prevent the JavaScript code from proceeding with the AJAX GET request to fetch the tasks.

In short, CORS support is very easy to add to your ASP.NET Web API service, and it will allow it to be called from more than just your own server. That is the point of Cross-Origin Resource Sharing: to share resources between systems.

Summary

In this chapter, we covered a representative portion of our task-management service with automated unit and integration tests. The ASP.NET Web API team has developed, and is continuing to develop, the framework with testing in mind, and we hope we've encouraged and equipped you to take advantage of their efforts.

We also completed the picture, so to speak, by demonstrating how to consume our task-management service using a simple Single Page Application. Calling an ASP.NET Web API service is very easy with today's JavaScript libraries, as we showed with the use of KnockoutJS. We also showed how easy it is to enable your service to be called from a different domain, via the CORS standard and the recent addition of CORS support to the ASP.NET Web API.

This brings us to the end of our present journey. We've demonstrated how to leverage the features and capabilities of the ASP.NET Web API to build a RESTful web service from start to finish. We first explained the REST architectural style, and then we built on that knowledge, the ASP.NET Web API, and some helpful patterns, tricks, and techniques to go from a blank slate to a fully functional, secure, and tested RESTful service.

ASP.NET Web API will continue to evolve, so the end of this book is not the end of the overall story. It will be interesting to see what exciting new capabilities will become available if the Open Web Interface for .NET (OWIN) and project Katana (which is built on OWIN) become mainstream in the Web API development community. As an example, at that point, authentication filters, not message handlers, will be the preferred approach to authentication. You will no longer need to write your own authentication mechanisms for standard authentication schemes, because all of the standard authentication filters will be built into Katana. You can read about OWIN and Katana here: `http://www.asp.net/aspnet/overview/owin-and-katana/an-overview-of-project-katana`. And, of course, be sure to periodically visit Microsoft's official ASP.NET Web API site (`http://www.asp.net/web-api`) to stay abreast of the latest features and releases.

With that, we bid you a fond farewell, at least for now. It's time for you to get started on your next ASP.NET Web API project! May our paths meet again someday!

Index

■ R

Get the eBook for only $10!

Now you can take the weightless companion with you anywhere, anytime. Your purchase of this book entitles you to 3 electronic versions for only $10.

This Apress title will prove so indispensible that you'll want to carry it with you everywhere, which is why we are offering the eBook in 3 formats for only $10 if you have already purchased the print book.

Convenient and fully searchable, the PDF version enables you to easily find and copy code—or perform examples by quickly toggling between instructions and applications. The MOBI format is ideal for your Kindle, while the ePUB can be utilized on a variety of mobile devices.

Go to www.apress.com/promo/tendollars to purchase your companion eBook.

10330320R00155

Printed in Great Britain
by Amazon.co.uk, Ltd.,
Marston Gate.